WITHDRAWN
L. R. COLLEGE LIBRARY

W9-BBP-156

A Practical Approach to Costume Design and Construction

VOLUME I

CARL A. RUDISILL LIBRARY
LENOIR RHYNE COLLEGE

A Practical Approach to Costume Design and Construction

VOLUME I

Fundamentals and Design

Beverly Jane Thomas
Florida Atlantic University

ALLYN AND BACON, INC.
Boston   London   Sydney   Toronto

Frontispiece: Historical source, the Duc du Berry's *Book Of The Hours* (left), and the finished costume as used in Shaw's *St. Joan* (right).

Illustrations in this book were drawn by the author.

Copyright © 1982 by Allyn and Bacon, Inc., 470 Atlantic Avenue, Boston, Massachusetts 02210. All rights reserved. No part of the material protected by this copyright notice may be reproduced or utilized in any form or by any means, electronic or mechanical, including photocopying, recording, or by any information storage and retrieval system, without written permission from the copyright owner.

Library of Congress Cataloging in Publication Data

Thomas, Beverly Jane.
    A practical approach to costume design and construction.

    Bibliography: v. 1, p. 227 v. 2, p.
    Includes indexes.
    Contents: v. 1. Fundamentals and design—v. 2. Design and construction.
    1. Costume design. 2. Costume. I. Title.
TT507.T466   792'.026   81-7950
ISBN 0-205-07273-9 (v. 1)   AACR2
ISBN 0-205-07367-0 (v. 2)

Managing Editor: Robert Roen

Printed in the United States of America.

Printing number and year (last digits):
10 9 8 7 6 5 4 3 2 1   86 85 84 83 82 81

*To my students, past and present,
who asked the questions that brought this book about*

792.026
T36P
133306
aug. 1985

Contents

Preface

Several years ago as the guest speaker at a theater conference, I was asked to lecture on costume construction under the dubious title "How to Make a Silk Purse out of a Sow's Ear." It can't be done nor should it be. Not one wants to see a sow's ear in the spotlight.

This book will show you how to choose the right "purse," how to construct it, and even how to fake the silk or fit silk into the budget. The aim of this book is to put between two covers all the practical knowledge I've gained over the last almost twenty years. Most of it was gained by trial and error. The object of this book is to help speed up the process, so that you will find costume design less of a trial and make fewer errors in costume construction.

I was once asked what it takes to be a costume designer. At the time I answered, "Patience. Infinite patience." Over the years I have amended that to include a love of history, a curiosity about people as manifested in their self-adornment, an undying love of theater, an ability to sacrifice individual ego for the good of the cooperative whole, a thorough knowledge of sewing, cutting, and textiles, and the ability to illustrate an idea from one's own mind, so that it is easily recognizable in the mind of the director, pro-

ducer, playwright, actor, and so forth. In other words the costume designer must be part historian, anthropologist, artist, engineer, draftsman, psychologist, economist, and still retain a sense of perspective and humor.

How does one become a costume designer? I am a firm believer in education. I hold a Bachelor of Science in Speech degree from Northwestern University, a Master of Fine Arts degree from Carnegie Mellon University (in my day Carnegie Tech), and a certificate in French from the Alliance Française in Paris. If you desire a college education, there are several paths to follow. Various colleges and universities offer differing programs. The most common are the B.A. (bachelor of arts) degree or the B.F.A. (bachelor of fine arts) degree in a theater major. The B.A. degree usually has a language requirement and is a more academically diversified course of study. The B.F.A. degree is a more specified course with a higher concentration in the major field. After graduation all you have to do is get a job and work like the devil.

If you wish to teach at a college level the M.F.A. (master of fine arts) degree is required of the designer. Master of arts (M.A.) degrees are offered, but again that is a more generalized degree and does not give the specific discipline the designer often requires.

There are also several well-qualified fine and commercial art schools in this country, which give an excellent background in fashion history, design, pattern drafting, cutting, and so forth. Several of these work in conjunction with universities in their area and give degrees. All give some sort of certificate of matriculation.

If you wish to design in the New York commercial theater or the Union houses throughout this country, then you must belong to the United Scenic Artists. This is a "union" or professional guild and one must pass an entrance examination

My own opinion is that a university education broadens one's intellectual horizons much more than the strictly commercial course. It takes many diversified pursuits to alloy into one thing called a "theatrical designer." But college is expensive and is not temperamentally suited for everyone. You must choose your own path.

Please remember this: a college education never promises job security. It is a broadening of the thinking process that enables one to survive this life more equitably.

If you are looking for job security, you shouldn't be in the theater at all! There is none. No matter how hard you work, you have to prove yourself with each show. In the long run it isn't just talent or education that spells success; it's what my grandmother used to call "stick-to-it-iveness." I call it just plain "glue." On the other hand, life is too short to spend it at a job you hate. You'll never know how much glue you've got until you try.

Last year at the graduation exercises the father of one of my best design students expressed great regret that his daughter was not going to be an English teacher. I reminded him that there seems to be too many teachers at the moment and very little hiring was being done. After all, if one is going to be unemployed, one might just as well be "unemployed" at something one enjoys.

Are you the mother of a budding ballerina and have gotten yourself roped into making thirty tutus for the dance recital next month? Are you the high school English teacher who's just been shanghaied into producing a Midsummer Night's . . . "Nightmare" for the school play? Are you a member of a community theater and have just struck your tenth Neil Simon one-set, modern dress show and would like more of a scenic challenge? Are you the undergraduate theater major, who knows the difference between Shakespeare, Shaw, and Sheridan, but needs a portfolio to prove it? If you fit these or any similar circumstances, you are the person to whom I am speaking.

When I was asked what I was going to name this effort, I was very tempted to call it "Glitz and Brass," a parody of that delightfully accurate song in *A Chorus Line.* Put an ordinarily dressed person on the stage and something is missing. A dress does not a costume make. It needs thoughtful help to punch it up, make a character statement, or give it "pizzazz"; thus the "glitz."

"Brass" is what is takes to sell it. "Chutzpah" is another great word for the same thing. Designers must be able to sell it just as much as any actor. The difference is that the actor sells himself. The designer sells ideas. It has always been a great comfort at the end of a busy day to put my sketches back in my portfolio case, zip it up, and go home. The actor must live within his portfolio.

One of my first design professors privately called actors "the glory seekers." Let's face it, we are all glory seekers. Why else would a relatively sane person elect to go into the theatrical profession? The hours are ridiculous. During your starting years the pay is a joke and it takes five to ten years to attain a firm foothold. Some of the people you must work with have egos a mile wide. It's the only art form that is a collective whole. You can never say "that's my production" the way the artist can say "that's my painting."

Ah, but when it works it is indeed glorious. Actors and actresses don't get all the applause. The actors merely walked across the stage and stood in a double line. My costumes for the Ascot Gavotte scene in *My Fair Lady* (Franky Park Music Festival Theater in Fort Wayne, Indiana) got a standing ovation every performance. I designed the whole thing in shades of blue with the female chorus in pairs, negative and positive. Eliza wore a white lace over turquoise taffeta creation with the palest of turquoise chiffon draped around the sheath. Her hat had two white stuffed herons eating opalescent grapes. It was worth every bloody finger and blistered palm I'd acquired from shoving needles through multi-layers of buckram.

Actors get a thrill knowing that the audience is hanging on every word. It gets so quiet you can hear a pin drop. I got the same kind of thrill during a production of *The Tempest* at Florida Atlantic University. When Caliban made his first entrance, he was so glitteringly strange that an audible "Ah!" swept the audience like a wave sweeping the shore. During Trinculo's "man or fish" speech he lifted the hand of the sleeping Caliban. You could always hear someone whisper, "Look, webbed fingers!"

This book deals primarily with the practicality of design. It is impossible to separate the practical entirely from the philosophy behind it. The philosophy is, of course, my own. It is what works for me. Please remember that there are no absolutes in life. I am merely trying to show pathways to an end result.

Please remember also that circumstances vary according to place, situation, and time. There are great similarities between the resident theater (opera or ballet) companies and the university theater situation. Repertory theater has its own special requirements. Stock has its specific problems. The long-running production has problems peculiar to it. Wherever possible, I shall try to account for particular situations, but no one can predict them all.

The words "professional" and "amateur" when used in conjunction with "theater" have long been out of date. Anyone who recieves money for doing a job is a "professional." For this book I should prefer to divide the theatrical situation into the "commercial" and the "noncommercial." The commercial theater is that which lives, primarily, off its box office receipts. This includes most resident theater companies (whether repertory or not) stock, and long-running shows, such as Broadway and national touring companies. The non-commercial theater generally includes community and educational theater, whose primary objective may not be commercial success in the strictest sense of the word. This may also, in part, apply to certain resident companies, particularly those that attempt to do culturally improving shows that do not have broad commercial success, such as Shakespeare, Moliere, and the classics.

Construction techniques will be handled in another volume entitled *A Practical Approach to Costume Design and Construction: Volume II: Construction.*

Now that we've been properly introduced, let's get this show on the road.

B.J.T.

Acknowledgments

Special thanks go to Sandra Allen, Bobbie Smith, Malcolm and Daniel Hensley for help in cataloging research; to Dikran Harijan for his excellent experiment with leather masks; and to Barbara Bell, Maria Marrero, and Missy McArdle for all the help in the trial and error processes I've developed over the last eight years.

I want to give extra special thanks to Harold Barris-Meyer, without whom this project would never have been completed.

A Practical Approach to Costume Design and Construction

VOLUME I

ONE

Fundamentals and Design Precepts

In this section will be explained the costume designer's roll in the hierarchy of theatrical personnel as well as some of the basic design elements. These are the tools of our trade, all of which culminate in the design concept.

It may come as a surprise to some that the chapter on the sketch itself is in the third part of this book, Research and Organization, rather than under Design. The sketch is only one more step in the organizational process of getting the actor properly clothed for his stage appearance. In other words, it is a means to an end; not the end itself.

I am constantly asked two fundamental questions by laypeople. The first is, "Is costume designing an art or a craft?" The second is, "Is there a difference between the costume designer and the fashion designer?"

Costume designing is both an art and a craft. In the sense that it has commercial value, it really becomes a commercial art. The actual designing is the artistic part. Getting the costumes on stage becomes the craft. You may not be involved in both ends but it is necessary to understand both thoroughly.

There is no basic difference between the costume designer and the fashion designer. The fashion designer often bases the latest haute mode on his or her knowledge of period costume; the costume designer is often called upon to invent haute mode for the stage. Many designers do both. This is easier to do in New York, southern California, or south Florida, areas that have large garment manufacturing centers. To paraphrase Gertrude Stein, a dress is a dress is a dress.

1

The Theatrical Chain of Command

If you were to draw a family tree of your theatrical family it would look something like the figure below.

If you are producing a musical, choreographers and musical conductors need to be added. These two positions, like that of the actors, are directly responsible to the director during rehearsals and to the stage manager during production.

In the resident company situation the producer is often called the "arts manager" or the "fine arts coordinator." The role of producer falls to the chairperson in most university theater departments. No matter what you call it, the job is essentially the same. The producer selects the play, hires the director, and is responsible for finding and controlling the money and keeping his or her angels happy. The producer must ap-

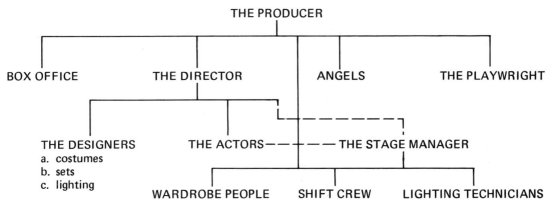

Figure 1–1. *Theatrical Family Tree*

prove the director's selection of the designers, the stage manager, and the actors.

On Broadway the stage manager is often held directly responsible to the producer in a checks and balance system of the directorial position.

The Designer's Obligation to the Producer

The designer's obligation to the producer is not as much an artistic one as an economic one. In an ideal relationship, the producer, director, and designers should decide on the budget together. Most resident companies and university theaters work on a yearly budget; it is then up to the designer to spend on each show as he or she sees fit. Occasionally a designer is asked to bid on an independent job. He or she then designs it and submits a budget estimate. Often a designer will be hired for a show and given the budget. It must be designed accordingly.

However one arrives at it, it is the designer's obligation to stay within the budget as much as possible. There are always those unforeseen events that make this impossible. It is wise to keep in mind that the most frequently employed designers are not necessarily those with the most talent. They are those who do the most within the confines of the budget.

In the unionized commercial theater the producer is also responsible for the construction of both set and costumes. Once these items have been designed and the fabrics or construction materials chosen, it is out of the designer's hands. Designers retain approval rights. They are often called upon in a consultant capacity, but if their designs are being constructed in union shops, they have no right to touch their own work. Exceptions are made if they are members of that particular union, of course. Most union shops will accept scaled pattern drawings from costume designers just as the scene shop accepts construction draftings and paint elevations from set designers. This will be discussed in great detail in Chapter 12.

Many resident and university theaters maintain their own shops. In this case the management of the shops falls to the resident designers. In the long run it is far less expensive to build for yourself than to rely solely on rentals. This matter will be discussed fully in Chapter 7.

The Designer's Obligation to the Director

The director holds the artistic reins. His is the overall concept to be conveyed. Your obligation to him is to help realize the concept on the visual level. (See Chapter 3.) Once that concept has been achieved and the sketches notated with final approval, there is an obligation to have the finished product actuate that sketch. There is no room in "show biz" for that old adage "Realization is anticipation disappointed."

The Costume Designer's Obligation to Fellow Designers

There are times when one person designs both sets and costumes, but it is more usual to use two people. Two heads are not always better than one on the conceptual level, but the two jobs may be too demanding for one person. This is particularly true in the stock, resident, and university theater situations, in which designers run their own shops. No one can be in two places at the same time. One shop or the other suffers from a lack of communication and/or supervision.

The costume designer and set designer have an obligation to each other to arrive at a unified scenic element. Neither part should overshadow the other. No sense of personal competition should be allowed to interfere with this. After all, these two people speak the same language.

Many people ask the difference between the costume designer and the set designer. Essentially, there is no difference. I have done both;

but given a choice, I prefer costumes to sets. It doesn't matter which I design; my preference comes in the actual construction segment. I do not like carpentry; I'd rather sew. (Then, too, I have a dreadful fear of a band saw.)

I have a private theory concerning the differences in the thinking process required by the two sides of the scenic coin. It is the difference between inductive and deductive reasoning. The set designer must go from the whole to the specific; the costume designer goes from the specific to the whole.

The Designer's Obligation to the Actors

Except in those cases in which an actor's contract requires costume approval, the designer is not legally obligated to the actor. An obligation exists nonetheless. It is the actor who wears the costume.

The function of the costume is to enhance the character, to make a statement about his station in life, his view of himself, and his relationship to the other characters. The costume should also help the actor to achieve such a portrayal, plus any demands of period, time, or place by freedoms and restrictions of bodily movement.

The costume must allow the actor the freedom of movement necessary to the requirements of period and action. Returning from the ball, Romeo has to climb that balcony. Regardless of the chosen period, his costume must allow for great limb stretching. It's no use giving him a cloak. It's bound to get "hung up" on a branch or balustrade. On the other hand, the male actors of a restoration comedy must wear the proper 2½-inch heeled shoes to achieve that special movement that gives the period and play its specific grace.

In 1978 on public television Beverly Sills gave an interview after a Wolftrap performance of *Roberto Devereau*. She stated that one of her Queen Elizabeth costumes weighed fifty pounds. The interviewer asked her if the weight made singing difficult. She answered that she would not feel "in character" without it. One must keep in mind that the gems of her jewel-encrusted gown were glass and the pearls plastic. Imagine how the real gems and pearls must have weighed down Elizabeth I. Sir Walter Raleigh probably spread his cloak over that puddle to prevent her from drowning.

One of the obligations the designer has to the actor is to get any restricting costume pieces to him as early in the rehearsal period as possible. It does not have to be the actual costume; a workable substitute will do. Such pieces would include the aforementioned shoes, as well as hoops, corsets, padding, bustles, bum rolls, capes, cloaks and sometimes masks, hats, gloves, eyeglasses, pocket watches, etc. All actors should have leotards and tights, and actresses should add floor-length rehearsal skirts to their work-a-day wardrobes.

The designer is also obliged to try to please the actor as much as possible within the confines of concept, period, and scriptual specifications. We all have our personal preferences, but these should be made known in the conceptual phase of production, not after the sketch has been finally approved, the costumes built, etc.

Once, an actress playing Queen Gertrude in *Hamlet* asked me not to put her in purple. She said she once had a purple dress that she wore four times, and each time disaster occurred, including the death of a loved one. She said she was not sure it was the dress or its color, but she did not want to take any chances.

There are times when the best laid plans "gang aft' a glee" and a finished costume just does not work. My own list of nightmares includes M. Cummiere's *(Marat/Sade)* directoire suit of gorgeous black panné velvet which continued to grow daily. I had to take it apart and quilt stitch each piece to its construction lining.

All designers have experienced the "odd man out" problem. A change of gel color suddenly can punch out the wrong color, or the tallest actor in the crowd somehow gets the only hat with a magenta feather. It will be solved, as will any ill-fitting problems, during dress rehearsals.

The actor also has an obligation to the designer to try to make things work. He is not the best judge of his costume because he does not sit in the audience; he cannot see the whole picture. He may want to look resplendent at all times, even when playing a witch of Endor. (This is particularly true of the less experienced actor.)

Some times an actor will dislike a particular part of his costume: his hat, for example. He will hold it, "forget it"(?), and do almost anything with the damned thing but put it on his head. The costume then looks incomplete and so does the character, and this makes both actor and designer look idiotic. It all boils down to mutual trust. Good designers will do everything in their power to help the actor look his part. The good actor will use the costume to its fullest possibilities.

You've all heard that show business saying, "It's not what you know, but who." The truism of this comes from adding, "whom you trust." If you establish a good trustful working relationship with someone—be he actor, director, or fellow designer—you enjoy that feeling. When you get a job and the producer is looking for someone in the other capacities, you will naturally suggest working again with the aforementioned person.

The Designer's Obligation to the Play

The designer's obligation to the play is the essence of the occupation. He or she must bring to visual life the character and times, mood, and theme of the play itself. This is done through all the design elements at his or her command.

2

The Elements of Design

Stated simply, the design elements function to help the audience identify, clarify, and intensify, through eye appeal, the intellectual and/or emotional perception of the play's action. For the costume designer this is done on two levels, the individual costume and the overall costume scheme. Both of these effects are achieved by the various elements of design—line, color, texture, movement, mood, composition, balance, and period. As we discuss these elements, please keep in mind the duality of our purposes. Although these elements work both generally and individually, there may be times when they may be at cross purposes.

We all learn best from our own mistakes. One of mine occurred during a production of Shaw's *St. Joan.* I had based my color scheme on the heraldic colors of Plantagenet England and Capet France. In two scenes I felt the need of a fresh color to enliven the mood. The first was the wind-changing scene between the Bastard of Orleans and Joan. I used green for Orleans and his page. He appears only in that scene and the coronation scene, so I felt that one costume would probably work with accessory changes. He didn't have very much to do at the coronation, but that didn't matter. Even if he only twid-

dled his thumbs, he was the only man in green amongst all that blue, white, red, and gold. The eye gravitated to him at all times. Between the second and third dress rehearsals I made him a second costume. This was a case of sublimating the individual costume for the good of the whole scheme.

Line

The first element of design is line. There are basically only two types of line, a straight line and a curved line. What you do with it is all important. You can converge (Fig. 2–1.1) or enclose (Fig. 2–1.2). Converging straight lines form angles; converging curved lines form arches. Enclosing straight lines form rectangles and triangles; enclosing curved lines form circles and ovals.

Then there is the meandering line, either a series of straight lines going in different directions (Fig. 2–1.3) or a curved one (Fig. 2–1.4). Lines are used either in repetition (Fig. 2–1.7) or in progression (Fig. 2–1.8). Horizontal lines accentuate width (Fig. 2–1.6) and vertical lines accentuate height (Fig. 2–1.5).

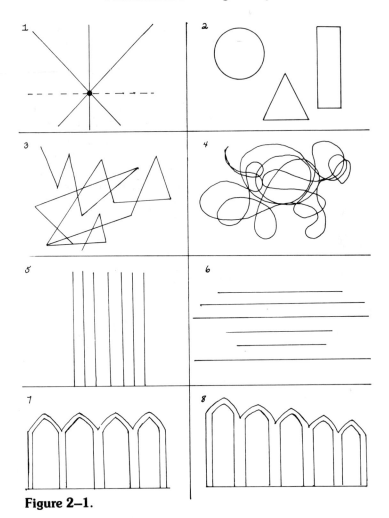

Figure 2–1.

Color

The second element of design is color. That particular word takes in everything that is not black or white. Technically speaking, neither black nor white is a color. Black is the presence of all pigment; white is the absence of all pigment. Therefore, the word "hue" is used to denote those "colors" on the color wheel.

There are primary pigment hues of red, yellow, and blue. These mixed together give the secondary hues. Red and yellow make orange; blue and yellow make green; red and blue make violet. When you mix a primary and a secondary you achieve an intermediate hue: red and orange make red-orange; red and violet make red-violet (called magenta), etc. These hues are marked on the color wheel by P for primary, S for secondary and I for intermediate. A color wheel, an intensity chart, and a grey scale chart appear in Figures 2–2, 2–3, and 2–4. An excellent source for this is Alexander Pope's book *The Language of Painting and Drawing*.

Remember that the primary hues for light and pigments are slightly different. Light primaries are red, blue, and green. On the second-

Figure 2–2. *Values on the Grey Scale*

ary level, green and red make yellow, red and blue make violet, blue and green make turquoise. Also, black is the absence of all light. White light is achieved by using all three light primaries together.

The hue called "brown" is neither fish nor fowl, so to speak. The easiest way to mix brown is a primary and a secondary in equal proportions: violet and yellow or green and red (see Fig. 2–2). You can also mix all three primaries in unequal proportions. Theoretically, if you mix equal proportions of the three primaries you would get black. Therefore, brown is an imperfect black. It is classified as a neutral, along with greys, black, and white.

Intensity is a term that describes the level of pigment in any given hue in relationship to black or white. A pure hue is undiluted pigment and therefore the most "intense." This, then, works in direct correlation with the values of the grey scale. Any hue mixed with white becomes a "tint." Any hue mixed with black becomes a "shade." Therefore, the color we call pink is a tint of red, and burgundy would be a shade.

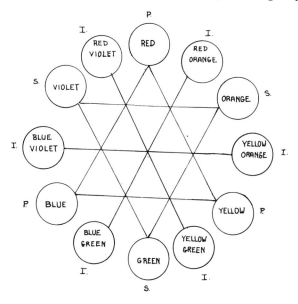

P. = PRIMARY HUES   S. = SECONDARY HUES   I.= INTERMEDIATE HUES

Figure 2–3. *The Color Wheel*

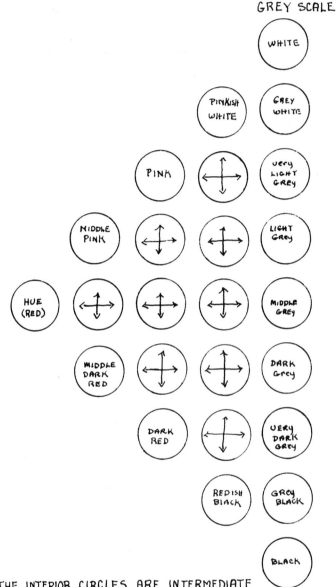

NOTE: THE INTERIOR CIRCLES ARE INTERMEDIATE
    VALUES, ACHIEVED BY MOVING EITHER VERTICAL-
    LY OR HORIZONTALLY

Figure 2–4. *Intensity Chart*

All paintings and design are predicated on the relationship of light to dark, tint to shade, black to white, negative to positive. This relationship has been named "chiaroscuro." The principle that goes with this is dark recedes or seems to pull away, while light proceeds or seems to come forward.

Tone

The word tone, when speaking in the language of the artist, seems to take in a wide variety of hues, tints, and shades. For the purposes of the designer I prefer the word tone to indicate an overall look to a hue or group of hues. For example, when talking about "jewel tones" one is discussing that quality of depth, brilliance, and clarity of color one finds in gemstones, such as jade, emerald, ruby, sapphire, amythest, and topaz. When talking of the "tone" of the design concept, you might describe something that was neutral in tone. This does not mean that no primary or secondary hues were used; it merely indicates that those hues used were sufficiently greyed down to give a neutralized look.

Now we must think about various color schemes, in other words, colors in relationship to one another. There is a *neutral color scheme,* although the term does have its paradoxical quality. It is simply an arrangement of values on the grey scale, including browns and creams, as well. There is the *monochromatic color scheme,* made up of tints and shades of only one color. There is the *harmonic color scheme,* made up of colors in close harmony on the color wheel, such as red, red-orange, orange, yellow-orange, and yellow. Finally, there is the *complementary color scheme,* picking two colors opposite each other on the wheel, such as orange and blue, red and green, or yellow and violet, usually a primary and a secondary. There is also a *warm color scheme* and a *cool color scheme.* Warms are magenta through yellow; cools are yellow-green through violet.

Texture

Texture is simply what an object "feels" like. In design it is how it looks like it might feel. Stage lighting and distance play tricks on the eye, and the way something actually feels has nothing to do with how it looks. Objects and fabric look either rough or smooth, heavy or light, hard or soft. For example, homespun, osnaberg, monks cloth, rope, burlap, and shantung look rough. Satin, velvet, silk, and chiffon look smooth, but satin and velvet also look heavy. Chiffon and shantung look light. Leather, bone, and metals look hard. Feathers, fur, and chamois look soft, but chamois is also a leather. Certain periods have a soft look, usually ones with drapery. Certain periods have a hard look, usually ones with close, form-fitting garments.

Movement

Certain fabrics and lines have inherent movement to them. The serpentine line seems to have a gentle, smooth movement. The angular line has an abruptness to it. Balls roll smoothly, boxes jerk and bump. Flowing drapery moves well, usually because the best drapery is done with lighter weight, flexible fabrics, but heavy velour has a dignity to its more voluptuous folds. Stiffened and padded costumes tend to restrict movement or confine it, as do certain hoops, corsets, and bustles.

Then there is what I call the "glissando" movement; in musical terms it is a slide with notes sounded in rapid succession. In terms of the ballet it is a smooth, follow-through, gliding movement. In costume terms it can best be exemplified by either the Victorian hoop skirt or the Elizabethan, with its bum roll or Spanish Farthingale. The feet cannot be seen moving, but the body seems to sweep along as if by magic. For men the sweeping gestures of the Cavalier period have that same effect.

Often form-fitting costumes seem to give a stiff and upright movement. This is particularly apparent in military uniforms. On the other hand, there is nothing more form-fitting than leotards and tights, which certainly allow the body complete freedom of movement, while having no inherent movement of their own.

Mood

Mood describes a particular state of mind or feeling. It has an emotional content. In design terms it is that emotionality most generally perceived in the visual elements. This occurs in primarily two directions—that psychology perceived in the use of line and color.

Emotions are always subjective, yet our culture puts upon us certain universalities which we all seem to share. Most European or Americans associate death with the color black. To an Oriental, white is associated with death. In our society white is associated with purity, sterility, and virginity; brides wear white. For years hospitals were white; nurses and doctors wear white. Red is associated with blood, such as the Red Cross, or evil, such as the devil or prostitutes. Pastel tints or pink and blue are associated with young babies. Yellow is a "sunny" color. Green seems to represent hope, springtime. The list goes on. The ancient Egyptians thought the color scarlet to be evil. Red is the vestment color for the Passion of Christ. Phillip IV of France made prostitutes dye their hair red. From where do these ideas come? Who knows?

I once wanted to find out how people emotionally reacted to color and if people in the arts perceived them differently than the layman. One item constantly surprised me and that was the response to the color lilac or lavender; invariably women of any age responded by saying "old ladies." Men did not have that response at all. Psychologists might tell us it is all conditioning.

There also seems to be a psychological perception to line; in its most general terms the curved or serpentine line seems more soothing than the angular or straight line. On the other hand, there is a cleanliness and directness to the straight line that a curved line does not possess.

There is even an emotional content to dark and light. Darkness brings fear and foreboding; light brings a feeling of safety and happiness.

Composition and Balance

Composition is the arrangement of design elements in a pleasing order; a balance of weight, line, color, and texture. Things are either composed symmetrically (Fig. 2–5) or asymmetri-

Figure 2–5. *Symmetry*

Figure 2–6. *Asymmetry*

cally (Fig. 2–6). "Symmetrical" means that design elements are distributed evenly from a central point; "asymmetrical" occurs when the balance point is not centered.

Focus

By the use of the design elements we achieve "focus." Focus can be the balance point. It can be the point of convergence of line. It can be the center of enclosure of line. It can be the man in green in an otherwise red and blue color scheme. It is the visual means of drawing the audience's attention to a specific character or movement.

Period

Artistically speaking, period is not an element of design, but the designer should think of it as such. You must be aware that certain periods have inherent freedoms and restrictions that may definitely affect the design concept. (See Chapter 5 for a table of costume periods and their approximate dates.)

Often the period of a play is not open to question. St. Joan died in 1431. If you are doing Shaw's play you have to make sure you are in that period. Conversely, excluding his histories, most of Shakespeare's plays can be set in almost any time period. It is up to the director and the designers to choose. It may depend on the type of movement desired. If the director wants fluid movement and/or a flowing line, the Elizabethan period would not be the best choice because of too much restriction of padding, ruffs, farthingales, and corsets. The Greek, Roman, Empire, or Gothic periods might be a more reasonable choice.

I designed *Hamlet* for a director who said, "If Hamlet had been sent out of a barbarian environment into an enlightened one, and then returned, only to have barbarianism thrown upon his again in the form of his father's murder, his subsequent indecision and vascillation would be even more pronounced." How do we represent that visually?

The one indisputable fact was that Hamlet was a Prince of Denmark. Denmark was once Viking. The Vikings co-existed with the Byzantine Empire. They even sent a group of mercenary soldiers to the Byzantine Emperor (see Byzantine silhouette general description). That would let us pit the hard line and textures of the Vikings (all that iron, bone, fur, horns, and so forth) against the softer lines and textures of Byzantium (silk, embroidery, gold, jewels, and drapery). This was how we began to arrive at what is termed a "design concept."

3

The Costume Plot

With any new design assignment the very first requirement is to read the script. You should sit down, put your feet up, and read it once straight through, strictly for the enjoyment of it. Allow it to make an initial impact on you. This is particularly valuable with a script that has not been previously produced or that is totally unfamiliar to you.

Then read it again with pencil and paper handy and make a costume plot as you go. The costume plot is your road map. It allows you to plot your trip, so to speak. A good costume plot should tell you who wears what, when, how often, how many chnges there are and where they occur. It should also detail time, place, and character. It will show you how many total costumes are required and allow you to begin making budgetary estimates. Never go to a first production meeting without a costume plot. It is as disastrous as going unarmed to the O.K. Corral.

Occasionally I have done costume plots in color. This was helpful for *St. Joan* and *Romeo and Juliet.* In both cases I wanted to show the protagonists and the antagonists clearly, and colored squares were very useful, but this is the exception and not the rule.

For the most part I use a form like the one shown in Table 3–1 for *Catch Me If You Can,* a nice tight, modern dress murder mystery. I also used this form for the slightly more extensively costumed play, *The Royal Family* (see Table 3–2).

Basically, the characters are listed vertically down the left hand side. The Acts and Scenes go across the top, making vertical columns and a written *brief* description goes in the proper box. When a character does not appear in a scene, the box is empty. If he or she wears the same costume as in the previous scene, the word "same" is written. After the costume plot is charted, counting the squares with notations will give you the total number of costumes. You know when the fast changes come, as well.

Some plays are not even that demanding. *The Fantasticks* (Table 3–3) is set in the imagination. The time is anytime. Each character wears one costume, except Matt, who needs two shirts originally alike. One is tattered to symbolize the school of hard knocks from which this latter day Candide graduates. A good many of Moliere's plays are simple, one-costume-per-person shows, and can be done this way. Even some of Shakespeare's plays require very little more. For an example, look at the plot for *Love's Labor's Lost* (Table 3–4).

Operas, musicals, and historical dramas (whether Shaw, Shakespeare, or Maxwell Anderson) seem to require the most extensive costume plots. *Little Mary Sunshine* (Table 3–5) is

Table 3–1. Costume Plot *Catch Me If You Can*

PLACE: Vacation house—New York State

CHARACTERS	ACT I Labor Day 8:30 p.m.	ACT II Sc. I Later that night	ACT II Sc. II Next morning	ACT III Ten minutes later
1. Dan Corban	slacks, ascot, shirt, cardigan, loafers	same; grabs coat when he goes for car	same slacks, loafers, new shirt, open at neck; no sweater	same as II-II
2. Inspector Levine (Jewish Columbo)	dark suit, black shoes, felt fedora, raincoat	same	same	same
3. Luther Kelleher, priest	black suit, clerical dickie, black shoes, black coat, and black hat	same	same	same
4. Elizabeth Corban	three-piece pants suit and blouse, scarf, low shoes, shoulder bag	sexy caftan or lounging outfit	same slacks, shoes purse, new overblouse, belt, different jewelry	same as II-II
5. Sidney, deli owner (dies of knife wound in chest; have double costume)			black slacks, black shoes, white shirt, black bow tie, white butcher coat, and apron	
6. "Mrs." Parker (?), gorgeous blonde and nobody's wife				clinging pants suit lots of chains and hoop earrings
7. Everett Parker, Mr. Cool type, but sporty				three-piece business suit, boutonierre, white shirt, expensive tie, and cuff links
Costume Total: 11				

Table 3–2. Costume Plot *The Royal Family*

PLACE: Fanny Cavendish's apartment—New York

CHARACTERS	ACT I—Nov., 1926	ACT II—Nov., 1926	ACT III—Nov., 1927
1. Della	maid's uniform	same	same
2. Joe	houseboy's uniform	same	same
3. McDermott	boxing attire	fencing attire	
4. Herbert Dean	business suit, matching vest, coat, hat, tie, dark shoes	same, with contrasting vest and new tie	another business suit and tie; same coat and hat
5. Kitty Dean	smart walking suit, coat, hat, purse, gloves, shoes, and dark stockings	tea time ensemble	walking suit of Act I with new blouse and hat, fur scarf
6. Oscar Wolfe	suit, coat, homberg	same	same
7. Gwen Cavendish	riding clothes, changes to tea dress, coat, scarf	negligee	smart suit, hat, purse, gloves, etc.
8. Perry Stewart	riding clothes	business suit	same suit; add hat and coat
9. Fanny Cavendish	long, matronly at-home dress	tea dress, change to gorgeous wrapper	long tea gown
10. Julie Cavendish	afternoon dress	smart suit, fur scarf, hat, purse, gloves	long tea gown
11. Tony Cavendish	fur-collared polo coat, fedora, suit, ascot	fencing garb over fisherman's turtleneck and white flannels; changes to underwear and robe; changes to bellboy	parka, Tyrolean hat; something bizarre
12. 2 Hallboys	bellboy outfits		same as Act I
13. Chauffeur	chauffeur's outfit		
14. Gil Marshall		conservative three-piece business suit, carnation in buttonhole	same suit; new carnation; new tie
15. Gunga			new suit, parrot on shoulder, turban
16. Miss Peak			typical English nanny's outfit
Total: 35 outfits			

Adapted from The Royal Family *by George S. Kaufman and Edna Ferber. Reprinted by permission of Anne Kaufman Schneider and Leueen MacGrath, and by Harriet Pilpel as trustee under the will of Edna Ferber.*

Table 3–3.   Costume Outline   *The Fantasticks*

CHARACTERS	Place: Imagination Time: Now
1. El Gallo	Caballero suit, hat, and boots
2. Matt	Two shirts alike (one tattered for 2nd Act), slacks, bow tie, sweater vest, tennis shoes
3. Louisa	Pretty, almost little girl dress, full petticoat, ballet slippers
4. Matt's father	Boater, slacks, shirt, vest, bow tie, arm garters, black shoes
5. Louisa's father	Derby, cardigan, slacks, shirt, regular tie (loose at neck), black shoes
6. Mime	Top hat, black and white parti-tights and leotards
7. Old actor	Bits and pieces of various period costumes; skull hung from belt
8. Indian	Red longjohns, loincloth, beads, feathers, braided yarn wig

Table 3–4.   Costume Plot   *Love's Labours Lost*

Characters:
1. Ferdinand, King of Navarre
2. Biron ⎫
3. Longaville ⎬ Lords attending Ferdinand
4. Dumain ⎭
5. Don Armado
6. Sir Nathaniel, a curate
7. Halafernes, a schoolmaster
8. Dull, a constable
9. Costard, a clown
10. Moth, a page to Armado
11. A Forester
12. The Princess of France
13. Rosaline ⎫
14. Maria ⎬ Ladies attending the Princess
15. Katherine ⎭
16. Jaquenetta, a country wench
17. Mercade, attendant of Princess
18. Two Blackamoors
19. Boyet, attendant of Princess

Note 1: Armado, Moth, Dull, Halafernes, Sir Nathaniel, and Costard are all in the play-within-the-play.

Note 2: King and three lords pretend to be Russians.

Time: Anytime and all on one day.

Place: A wooded glen.

Costume Total: 30

Table 3–5.   *Little Mary Sunshine*

Characters	Act I Sc. I (Front of the Inn, a summer afternoon)	I II (The Garden)	I III (Front of the Inn)	I IV (Primrose Path)	I V (Front of the Inn)	Act I Notes	Act II Sc. I (Front of the Inn, that evening)	II II (Point Look-Out)	II III (C. Brown Bear's Tepee)	II IV (Girl's Bedroom)	II V (Primrose Path)	II VI (Point Look-Out)	II VII (Front of the Inn)	Act II Notes
1. Chief Brown Bear	①				①	Big Chief = ①			①				①	①
2. Corporal Billy Jester	①			①	①	Ranger = ①	②		③			③		② evening attire / ③ buckskins
3. Captain Jim	①	①			①	Ranger = ①	②						①	② evening attire
4. Pete	①		①		①	Ranger = ①	② / ①	①						① ② evening attire
5. Tex	①		①		①	Ranger = ①	② / ①	①						① ② evening attire
6. Tom	①		①		①	Ranger = ①	② / ①	①						① ② evening attire
7. Hank	①		①		①	Ranger = ①	② / ③	①						① ② evening attire
8. Chuck	①		①		①	Ranger = ①	② / ①	①						① ② evening attire
9. Buster	①		①		①	Ranger = ①	② / ①	①						① ② evening attire
10. Slim	①		①		①	Ranger = ①	② / ①	①						① ② evening attire
11. Little Mary Sunshine	①	①			①	Gardening dress = ①	②			①				② party dress
12. M. Ernestina		①			①	Tyrolean dress = ①					①		①	①
13. Cora				①	①	Calico = ①	②			③				② party dress / ③ nightgown
14. Henrietta				①	①	Calico = ①	②			③				② party dress / ③ nightgown
15. Millicent			①		①	Calico = ①	②			③				② party dress / ③ nightgown
16. Mable			①	①	①	Calico = ①	②			③				② party dress / ③ nightgown
17. Maud			①		①	Calico = ①	②			③				② party dress / ③ nightgown
18. Gwendolyn			①		①	Calico = ①	②			③				② party dress / ③ nightgown
19. Nancy Twinkle				①	①	Maid = ①				②	①	③	②	③ M.H. Cape / ③ Buckskins
20. Fleet Foot					①	Very old Indian = ①	①							①
21. Yellow Feather												①		① Buckskins ①
22. Gen. Fairfax							①				①		①	① motoring outfit

a modest musical; it has a cast of twenty-two, including a "chorus" of rangers and seminary ladies. However, it has several within-scene changes. The small circled numbers in the right

hand corner of the box signify the costume: 1 = first costume seen; 2 = second costume, and so forth. The inter-scene costume changes are indicated by an arrow to lower left and the cos-

Table 3–6. Costume Plot *Kismet*

Characters	Act I Sc 1	I–2	I–3	I–4	I–5	I–6	I–7	Act II Sc 1	II–2	II–3	II–4	II–5	II–6	II–7
Poet-Haji	1	1	1	2			2		2		2	3		3
Iman of Mosque	1													
Four Muezzins	1		1		1			1	1					
Three Brigands	1	1												
Three Beggars	1							1	1					
Two Dervishes								1	1					
Omar	1		1		1			1	1			1		1
Marsinah	1		2		2					3	3		3	3
Four Merchants	1		1					1	1					
Jawan		1					1							
Four Street People	1						1	1						1
Two Street Dancers			1		1			1	1					
Informer			1	1										
Two Spies										1				
Three Bangle Sellers			1		1			1	1					
Two Policemen			1	1	1		1	1	1	1		1	1	1
Grand Wizard			1				1			2	2		2	2
Two Wizard's Guards			1				1			1	1			
Lalume			1				1			2	2			3
Lalume's Two Male Attendants			1				1	1	1					1
Calif			1		1	1	1	2	2		1		3	3
Three Princesses of Ababu			1									1		
Four Slave Girls				1		1		1	1					
Four Harem Girls											1	1		1
Peddler			1		1									
Male and Female Servants			both 1	male 1							fe-male 1			
Princess Zubbediya					1									1
Her Ayah					1									1
Prosecutor							1							
Widow Yusseff									2					
Four Diwan Dancers														1
Six Male Nobles														
Six Female Nobles														

Table 3–6.   (cont.)

TIME: One day in Bagdad

PLACE:	Act I–Sc. I	Steps of the mosque
	Act I–Sc. II	A tent outside the city
	Act I–Sc. III	The caravan bazaar
	Act I–Sc. IV	A side street
	Act I–Sc. V	A garden
	Act I–Sc. VI	A side street
	Act I–Sc. VII	Throne room—Wizard's palace
	Act II–Sc. I	Route of Calif's procession
	Act II–Sc. II	A garden
	Act II–Sc. III	Anteroom to Wizard's harem
	Act II–Sc. IV	Rooftop of Wizard's palace
	Act II–Sc. V	Corridor of Wizard's palace
	Act II–Sc. VI	Anteroom to harem
	Act II–Sc. VII	Throne room—Calif's palace

Costume totals: 87 costumes

tume indicated. Therefore, the rangers change from evening attire back to their "fighting" clothes in the middle of Act II, Scene I. Those twenty-two characters wear a total of forty-nine costumes.

A musical on the more traditionally lavish scale is *Kismet* (see Table 3–6). Here approximately seventy-seven characters wear a total of eighty-seven costumes. In this case, the costume plot was done for a specific organization that told me how many guards, nobles, harem girls, etc., they wished. This system is essentially the same as the one for *Little Mary Sunshine*, but because of the extensive number of scenes and the large cast list, time and place information had to go on a separate sheet.

Every now and then you will do a show so often that you have it practically memorized. (In my own case it has been *My Fair Lady* and *The Sound of Music*.) You no longer need costume plots for these, but you may need to sit down and write a quick summary. I have included one of these for *The Sound of Music* (Table 3–7). Keep in mind, however, that the number of nuns, party guests, etc., will change from production to production. The costume plot gives

your basic scriptural requirements. You may have to change this for one reason or another.

The size of the stage can change things. The last time I did *The Sound of Music,* it was for an arena stage $20' \times 18'$ square. Just having the Trapp Family onstage together was a crowd, let alone twelve nuns. On the other hand, your stage may be able to accommodate the Triumphal March of *Aida.*

Another consideration may be budget. We did *Little Mary Sunshine* at the end of a long and expensive season that included a bizarre production of *Blood Wedding, Taming of the Shrew,* and *The Good Woman of Szechwan.* Fortunately, *Little Mary* is set at the turn of the century, a period we have quite profusely in stock. By pulling and eliminating the nightgowns in Act II, Scene IV we could cut our budget in half. We also found an extra, unpaired Ranger, who was eliminated. For more on budgeting see Chapter 9.

In many published scripts, particularly those still under copyright, you will find a costume plot in the back. These are published from the stage manager's script in the professional (usually New York) production. The question always arises,

Table 3–7. Costume Plot   *The Sound of Music*

Maria:	Postulant, ugly arrival dress, dress out of draperies, nightgown, party dress, wedding dress, singspiel dress, Tyrolean cape	8
Children: 5 girls: 2 boys:	sailor outfits, draperie outfit, nightgowns nightshirts, wedding outfits, singspeil outfits, Tyrolean capes	49
Mother Abbess Ten nuns Two postulants	} 13 habits	13
Rolf:	Tyrolean outfit, brown Hitler youth outfit	2
Captain Von Trapp:	everyday uniform, sports suit and ascot, dress uniform, singspiel outfit, overcoat, evening tails, smoking jacket	4
Baroness:	afternoon ensemble, evening gown	2
Uncle Max:	nicker suit, evening tails	2
Party guests: 3 female:	3 evening gowns	3
3 males:	3 evening tails	3
Housekeeper:	1 outfit	1
Butler:	tails with striped vest	1
Two SS Men:	dark suits and leather coats	2
Lady at Singspeil:	Tyrolean dress	1
Total Costumes:		91

"Should I use that or do my own?" That, of course, is a totally subjective matter.

I personally am so used to doing my own that I forget the published costume plots are there. I originally decided against using them years ago, because it always seemed like cheating. It wasn't creating, but merely recreating. Often we came to the same conclusions, that unseen fellow designer and I; just as often, I found different ways. In certain instances, generally when the director and I have agreed on a new and different approach, I purposely ignore the written costume plot.

There are two exceptions to this rule. Exception #1 is summer stock. When you are doing one show a week, time is at a premium. Exception #2 is a little more complicated and *The Royal Family* is a good example. Essentially, it is a look at a theatrical family, supposedly mod-

eled on the Barrymores. The play was originally produced during their heyday and I felt the original designer may have been closer in life experience to that period than I could merely absorb through research. I found their costume plot helpful, particularly in regard to Fanny and Tony. It really comes down to circumstances and personal preference.

When I am trying to really sell an idea I will make a secondary "fabric plot." It is arranged much like costume plots shown in Tables 3–1 and 3–2, only in each block I glue fabric swatches and sometimes prices. Even first and second choices may be included. This is not necessary for a first production meeting, but it certainly helps for design conferences. Once a fabric selection has been finally approved, have it initialed or notated in some fashion. This saves time and agrument in the future.

4

How to Arrive at a Design Concept

All the Rules and When to Break Them

Once you have assimilated the elements of design, you will see that you have unconsciously made some "do's and don'ts" for arriving at a design concept for an individual costume. If you want to minimize a fat person's size, you would use vertical lines and dark colors and avoid large prints or plaids. If you want to make a tall person look shorter, you would use horizontal lines. A skinny person looks less so in full clothing and bright colors. Those are a few of the 'do's".

Here comes a parade of "don'ts." Never put a fat person in tight clothing. Never put a short person in full, puffy lines. Never put a short woman in a big hat. Never put anyone in ill-fitting clothes.

One could just as well say never wear scarlet to a funeral, yet Mary Queen of Scots did, to everlasting effect. (See Elizabethan General Description). You would never put a bride in black, but that might work best for a production of Lorca's *Blood Wedding*. In other words rules are made to be broken when breaking them is for a specific purpose.

How to Talk to Directors

With all this in mind you are ready to sit down with the producer, director, and fellow designers and hash out an overall design concept for the entire production. This can be the most exciting time of the project or the most disastrous. One director actually said to me, "Well, . . . ah . . . I don't really know what I want, but I'll know it when I see it." This is not exactly what you would call helpful. On the other hand, when planning an upcoming production of Goldoni's *A Servant of Two Masters*, the director might say he would like a carnival in Venice effect, and we should aim for a look like the paintings of Pietro Longi. That could be a masterful stroke.

Sometimes a little nothing can start the wheels rolling. At the end of the summer season of 1975 we were sitting backstage after strike night, polishing off the last of the beer while sorting nails. We had just announced that we would open the 1976 summer season on July 4th with *The Music Man*. I said, jokingly, "Why not do the whole show in shades of red, white and blue?" The director said, "What else!" The set designer said,

"Whoever heard of an all blue train?" By the next season it was no longer a joke and it was certainly one of the most fun concepts with which I've played. Granted, it would only work for the Bicentennial, but an exterior stimulus beyond the realm of the play itself can often be valid.

The pivotal point for the design concept of *The Tempest* could be "magic": Prospero, the magician, is a mover of storms and mountains, monsters and fairies. Ariel could fly like Peter Pan. The mountain might magically move. Magic hats would appear and disappear, along with banquet tables and serving beasts and shapes that go bump in the cave. Have Prospero disappear, leaving only magic dust behind. What is the color of magic? Things are the color they are not supposed to be. Put Ariel in turquoise and plum, Caliban in greens and blues. The lovers could wear blues, and even the logs that Ferdinand carries could be blue. Make the mountain turquoise, green, and lavender, as well as all those island inhabitants. The shipwrecked visitors, however, should be different. They are in "real" colors of earth—browns, rusts, earthy greens, and golds.

Anything that unifies the design elements to a cohesive whole works, if every aspect follows through. It is no good if the set goes one way and the costumes another. Neither does it work if even a brilliant visual concept is out of synchronization with the acting and/or blocking. Have you ever seen a set with five doors, but the actors only used four? Didn't you spend most of your time wondering about that fifth door?

When working with a new director, one can play a sort of word association game. Let's say we are about to design Ibsen's *Hedda Gabler*. You might ask the director, "If Hedda were a flower, what would she be?" (A thistle or, perhaps, a Venus's Fly Trap.) If she were a piece of music, who would have composed it? (Debussy, perhaps, or maybe Grieg's "March of the Trolls" from the *Peer Gynt Suite*.) A writer? (What a pity she was too early for Sartre's *No Exit*.) A color? (Brown and red.) In this way a picture begins to

emerge. She is the pivotal point of this play. Other characters would elicit other responses. Thea might be a daisy or Rubenstein's insipid "Welcome Sweet Springtime," for example. This is a way of getting at intangibles. Some directors do not care about the in-between elements, as long as they get the right effect for the various climaxes or dramatic moments. If that is achieved, the rest is up to you.

Some directors have certain color prejudices and will tell you they don't like a costume only because it's green and they can't stand green. It's nice if they tell you they can't stand green to begin with, but often they are not aware of it themselves and you have to be intuitive enough to discover it. Little things like what colors he wears or never wears, how his office is decorated, and what kind of paintings he has on his walls are excellent clues, not only to his preferences in color, but line as well.

Often a stimulus comes from a line in the play. In Shakespeare's *Love's Labours Lost* Don Aramado says "Green indeed is the color of lovers, but to have a love of that color! Methink that Samson had small reason for it. He surely affected her for her wit." There are four pairs of lovers in that play. The setting is a forest glen. What would be more natural than a color scheme of greens. The set designer chooses springtime with a blossoming tree. You might combine green with one springtime flower color for each of the three pairs; yellow, pink, and blue. For the King and the Princess you pick lilacs, mauves, and browns because you want them to stand out. Take this idea to the director. Take fabric samples with you and both of you can play around with grouping them in various combinations.

You might see a painting that for some reason strikes you as being right for a particular play. Take it or a picture of it with you to the director. Take anything that will open discussion.

A directorial concept may be superimposed onto a play. The director may see that play, not only for what it states, but for what it alludes that he may wish to convey to the audience. He may see *Tiny Alice* as an allegory of good and evil, or the re-crucifixion of Christ with Alice as the Lilith of Creation, the devil tempting Christ. You both need to kick that around until a physical solution is found.

The key word is communication, and therefore whatever stimulates this exchange if useful, whether it is a picture, fabric sample, observations, or intellectualizing. When this communication stops, disaster strikes. Get as much as you can in the way of concrete facts established in the pre-sketches stages.

This is the time to talk with your pencil. Doodle in some rough sketches for him. Discuss period, the type of action he envisions, color, line, and draw as you go. If he likes something, have him initial it, so that both of you remember it later.

Good directors must have a concept of space and line, if only for their own blocking. They may not know what the difference is between Pumpkin hosen and Cannions, but you can quickly show them.

A costume designer might take some old costumes to early conferences. "Look, velvet moves this way, but it won't float or look airy. Is this what you're after?" You as the designer may come up with the directorial concept based on a strong visual picture. Several years ago I was asked to design costumes for a production of *Godspell*. The hippie movement had died out and I got the idea to do it as a circus with Jesus as the starring aerialist and Judas as the ringmaster. The director liked the idea so well that she asked me to also design the set. I included a workable trapeze upon which Jesus was crucified. The audiences loved it and the critics raved. Remember, just as you get stimulation from the director and other designers, they should get it from you.

An old American Indian adage says, "You can't judge a man until you have walked a mile in his moccasins." This brings up a point vital to communications. The more jobs you have done in the theater, the better your chances of com-

munication. You've been the actor who missed an entrance because a seam split. You've been the director who wants the King to have focus, but the jester's bells keep ringing. You've been the set designer who was told that five doors were needed, but only four were used. From all of this you learn.

Before you leave, get a firm budgetary commitment from the producer. Work this out together with the aid of your costume plot. Budget does affect design concept. Some periods require more fabric and trim than others. That may have a great deal to do with the concept.

If you are in a repertory or university situation, you may pick a certain period because you have a lot in stock from which you can pull and thus keep the budget low. On the other hand, you may pick a certain period, because you do not have it in stock and it will help to fill out the wardrobe.

Now you are ready to go digging in the library and do some sketching. Before you do your final sketches, set up several appointments with the director for viewing rough sketches and research material. The two of you must work very closely. Final painted sketches take time to do well. You want to have as much concrete approval as possible to avoid having to waste time doing final sketches over. Remember, a costume sketch, even a supposedly "final" one, is still a *working* drawing. That old Burns poem about the best laid plans of mice and men, etc., became an adage by virtue of its veracity. Sometimes, in spite of the best planning, things go awry.

Both you and the director see a tall, skinny person for a certain part, but the best available actor is short and chubby. You have wanted a certain fabric, but it's unavailable. You think an effect will work a certain way, but under the lights it does just the opposite. These are exciting give-and-take situations and should be viewed by both you and the director as challenges rather than obstacles. The change in actor type could give a whole new outlook to the part. A new fabric might be more exciting; a little dye may help the effect or may lead to a new effect. Try to avoid becoming any more locked into a concept than time and money dictate.

What do you do whan all this fails and you can't seem to communicate with the director and/or other designers? If it's a job you're bidding on, you probably won't get it and don't cry over it. It saved you a lot of heartache. There is always another show. If it has already been contracted, grin and bear it and don't accept future contracts from the same source. Avoidance is the keyword.

If you are in a reportory, stock, or university situation in which you must work together again, hold what some universities call a "post mortem." After the show is over, sit down and talk out the problems. State them honestly and try to be aware of the pits so that you don't fall into them again.

TWO

Basic Period Silhouettes

To aid you in period identification, a silhouette of a male and a female figure for each era is given along with some historical data concerning events, originators of styles, fabrics, and color information. I have also attempted to add a little of the why, to the who, what and where. Of course, the "why" is always a bit subjective.

I believe that man's fashion is an outgrowth of philosophy at any given moment. It is a reflection of the world. People gave up wearing clothes merely as protection somewhere in the prehistoric past and started to decorate their bodies as they did their caves. Perhaps they simply traded mere physical protection for ego protection. As we shall see, clothing became a means of expressing wealth, status, social position, and in several cases, social protest.

These silhouettes are composites of various sources, a skirt here, a hat there, except where specifically indicated. Most of what we know about what people wore in "the olden days" is derived from paintings and artifacts left to us by the wealthy, who could afford them at the time of origination. Therefore, more is known about the rich of each generation than the poor. The

rich had their portraits painted, acquired beautiful things, kept favorite items of clothing in scented chests, and even left stone effigies of themselves on their tombs. They could easily afford not be to forgotten.

The poor wore their clothing to rags and were lucky to be adequately fed and sheltered. Since human nature has not changed very much, we can presume that the poor copied the rich to the best of their affordable means. Records show that clothing was often willed to the younger generation and the cast-off system is ages old.

There is nothing more aggravating to an expert than a purposeless anachronism. In a recent production of The Taming of the Shrew, done in passable Italian Renaissance of 1500, Petruchio entered wearing cowboy boots. Another pet peeve is zippers in dresses before 1900 (see silhouette figures of 1880s). It does absolutely no good to say that the ordinary person would not know the difference. That equates the "ordinary person" with the uneducated and/ or unobservant.

Uneducated and unobservant people do not usually go to the theater, and if they do it is our *job to elevate their knowledge. This is not to advocate using points for tying garments together. Use modern techniques wherever possible as long as it looks correct. For example, having an actor wear tights under his breeches instead of stockings does not change the outward appearance of the line at all. At the same time it is more comfortable for the actor, who does not have to fuss with garters or points. You have simultaneously eliminated baggy knees and sagging ankles.*

The key word here is "purposeless." You may wish to score a comic point with an anachronism. Fine! Consideration of a fast change may demand a zipper, but is there any reason why it can't be masked? After all, accuracy costs nothing but a little time in the library or museum.

Several museums have excellent costume collections worth mentioning. Here in the United States are the Brooklyn Museum collection and the Metropoliton Museum of Art in New York. The Musee des Art Decoratif in Paris has some exquisite hand props and jewelry. The Victoria and Albert Museum in London has a fine costume collection, as does the Assembly Room Costume Museum of Bath, England. The old fortress of Milan, Italy, has a superb armor collection. These are just a few.

Included in this section is a Table of Periods for quick and easy reference. The list contains the stylistic names and their approximate dates, but some may be confusing. Let us look at the Puritans for an example. In style they were a reaction to both James I and the Cavaliers, starting as early as 1610 in England and continuing to 1700 in America. During the 1640s and '50s they became part of the Cromwellian forces.

Further down the table you will see that Regency co-exists with the Directoire and Empire in France and a seemingly unanchored Neo-Classic period. George III had several periods of madness toward the end of his reign. His son, George IV, acted as the unofficial king until it became evident the George III simply could not reign. Then the son was officially declared re-

gent in 1811, but his influence was felt stylistically as early as the 1790s. The Neo-Classic movement was purely a stylistic one as were the later ones: American Gothic, American Gingerbread, Art Nouveau, and Art Deco. For cross reference purposes one needs to be familiar with all of these.

Where does one period stop and another start? It would be foolish to attempt to be definite. Time, even measured by changes in fashion, is a continuum. There are no absolutes. Therefore, in choosing dates I have tried to be as open ended as possible. I have also tried to show both the English and French names (and later, American ones) for what really amounts to the same time slot. For example, what is referred to as Restoration in England is also called Louis XIV or Baroque in France. Louis XIV is not a very efficient name for a period of fashion because during his lifetime the fashions went through two distinct styles. To represent this the names Middle and Late Baroque are used. There is no early baroque on the table; in both England and France what amounts to early baroque was called Cavalier.

As to the fashion continuum, it is obvious that the ancient world includes Eygptian, Greek, and Roman. When the barbarians overran Rome, Roman culture was sustained in Byzantium. The rest of Europe entered the "dark ages," which stylistically is called Romanesque. Charlemagne united these two worlds once more in the tenth century. Therefore Romanesque and Byzantine, although differing in style, occupy the same period of time.

Chapter 6 includes a section on ecclesiastical vestments and garments along with the Byzantine fashions because they stem from this time. This information is included because the list of operas and plays that require costumes of this sort increases yearly. To name just a few, there are Tiny Alice, Hadrian VII, Beckett, Murder in the Cathedral, St. Joan, The Lark, Henry VIII, A Man for All Seasons, Dr. Faustus, Tosca, Manon, Dialogue of the Carmelites, Soeur An-

gelica, The Sound of Music, Cyrano de Bergerac, The Devils of Loudon, Marat/Sade, *and* Romeo and Juliet.

After each silhouette and description is a section marked "Best Sources". These are sources I have found most helpful. Some of them, such as Godey's Ladies Book, can be found in the libraries of the older, more established cities. *Also included is a section on some well-known playwrights, composers, and theatrical trendsetters, because it is to these that we owe our jobs and our inspiration. They are our touchstone.*

Periods and Their Approximate Dates

Ancient	Adam to 1 A.D.	Late (French) Rococo	1760–1789
Egyptian	4000–30 B.C.	Georgian	1714–1790
Greek	3000–100 B.C.	Neo-Classic	1750–1820
Archaic	600–480 B.C.	Republican	1789–1795
Golden Age	480–400 B.C.	Directoire	1795–1806
Hellenistic	400–100 B.C.	Empire	1806–1820
Roman	800 B.C.–450 A.D.	Regency	1790–1820
Republican	800–44 B.C.	Federalist	1776–1812
Imperial	44 B.C.–450 A.D.	Romantique	1820–1840
Byzantine	400–900	Early Victorian (crinoline)	1840–1850
Barbarian	400–1000	July Monarchy	1840–1848
Romanesque	400–1200	Early Victorian (belled hoopskirt)	1850–1860
Early Gothic	1200–1300		
Middle Gothic	1300–1400	Second Empire	1848–1878
Late Gothic	1400–1485	Ante-bellum	1840–1861
Early Italian Renaissance	1450–1500	Middle Victorian (fishtail hoop)	1860–1870
Late Italian Renaissance	1500–1600		
Flemish-Burgundian (transition)	1485–1525	Middle Victorian (bustle)	1870–1878
		American Gothic	1870–1885
German Renaissance	1490–1600	Late Victorian (sheath)	1878–1882
English Renaissance	1485–1603	Late Victorian (bustle)	1882–1890
Tudor	1485–1558	American Gingerbread	1885–1900
Elizabethan	1558–1603	Late Victorian (belled skirt)	1890–1900
Spanish Renaissance	1506–1600		
French Renaissance	1525–1600	Second Republic	1878–1890
Elizabethan-James I (transition)	1603–1620	Fin de Siecle	1890–1900
		The Gay '90s	1890–1900
Cavalier	1620–1650	Edwardian	1900–1914
Puritan (English-American)	1610–1700	La Belle Epoch	1900–1914
		Turn of the Century	1900–1914
Cromwellian Commonwealth	1649–1660	World War I	1914–1920
		The Roaring '20s	1920–1930
Dutch Baroque	1600–1700	Depression '30s	1930–1940
Spanish Baroque	1600–1700	World War II	1940–1950
Middle (French) Baroque	1660–1690	The "New Look" '50s	1950–1960
Late (French) Baroque	1690–1720	The Hip '60s	1960–1970
Restoration	1660–1714	The Eclectic '70s	1970–1980
Early (French) Rococo	1720–1760		

5

The Ancient and Classic World

According to the story in Genesis, Adam and Eve needed no clothing until they gained knowledge and their knowledge made them look upon the naked body with shame. Also, they were cast out of perfect paradise (where it never snowed or got cold) into the cruel world and they therefore needed something for self-preservation. There it is—the two-edged sword of fashion—protection and survival on one side and pride on the other, because pride is the obvious reaction to shame. One way of expressing this pride is adornment. It also shows individuality. (Eve may have put a flower in her hair even before she ate the apple.)

The cave dwellers wore bones of interesting shapes. The American Indians adorned themselves with feathers and beads made of colored stones and bones. After the necessities of warmth and protection were solved, vanity became the criteria. Ancient people were just as prone to vanity as we are today.

Figure 5–1. *Ancient—Adam to 1 A.D.*

Ancient—Adam to 1 A.D.

A Cretan Lady—1700 B.C.

The woman in Figure 5–1 could be Medusa or Megiera, a Cretan priestess of the snake cult, a gorgon. Anyone who gazed on a gorgon was turned to stone. Except for the exposed breasts, her dress is very reminiscent of something mid-Victorian. It consists of a very tight bodice and sleeves and a three-tiered skirt. She wears a somewhat Greek-looking diadem, and her hair is arranged in a series of heavy rolls. To be an absolutely accurate gorgon her hair would be snakes, but in reality this is unlikely. Lastly, she seems to wear a metallic netted apron-like device that extends from the waist over the abdomen.

An Assyrian Man—1500 B.C.

The man in Figure 5–1 is an Assyrian King. On his head he wears the high crown with cone that designates his office. His hair and beard are arranged in carefully groomed curls. He wears a simple T-shaped tunic over which is wrapped a fringed rectangle that has been belted. A strap from one corner of the rectangle seems attached to this belt, which starts the wrapping.

The Assyrian women dressed in a similar fashion. They wore boots for hunting and both sandals and shoes. Both men and women wore earrings and many bracelets. The Assyrians were deft at weaving and loved patterned fabrics, and as this king displays, the more pattern, the better.

General Description

One cannot possibly cover every small culture of ancient times. These two widely divergent cultures have been chosen because they are among the most interesting from a fashion viewpoint and because separately and unknown to each other they make a certain statement about fashion and ancient times in general.

The Cretan culture seemed matriarchal; the Assyrian was definitely male-oriented. Yet both employed in their surroundings, as well as in their fashions, a tiered look. His skirt, as well as hers, consists of three layers. Both show a high degree of ornateness, thus belying the theory that ancient people were clothed simply and had little knowledge of cutting and fitting.

Best Sources

Crete: Cretan Statuary and the wall paintings from the palace of Minos, Knossos.
Assyrian: Assyrian bas-relief and statuary.

Egyptian—4000 to 30 B.C.

The Pharaoh

The pharaoh in Figure 5–2 wears the crown of United Egypt at which time the upper and lower kingdoms came under one leadership. The white interior symbolizes Lower Egypt and

Figure 5–2. *Egyptian—4000 to 30 B.C.*

the red exterior, Upper Egypt. The color red (vermillion or scarlet) was considered an unlucky, evil color. Therefore, the red of this crown was either a magenta or a terra cotta.

He also wears a tied-on beard, a ceremonial symbol, and carries an ankh, the symbol of everlasting life.

He wears a wrapped loincloth of fine linen or cotton and a decorative belt that has a stiffened and decorated triangular wedge suspended from it. He also wears a beautifully decorated and jeweled collar. His feet are bare.

The Princess

The princess in Figure 5–2 wears a cobra circlet over her much-braided wig. Each braid has a gold casing and several gold bands and there are many tiny braids to the wig, creating a very dazzling effect. On the crown of her head is a cone of perfumed grease that would slowly melt, leaving a pleasant scent whenever she moved.

Like her brother, she wears a jeweled and decorated collar. Her skirt is of knife-pleated linen gauze. A cape of it goes around her shoulders and tucks into the skirt front. She, too, wears a decorated hanging belt. Her feet are bare.

General Description

The key to Egyptian fashion was comfort. Since Egypt is a hot country, the most popular color for everyone, Pharaoh, priest, or slave, was white. The best color to reflect heat is white. The Egyptian color that symbolized death was black. As stated before, red was considered evil. Other popular colors were blue, green, terra cotta, yellow, turquoise, and plum.

Because of the heat, the naked body was also fashionable. Dancing girls danced nude. The upper torso of woman as well as men was often bared. Even hair was shaved off by both men and women. Wigs and hats were worn instead. Feet were bare while indoors; sandals were worn for protection out of doors.

The Egyptians were highly skilled artisans and turned out beautiful gold jewelry of every sort, sometimes augmented with enamel work, sometimes with semi-precious stones, and sometimes with glass. Glass was considered precious. It was found in the desert. The Egyptians knew how to melt it and reuse it, but did not understand how to manufacture it. Because it could be found after lightning struck the sand, it was considered a gift from the gods. Other stones favored by the Egyptians were turquoise, carnelian, lapis lazuli, malachite, amethyst, garnet, and tiger-eye.

The Egyptians wore crowns, bracelets, anklets, necklaces, rings, and brooches. They had several favorite decorative motifs—the lotus flower (see the princess's collar and the Pharaoh's triangular wedge), the wings of the vulture (the Pharaoh's collar), the cobra, the scarab (the beetle), and the palm leaf. These motifs can be found on their wall and pillar paintings, as well as on jewelry and artifacts.

Sometimes a long, loose robe was worn over the loin cloth by both men and women. Women often wore a high-waisted, narrow skirt held up by shoulder straps but leaving the breasts bare. Priests wore leopard skin, including head, tail, and paws. When priests prepared a body for burial, they wore jackal-head masks.

A pale skin was prized by the ladies. They spent much time and money on make-up. A lead-based foundation was used to whiten the skin. Large amounts of eye shadow, generally green or blue, decorated the upper lid. Kohl was used to rim the eye and eyebrows. Rouge was then applied. Cleopatra is said to have bathed in milk and used powdered gold dust on her eyelids. Perfumed oils were used in great profusion, as was henna to redden the palms and soles of the feet.

Best sources

Tomb artifacts and paintings, particularly those of Tutankh-amun.

Ancient Greek—3000 to 100 B.C.

The Warrior—480 to 400 B.C.

The soldier in Figure 5–3 wears a bronze helmet with horse hair plumage and bronze greaves. He carries a short sword and round shield decorated with the "scroll" motif (sometimes called "wave"). He wears a leather cuirass laced over a short chiton. He is barefoot.

The Girl—480 to 400 B.C.

The girl in Figure 5–3 wears a simple gold or bronze circlet around her hair, which has been pulled back and is held by a cord at the nape of the neck. Her Doric chiton is pulled up in the peplos manner and fastened at the shoulder by two rounded pins. In earlier times these would

Figure 5–3 *Greek   3000 to 100 B.C.*
             Archaic   600 to 480 B.C.
             Golden Age   480 to 400 B.C.
             Hellenistic 400 to 100 B.C.

have been two metallic circles through which the fabric ends were pulled and held by very sharp, straight pins, similar to the hat pins of today.

She wears a double girdle or two belts, neither of which can be seen. The first creates the "peplos," or what we would today call a peplum; the second creates the "kolpos," the bloused-over effect at the waist. This chiton has been bordered with the "laurel leaf" motif. She, too, is barefoot, but sandals were frequently worn.

General Description

The basic philosophy of Greece at this time sought the truth in all things. This accounts for the Greeks' love of the uncluttered line and sense of summetry and balance. Men and women wore basically the same things, although women had a little more variety. The three basic items of clothing were the chiton, the himation, and chlamys, all rectangular pieces of cloth. There is a great similarity between the Greek himation and the wrapped garment of the Ancient Assyrian kings. After the Persian Wars they adopted the T-shaped tunic.

Soldiers of an earlier time than that pictured in the silhouette fought wearing nothing but a chlamys and helmet. During a slightly later period the Persian influence gave them fish-scale plated armor, much like the Varangian Guards of the Byzantine period (see Barbarians—General Description).

Men wore short chitons, belted in the middle. Women had two versions. The Doric, which we have seen in silhouette, was generally less full than the Ionic. There was a very slim version of the Doric, which was allowed to open to the knee on one side for ease of walking. It also was simply belted with no puffing of peplos or kolpos.

The Ionic chiton was full enough to create an almost long-sleeved look. Occasionally, the Doric was worn opensided and over the Ionic. Over this was draped the himation, an outer garment that took great skill at both draping and wearing, so that the drapery stayed where one wanted it. Men also draped the himation over chitons, sometimes over nothing. The chlamys was a short rectangular cape worn by both men and women.

Women wore their hair either naturally, or pulled up into a bun at the back of the head, or, as it was called in the 1950s, in a ponytail. A circlet was often worn; this gradually developed a peaked front that was called a stephane. In time this was worn further back on the head,

creating a crown-like effect, which finally developed into the Roman diadem.

In early Greece men wore long hair and beards, but this gradually lost out to short hair and the clean-shaven look for young men. A head band was often worn. The older man or scholar wore a beard to denote age and wisdom.

Little jewelry is seen on the vases and paintings of Greece until the Hellenistic period when anything and everything was worn. This coincides with the Roman-Asiatic influences.

White was the favorite color of the aristocracy. The ordinary people wore dull shades of green, brown, and grey, but certain bright shades were known to exist. For some reason blue was not used. Though indigo was grown as far back as around 1400 B.C. and there does not seem to be any evident taboo against it, one simply does not find it. The Greeks devised a purple dye from mollusk shells, which was considered the ultimate of dyes, but even it was used very little until Roman domination.

Certain motifs were used over and over. We have seen both the scroll and the laurel in our silhouette. The "key" motif is used in the Roman silhouette. There is also the meander (shown in Fig. 5–4.1), the dentil (Fig. 5–4.2), the egg and dart (Fig. 5–4.3), and the anthemion (Fig. 5–4.4).

The three periods of Greece can easily be seen through their types of columns (Fig. 5–5), going from the earliest and simplest to the most complicated and latest.

1.

MEANDER

2.

DENTIL

3.

EGG & DART

4.

ANTHEMION

Figure 5–4.

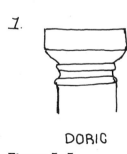

DORIC

IONIC

CORINTHIAN

Figure 5–5.

Best Sources

Greek vases and statuary

Well-known Playwrights

Aeschylus
Aristophanes
Euripides
Sophocles

Roman—800 B.C. to 450 A.D.

The Man—25 B.C.

The man in Figure 5–6 has won Imperial favor as identified by his laurel wreath. He carries

Figure 5–6. *800 B.C. to 450 A.D.*

a letter in his right hand. He wears a long tunic of a T-shape, called a Colabium, decorated by a border of a "key" motif at sleeves, neckline, and hem. He wears the white toga with the "purple" border called the toga praetexta over this. Unlike their Greek predecessors, the Romans thought it gauche to go barefoot indoors or out, and wore a wide variety of sandals.

The Woman—25 B.C.

The matron in Figure 5–6 wears what a Greek woman would call an Ionic chiton, which became a Roman lady's tunica. Over this is draped a "key" bordered palla, a female himation. (The male version was the pallium.) This palla is held onto the shoulder by a fibula (the Roman version of a decorated safety pin). Her hair is curled high on the forehead and supported by a diadem. Later this curly top would go to extremes and be combed over a wire frame. The back hair is held up by a semi-circular, perforated metal caul. She, too, wears sandals.

General Description

The Greeks originated; the Romans renamed and copied, almost wholesale. They took the Greek gods, architecture, and fashion, but they did improve upon a lot of things and were responsible for the dome, the curved arch, the toga, copper plumbing, and the importation of cotton around 180 B.C. They also took up painting as a fine art, using what we would later term realism and one-point perspective.

The uniqueness of the toga was that it was generally a gigantic semi-circle, usually about five to six yards long and about two yards wide at its widest point. At first, it was worn equally by men and women, replacing himations. Depending on its color and decoration, it had different significance.

There was the toga pura—all white (or cream) wool, shorter than others, used by any *free* citizen of Rome. The toga praetexta (illustrated) was the "purple"-bordered toga of public office. The toga candida was all white (bleached) worn by office seekers. The toga pulla was grey or black and was used for mourning. The toga picta was often embroidered and was worn for victory. The toga trabea was reserved for gods and emperors, who thought of themselves as gods (e.g., Caligula and Nero).

Gladiators wore the wrapped loincloth, which the Romans called a *subligaculum,* and various pieces of armor and studded leather, depending on weapon chosen. Those favored were the short sword, the trident and net, and the spear. Helmets were worn upon occasion.

The Roman soldier wore a brass or bronze molded and chastened cuirass, called a *lorica,* which was riveted to highly decorated leather strips that hung over the short tunic always worn underneath. This came to about three inches above the knee. Boots were worn to mid-calf, were of brown leather, and were called *caligulas.* Generals wore boots tied with red ties and short chaymers, called a *paludamentum,* of any length. Roman equestrians (the forerunner of what we would call the cavalry) wore a short purple-and-white striped tunic called the *tunic augustus clavis.* Slaves wore horizontal stripes and a leather collar around the neck with an iron ring in the center front so that they could be tied up at night. The Asian influence gave the kaftan to late Imperial Rome; Romans called it a *dalmatica.*

The Roman world can be divided into two sections; Republican Rome from 800 to 29 B.C. and Imperial Rome from 29 B.C. to 400 A.D. Republican Rome was simple in its philosophy and design. From 29 B.C. to about 200 A.D. was the Golden Age, which became progressively more frivolous, decadent, and disastrous. No country can long survive the excesses of decadence to which the Romans descended. Slaves were actually killed in the theater (a waste, not only of labor, but also memorization of all those lines). The Romans also staged real battles for amusement, and one must not forget all those lions! This descent into vulgarity can be seen in Roman fashions and artifacts.

Best Sources

Mosaics, statuary
Wall paintings of Pompeii and Herculeum

Well-known Playwrights

Plautus
Seneca
Terence

6

The Byzantines through the Romanesques

This time period is often called the "dark ages" because, in comparison to what had gone on before, these people seemed culturally deprived. Not only was the desire for the finer things in art and literature lost, but so was much work-a-day Roman knowledge. Can it all be blamed on the marauding barbarians? Even some of the nicknames of Romanesque kings shows a sad lacking in virtue: Pippin the Short, Charles the Bald, Louis the Sluggard (sometimes called "the fat"), and best of all, that well-known Saxon, Ethelred the Unready. One must compare this to Alexander, who was somewhere around five feet three inches tall and was known as "the great." The Byzantines fared somewhat better, but there were no new playwrights, no new arts, and not very much new in the way of fashion, just refinement of the old.

The one new stimulus seemed to come from Christianity, yet one cannot help but feel that its advent simultaneously impeded the arts as much as it progressed them. It was not until the Renaissance that classical foundations were regained. However, the desire for more had to

have been present. Great figures, both real and legendary, sprang up. King Arthur, Roland, and Beowulf fall into the latter category, but King Alfred and Charlemagne were real enough. It was indeed a paradoxical time.

Byzantine—400 to 900

The Man—500s

The man in Figure 6–1 wears the crown of an emperor, a flared diadem of gold bordered by pearls and set with large, square precious stones alternating with large round ones, mostly emeralds, which, if the mosaics are correct, were favored. Rubies and diamonds were also frequently used. The hair was cut short but somewhat full at the earlobe. Beards became popular around the 500s, but some men still remained clean-shaven.

This man wears a long tunic elaborately embroidered at hem, wrists, and neck. On the center front of his gown is a large square of em-

Figure 6–1. *Byzantine—400 to 900*

broidery set with precious stones. Such squares were also found on the rectangular cloaks and were called "tablions," often seen in ecclesiastical garments, as well. His cloak, called a paludamentum, fastened on one shoulder by a clasp, not unsimilar to the old Roman fibula. The bare arm and the bare legs of the Romans gradually disappeared. This man wears stockings and soft leather slippers.

The Woman–500s

The hair styles of Byzantine women like the one in Figure 6–1 stayed remarkably Roman. They often consisted of a series of knots, braids, and coils, but not as high as the old Roman style. Instead, coils were formed from side to side. On her head is an ornate diadem encrusted with precious stones and pearls. Ropes of pearls fall from it, as well. She also wears huge ornate earrings. Around her neck is a collar of gold and

precious stones. A series of teardrop pearls hangs around its bottom edge.

Byzantine ladies went in for the "layered" look. This woman wears an under tunica of fine combed cotton with shirred sleeves. Over this is a sleeveless tunica with an ornate gold and jeweled band at the bottom. Over all is the richly embroidered cloak, a vestige of the older Roman palla. It is pinned at the shoulder by a fibula. Like her male companion she wears stockings and soft leather shoes.

General Description

The people of Byzantium had their feet in two worlds simultaneously. One was the old Roman world, the other the customs and cultures of the Near East. It made for a gloriously rich civilization. The predominant color was metallic gold, which decorated everyone and everything in great profusion.

The mosaic art of this period has left us an excellent source of what the rich looked like. Once again, how the common person dressed is left to supposition. The favored colors were rich and somewhat dark hues of blues, coppers, browns, greens, plums, and "purple," which was reserved for the Emperor, as in Roman days. It was not the purple used by the Gothic people as royal, although this idea is surely a carry over from Roman influences. This "purple" was more of a cranberry or burgundy color. Chinese silk was used in great quantities; it was often unstrung and rewoven in a more sheer quality for veils and diaphanous fabrics. When this was done, a pastel tint of its former color remained. Gradually the process of growing and weaving silk was started in those sections of the Empire in which mulberry trees could be grown. Cotton was imported from Egypt and later grown and woven in Sicily and southern Italy. Wool was and remained the staple fabric.

The long gown was a symbol of wealth, wisdom, and station. Young men wore tunics to the knee for everyday life. Various length paludamentum (rectangular cloaks) were worn. Most of the time heads were bare. Sometimes a Phrygian-type cap was worn for riding or hunting. There is evidence that high boots of soft leather and studded with metal were also worn. The toga picta was worn into the late 700s by the Emperor and his council. This gradually became a long, narrow scarf that was wound across the chest and was known as the lorum. It was heavily embroidered and encrusted with jewels. It was only symbolic and eventually became the perogative of the Emperor alone. It lives on in a somewhat different form as an ecclesiastical garment (see Ecclesiastical costumes).

Women wore several variations to their gowns. One was an over tunica that was short-sleeved and mid-calf in length, showing the long sleeves and richly embroidered hem of the under tunica. The palla was sometimes worn as part veil, part cloak, or two pallas would be worn together.

The highly decorated collars worn by both men and women (and readily adopted by the West) are reminiscent of the collars of ancient Egypt. One cannot completely overlook the influence of the Coptic Christians at this time. The Copts were a group of native-born Christian Egyptians who refused to convert to Islam over many centuries. They were forced underground and developed an almost pictorial code of communication. For several centuries they kept in touch with their Byzantine fellow Christians, and a great deal of their motifs began to show up in the Byzantine culture. In 451 they split from Orthodoxy because of the Council of Chalcedon and its pronouncements concerning the nature of Christ. The Coptic sect is still prevalent in such divergent places as Ethiopia and Armenia.

From Rome came the Greco-Roman design (see Greek) motifs, including interlocking vines and leaves (see Roman), as well as the serpent and serpentine curves of the Norse. From Asia Minor came designs incorporating geometric patterns and animals of the hunt. Other symbols from early Christianity were also used in design. The earliest symbol of one Christian to another was the fish. The winged lamb, or just a plain lamb, was a symbol for Christ. Each author of the four gospels had a symbol—Matthew's was a winged man, Mark's a winged lion, Luke's a winged bull, and John's an eagle.

Figure 6–2 shows composite sketches taken from a Carolingian manuscript, *The Second Bible of Charles the Bald* (823–877). Charles was one of Charlemagne's sons. Strictly speak-

Figure 6–2. *Sketches from a Carolingian Manuscript.*

ing these designs may not be Byzantine, but they are so influenced by that culture one would be hard pressed to say where the Byzantine stops and the Romanesque begins. They transcend both cultures, as Charlemagne did by re-uniting them.

When the Church returned to Rome, it effectively split from the Church at Constantinople. For a while there were two Popes. (What had worked for the Imperial State of Rome five hundred years before was a dismal failure for the Roman Church.) Orthodoxy remained in much of the Middle East, Greece, Russia, and Middle Europe, and with it much of the Byzantine style of dress and design. Oddly enough, the Roman Church vestments owe their beginnings to Byzantium. The lorum, the stola, the tablion, the cope, miter, and chasuble can all be traced to Byzantium (see Ecclesiastical costumes). As we shall see, even the Romanesque

fashions owe much to Byzantium, but gradually they took on a life of their own.

Best Sources

Manuscripts of the early Coptic churches
Mosaics, particularly those in Ravenna, Italy
Russian icons

Ecclesiastical Garments and Vestments

Ecclesiastical garments are those worn by the clergy of the various Christian denominations. Although Protestant in philosophy, both the Anglican and Lutheran denominations still cling to essentially Roman Catholic vestments. Vestments are those items of apparel used in the church service itself or for church functions. Ecclesiastical garments are those worn by the clergy for every day. Figure 6–3 shows a few *composite*

Figure 6–3. *Ecclesiastical Vestments*

silhouettes of some church vestments taken from various portraits of people in the rank mentioned. No specific time is indicated, for with these vestments time seems suspended.

Lucy Barton, in *History of Costumes for the Stage,* believes that all vestments are Roman in origin. However, a far greater similarity can be seen between the Romanesque-Byzantine and these vestments, also the Gothic. In the sense that Roman evolved to Byzantine, Barton has a point, but the Byzantine is more direct, with practically no evolution required. The Gothic merely added to the Byzantine, while subtracting nothing.

The Pope

The Pope wears the three-tiered tiara that only the Pope may wear. This tiara came in around the 1300s. His cassock is white, with long, form-fitting sleeves. Over this he wears an alb bordered in lace and embroidery and fringed. It has belled sleeves and is a version of the dalmatica of Roman-Byzantine origin. Around his neck is the stole from the Byzantine lorum. Over this he wears an enormous semi-circular cape called the "cope"; it has a richly embroidered border on its straight edge. This was called an "orpherie," corresponding in shape and idea to the old Roman paenula.

The Pope generally wears all white, although the embroidery and stole correspond in color to the Church calendar.

The Cardinal

The cardinal wears a scarlet cassock that seems to have descended from a Byzantine kaftan-like garment, which can be traced all the way back to the Assyrians. Over this he wears a mantle shaped very like the Gothic peliçon. On his head is a biretta, which has appeared in various forms through the centuries, but is always square. The biretta is also worn by bishops and archbishops. All red became the official color for car-

dinals in the middle of the Gothic period. Color signifies rank.

The Archbishop

The archbishop wears the tall miter that came into being around 1300. Before that archbishops wore miters more like the bishop's. He, too, wears a cape with an embroidered orpherie. The exterior fabric of this garment is brocade; the interior is a solid, darker color. His inner robe is similar to the alb but has an overlapping front and a neck that is somewhat kimono-like. It is banded and belted in a cloth of gold. This robe is worn over a cassock just like the Pope's in cut. The archbishop carries an ornamental shepherd's crook called a crozier. He too wears a stole.

The Bishop

The bishop wears a miter of a somewhat lower and more squarish design. His cassock has a tablion of ornamental gold embroidery at the center front. Over this he wears the cotta, a garment similar to the alb but shorter and straighter in cut. This particular one is of a rich brocade with an embroidered and fringed border at hem and sleeves. Over this is the chasuble, egg-shaped in this case, also similar to the peliçon, but the chasuble preceded the peliçon by several centuries and therefore is more a descendent of the palla or the "collobium"; this was a transitional Roman-Byzantine garment, an enormous circle that seems to be slit on the radius for draping. This chasuble has also been richly embroidered and jeweled.

General Description

The Church calendar prescribed certain colored vestments for certain events. Green is the color used when no other color is prescribed; red is for Holy Week; white is for special Saint's Days, Christmas, and Easter; purple is for Advent and Lent. Until approximately ten years ago black was the color for the dead and dying, but it was changed to white to signify the Resurrection.

Though no longer used as a vestment color, black is used as a garment color. Priests are often associated with black suits and the "turned-around" clerical collar. This is actually a dickie-like garment of black with a stiffened white band around the neck and worn over a regular shirt, much like a vest. There are also detachable white collars that attach to a collarless black shirt, much like the regular men's shirt of the early 1900s. These turned-around collars are worn by Roman, Orthodox, Anglican, and some Lutheran clergy.

As one rises in the hierarchy of the Catholic Church, one wears the cassock (see Fig. 6–4). A priest's cassock is all black; a monseigneur wears a black cassock piped and buttoned in magenta with a magenta sash; bishops wear all magenta; cardinals wear all red; the Pope wears white. This is not a rule but merely a custom and

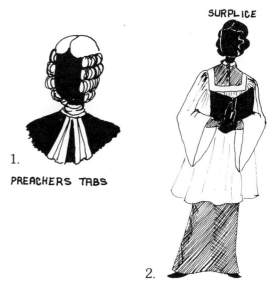

SURPLICE

1.

PREACHERS TABS

2.

Figure 6–5. *Preachers Tabs and Surplice*

is subject to change. Also in Fig. 6–4 is a low-crowned flat-brimmed hat. It is also worn by all members of clergy from monseigneur up. Color usually signifies rank.

Many Protestant denominations do not require their clergy to wear special clothing. The Presbyterians and Methodists at one time required their ministers to wear black and "preachers tabs" (Fig. 6–5.1) sometimes called preachers band. Many pastors today wear their academic robes in the pulpit. Choirs of many denominations wear a sleeveless cassock and a short alb-type garment called a surplice over it (Fig. 6–5.2). Many garments of the Orthodox Church are similar to those previously mentioned, but the high, truncated, conical hat is certainly its most distinctive item.

Figure 6–6 illustrates monastic garments called habits. These habits were everyday apparel at the time that a particular order was founded. The tradition of sameness and lack of worldly influences trapped these garments in an ecclesiastical time warp all their own. In the history of any order is the clue to what they wear. Again, these figures represent a composite, not any particular order.

Figure 6–4. *The Cassock*

Monastic Garments

The Monk

The monk in Figure 6–6 wears a hooded chaperone to which two long pieces of fabric are added in front and back, forming a sort of scapula. The edge of the hood has been stiffened, so that when it is down it forms a stand-up looking collar called a "cowl." Under this garment he wears a cassock tied around the waist with a rope belt. On his feet are sandals of either rope or leather.

If the hood were down, we would see the tonsure, a round shaved spot on the crown of the head. Sometimes a cap resembling a yarmulke was worn to keep that spot warm; this is called a tonsure cap.

The Nun

The nun in Figure 6–6 wears a stiffened toque-like headdress over her gorget. (In this case the word "gorget" takes on a slightly different meaning than in the Gothic military sense. It was a complete head covering with a hole for the face and ties in the back, not seen because of the veil.) A wimple is then worn around the neck and shoulders over her cassock-like habit and scapula. In this case, the scapula is a separate piece that hangs straight down from the shoulders, both in front and back. She wears a veil over the toque. Her inner sleeve is probably indicative of an under shift in the early days of the order, but it may also have been merely a fake lower sleeve. This nun wears soft leather shoes.

General Description

In any monastic order there is usually a progression of initiation, which is indicated by a slight differentiation in dress. For nuns one year is usually spent as a postulant, three years as a novitiate, and then a time for taking final vows. The rank of Mother Superior or Mother Abbess may be indicated by the type of veil worn, the color, the style of dress, or simply by some added piece of adornment. The cross on the scapula of the silhouette in Fig. 6–6 could indicate a Mother Abbess. The word "scapula" comes from the Latin word for shoulders, as this piece was only as wide as the shoulders.

Many orders take vows of poverty and exist only on what they themselves can produce. Therefore, they often grow their own flax and wool, weave it, dye it, and construct the garments. It often makes for a homespun look of uneven, somewhat bumpy fabric. This was called "monk's cloth." Today fabric manufactured to look like this is still called "monk's cloth."

Various orders picked various colors, but among monks creams, white, black, and browns

Figure 6–6. *Monastic Garments*

seem the colors most often used. Nuns have a little more selection. To the above grey, navy, and a very dark burgundy can be added. Some orders, such as the Dominicans, use black for cold climates and white for tropical ones. The fabrics chosen are generally highly serviceable ones.

The speed of twentieth-century life has taken its toll. The Sisters of Charity were those with the winged hats, but in Paris the hats became a traffic hazard, because the nuns had difficulty hearing oncoming automobiles. Many service orders have gone to modern dress as an aid to their jobs. Parochial school children can no longer rely on the clack of wooden rosary beads to indicated that retribution may only be one step around the corner.

Best Sources

Various Roman Catholic churches are exceedingly helpful when one is looking for specific information.[1] When I designed *The Dialogue of The Carmelites* in Pittsburgh, Pennsylvania, in 1965 a local Carmelite order graciously lent us its habits, complete with diagrams and explanation of how everything went together. The best advice is to go to the source.

Barbarian—400 to 1000

The Man—500s

The Viking warrior in Figure 6–7 wears the steel helmet with studded head band and bull horns, a symbol of virility that was supposed to cause great fear in the eyes of the enemy. He wears a short under tunic with tight sleeves, over which is another short-sleeved tunic of leather. Over this he wears a fur tabbard-like garment.

[1]I would like to thank both St. Joan of Arc and Ascension Roman Catholic Churches (Boca Raton, Florida) for their help with this section.

Figure 6–7. *Barbarian—400 to 1000*

His baggy pants are called "braies." These are drawn in and held up by leather straps wound around the leg. His shoes are of soft leather. Sometimes he strapped his lower arms; sometimes he wore metal cuffs, as in this figure.

His shield, usually round or oval, and a short flat sword were carried as almost standard equipment. His broad leather belt has a buckle with the lightning insignia on it. This was the mark of Thor, god of thunder and war. (See Norse mythological table.) The Nazis used it as the insignia for the S.S. during the Third Reich (even the swastika was once just an innocuous Arabic cross).

His last item of apparel is a necklace made of hide and bones and plaited hair worked together with a fine gold wire. Some evidence suggest that this might have been from his victim, like the bull's horn, to absorb the enemy's strength. More than likely it was from some valiant animal. Hair was generally shoulder-length, and beards were somewhat shaggy.

The Woman—500s

The Vikings invaded, among other places, eastern England and Scotland on a regular basis during the Dark Ages. One of the things they adopted from those they conquered was the art of weaving plaid, as the lady's shawl in Figure 6–7 shows.

She wears a woolen long-sleeved underdress and over this a chamois dress with short sleeves and laced up the front. Her shoes are of a sturdier leather. Her hair is worn in long braids like that of her Romanesque contemporaries, but instead of gold cords, hers are wrapped in leather strips. Her shoes are leather and much like the man's.

General Description

Two things were given civilization by the Vikings—excellent sailing vessels, which aided trade, explorations, and warfare, and knitting. No one knows exactly how old knitting is or how the idea got from one place to another, but the oldest evidence of it is in the Kon Tiki Viking Museum in Oslo, Norway. The Norwegians recently found a man in a bog of thawed tundra; he had been leatherized by the ground. Archeologists have dated him from around 2000 B.C. and he wore (also leatherized) knitted garments. It is believed that sailors were the first to crochet, an art they derived from repairing sails. The most prevalent design motif of the Viking culture is the serpent, which is remarkably like the serpent designs of ancient Mexico. Viking ships had serpent heads on their tall bows to ward off the monsters of the deep.

Figure 6–8.   *Fish Scale Armor*

How old is the art of weaving plaid? It too has no definite date. It is known that the earliest plaids were those of even weave and of only two colors. It is generally believed that the ancient people of Scotland were the first to weave plaid, but it was commonly used in the Viking culture as well.

Because of a group of Viking mercenaries employed by a Byzantine Emperor, we have a fairly good idea what they looked like. They were called the Varangian Guard and they found their way into several Byzantine mosaics. There is evidence that both Varangian and Byzantine soldiers sometimes wore armor made of a series of linked plates that looked like fish scales; so did that early Greeks. This is illustrated in Figure 6–8.

Best Sources

Byzantine mosaics
Stave churches

Romanesque—400 to 1200

The Woman—1100

The queen in Figure 6–9 is wearing a crown not unsimilar to her Byzantine contemporary. It is of gold and enamel work with gypsy set precious stones. Pearls edge the top and bot-

Figure 6—9. *Romanesque—400 to 1200*

tom. The crown holds a short veil in place. Her hair is worn in very long braids intertwined with golden cords.

She wears an undershift of linen, which has tight, long sleeves, over which is worn a very full gown with "angel wing" (my own term) sleeves.

On top of this she wears a kirtle (also kirdel or kirdle) of fine gold mesh. The neckline and arms are banded in leather studded and jeweled. Although this kirtle extends to her upper hip and even further in the center front, it is belted with a jeweled belt. Below that she wears what will later be known as a girdle (see early Gothic). It is a long knotted scarf. The word girdle comes from the verb "to gird"; to surround, to prepare for self-protection, as in the biblical expression "gird one's loins" (hips). Therefore, a girdle was originally a hip protector.

Over all of this she wears a fully lined and richly bordered mantle of a semi-circular cut. This, as well as the Ecclesiastical vestment called a "cope," were both derived from the early Roman toga.

The Man—1100

The king in Figure 6–9 wears a simple gold crown set with precious stones. It is worn over a cloth cap, not unlike a yarmulke. Unlike his Byzantine counterpart, this Romanesque man wears his hair long and flowing. By this time both cultures wore well-trimmed beard and moustaches.

This man, like his wife, wears to the ankle a long-sleeved woolen gown somewhat fuller than the shift. The cuffs are richly embroidered in gold and semi-precious stones. Next, he wears an ankle length short sleeved tunic, which has been belted and then pulled up to mid-calf length, while blousing over said belt. This is made of a soft wool, as well. A rectangular mantle of a double fabric is clasped with an enormous gold and jeweled brooch on the left shoulder.

The lining fabric is probably wool for warmth, while the outer fabric is a heavy silk encrusted with embroidery and banded on all sides by a gold border.

He wears stockings and richly embroidered slippers and carries a scepter.

General Description

Because of a lack of paintings, it is very hard to know what was worn in the Romanesque period. Our best sources are church statuary and tomb effigies. A conflict of research arises when one is told that two of the statues of Chartres Cathedral represent King Clovis I and his sainted wife Queen Clothilde. Clovis was a Frankish king and founder of the Merovingian dynasty who died in 511. His wife expired shortly thereafter. The church was completed several centuries later, but when were the statues actually done? Those several centuries seems to stretch fashion's credibility a bit far.

As with the Byzantine Empire, the prevalent design motifs were geometric in nature and encompassed certain early Christian symbols (see Byzantine silhouette and description). Yet northern Europe was also greatly influenced by the intricate ever-entwining circles and curves of the Celtic and Teutonic-Norse cultures. One of the best sources for decorative details of this is the Book of Kells.

When St. Patrick went to Ireland he founded monasteries. There the monks transcribed the first four books of the New Testament into Gaelic and beautifully illuminated this manuscript. Beside the design motifs, it gives an excellent idea of the Romanesque love of color, an almost pure pigment that would extend well into the gothic times.

St. Patrick is also held responsible for the in-

corporation of the Celtic Cross into Christian art (Fig. 6–10.1). The Franks introduced the trefoil cross in this period. The word trefoil is an Anglicization of the French *trois feuille,* meaning three leafed (Fig. 6–10.2).

During the late Romanesque era (after the Norman conquest) a style of mantle not unlike the ecclesiastical chasuble became fashionable for ladies. It was called a "peliçon" (see Fig. 6–11). At this time the peliçon was egg-shaped with a hole for the head (see Fig. 6–12). Some times a hood would be added. Often it was fur-lined. It would go through several transfor-

Figure 6–10. *Celtic and Trefoil Crosses*

Figure 6–11. *Peliçon*

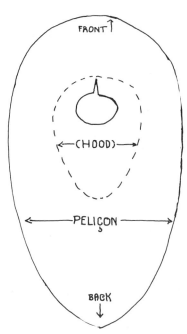

Figure 6–12. *Construction of Peliçon*

mations in the coming centuries (see Early Gothic).

The peliçon should not be confused with the pelisse illustrated in Figure 6–13. This was a mid-calf length overgown worn one way or another by Romanesque ladies from the 700s on. Sometimes it was worn with a belt at the natural waist, sometimes it was belted just below the breasts. In the 700s no belt was worn and the garment was of a somewhat straighter cut. There were short-sleeved versions, belled-sleeved versions, and the combination pictured here.

If it looks Russian or Slavic, this is not surprising. Byzantine-Romanesque-like garments were worn in Russia right up to the 1917 revolution. Many middle European folk costumes can be traced back to this era.

Figure 6–14 shows a Frankish knight of the mid-700s. His football-like helmet complete with noseguard is worn over an elongated gorget of squared metal plates that have been attached to an inner gorget of leather. Under this he wears

Figure 6–13. *Pelisse*

Figure 6–14. *Frankish Knight*

a tight, long-sleeved mid-calf length tunic. Around his upper hips and waist is a girdle of similar metal plating. He wears form-fitting, toeless leather boots and his toes are bare. His shield is a fascinating combination of riveting, woven strips, and studding.

The early Norman male favored a peculiar hair style that deserves recognition (see Fig. 6–15). The hair was brushed downward in all directions from the crown and then clipped in a circle even with the eyebrows and the top of the ears. Any hair below that on the back of the head was shaved off; however, those same gentlemen often sported gigantic walrus-like moustaches.

This may have been done for more comfortable wearing of the Norman armor shown in Figure 6–16. This Norman knight wears only half of the football for a helmet that has been banded and ribbed for added strength; the nose guard remains. His gorget and haulberk are made of a large linked chain mail and edged in studded leather. The haulberk has a slit up front and back for greater mobility. His lower arms are bound in leather strips over the sleeves of an inner tunic. He wears heavy woolen stockings and his legs are encased in leather straps for added protection. His gauntlets are of padded and quilted leather for either battle or hawking. Over his right hip a broadsword is suspended in a

Figure 6–16. *Norman Armor*

studded leather scabbard. He carries a battle ax in his right hand.

Although obviously the Romanesque people could have had the same fabric choices as the Byzantine and sometimes royalty did have costly silks and cottons, the staples were linen and wool. Leather and metals were used for armor and various furs provided warmth.

Best Sources[2]

Book of Kells
Carolingian manuscripts
Romanesque churches

[2]An excellent new slide program is available for viewing at the Pierpont Morgan Library in New York City, which is based on their excellent collection of Romanesque, Gothic, and early Renaissance manuscripts. There is also an excellent article on these manuscripts and their development in the February 1981 issue of *The Smithsonian Magazine.*

Figure 6–15. *Norman Hair Style*

7

Gothic

The thrust of Gothic thought was an upward movement to God, and God must have seemed very high up indeed. The architecture pointed heavenward and by the late Gothic period so did the fashions. This late Gothic period was called "high" Gothic, the quintessence of the upward thrust. It was also the basis not only for ecclesiastical structure but for feudal structure as well. The strong protected the weak and in return the weak slaved for the strong. This latter principle has been known as the code of chivalry.

The ideals of chivalry were threefold: might for right, the strong protector of the weak, and the honor of womanhood. The ideal women were the Rowenas of the world—blonde, blue-eyed, uneducated, and helpless. They were only good for child-bearing. In the great majority of our fairy tales, heroines are blonde and blue-eyed, and they all got married and lived happily ever after.

To examine the great similarity between the structures of the feudal system and of the Church, see Table 7–1, which includes French and English names, and female and church equivalents.

Table 7–1. Structures of the Feudal System and the Church

English	French	Female	Church
King	Roi	Queen	Pope
Duke	Duc	Duchess	Cardinal
Earl	Marquis	Marchiness	Archbishop
Baron	Baron	Baroness	Bishop
Lord	Seigneur	Lady	Monsigneur
Count	Comte	Countess	Priest
Knight	Chevalier	Dame[2]	Abbot
Squire	Esquire[1]		Monks
			Nuns
Page	Page[1]		Lay Brothers

[1]*There is no female equivalent to squires and pages, except perhaps a lady-in-waiting.*

[2]*The wife of a Lord, Count, or Knight may be addressed as "Lady." To be a "Dame" was an honor a woman earned in her own right.*

The most important historical events of this period, from a fashion point of view, were the Crusades. They gave purpose to the ideals of chivalry and new motifs to designs of heraldry, and opened up trade routes with Byzantium and the Near East. Cotton was imported from Italy. Silk was brought back from the "Holy Lands," a term the crusaders used for Byzantium. New weaving techniques were developed and imported first to France and then, thanks mainly to Eleanor of Aquitaine, to England. Combination fabrics were used, such as linsey-woolsey and "fustion," a linen-cotton blend. Velvets were imported at great expense. A new gossamer-like woolen fabric was called "lyraigne."

The peasant tended to use more stable fabrics like homespun, "carry-marry" (a nubby woolen), and russet, a fabric that got its name from its back dye, a color akin to Georgia clay.

Early Gothic—1200 to 1300

The Man—1215

The gentleman in Figure 7–1 might well be Ivanhoe or Robin Hood dressed for the signing of the Magna Carta (1215). He wears a long-sleeved, mid-calf length tunic of fine wool, which has been trimmed at hem, neck, and wrists with heavy gold embroidery. This tunic is worn over a "sherte" of linen in a darker shade. Combed woolen, hand-knitted stockings cover his legs. His shoes, although unadorned, are of the best quality leather.

The tunic is belted and from it is suspended a broadsword in its leather scabbard. Even a knight without armor needed this constant assurance. On top of all this he wears a hooded mantle of a heavy dark wool that has been bag lined in a lighter weight woolen of a contrasting color. Although we cannot see much of it, a gold corded embroidery embellishes the border of this mantle as well. It is held together by a

Figure 7–1. *Early Gothic—1200 to 1300*

brooch of gold filigree and enamel work, which characterizes much of Romanesque and Early Gothic jewelry.

The Woman—1215

The lady in Figure 7–1 wears an undergown of a dark "linsey-woolsey" fabric. It has long, form-fitting sleeves that somewhat cover the back of the hands and button at the wrists. Buttons were expensive and often made of bone, wood, or various metals. Lacing was popularly employed to save this cost. Under the undergown would be the ever practical shift, changed very little from its Romanesque predecessor.

The outer gown was known as a "bliaut" with belled sleeves. It has been slit up the sides and then laced to the waist to give more form to the figure. Both sleeves and hem have been banded with embroidery. Romanesque geometric and celtic designs are still the most popular. Around her hips she wears a girdle of leather that has been edged in gold, studded, and jeweled. Jewels were still unfaceted and held in "gypsy" settings—i.e., held by a ring of gold.

We know this lady is married, because her hair is bound and covered. Around her shoulders and throat she wears a wimple of soft linen. Her veil is held in place by a circlet of gold.

General Description

Heraldry gathered great momentum during the Crusades and some of the insignia of this time were the crusaders' plain, equally square, red cross (Fig. 7–2.1), the red cross of the knights' templar (Fig. 7–2.2) and the black Maltese cross of the order of St. John of Malta. (Fig. 7–2.3.)

Figure 7–3 shows a crusading knight. The style of the helmet has changed to one of an upside down bucket. The chain mail gorget is about the same as that of his Norman predecessor, but the chain mail suit is in two pieces—a short tunic with long sleeves and mail hosen. Sometimes each leg was separate and worn over stockings. The outer garment was the forerunner of the cyclas, which would later become the tabbard.

The peasant man generally wore a knee-length tunic over a "sherte" (to become shirt) and a wrapped diaper-like loincloth. A fashion for wearing stockings gartered at the knee and rolled down to it was seen in the countryside. Sometimes two pairs of stockings were worn

Figure 7–3. *Crusading Knight*

together, the outer one rolled down. A great variety of straw hats was worn as sun shields. Originally these were worn by themselves, but by the mid-Gothic they were often worn over the coif. In place of the bliaut, women sometimes wore an exceedingly full, sleeveless outer gown gathered to a circular yoke, not unlike the Hawaiian mumu. From the Germanic countries came a style of wearing a short, open-fronted jacket with tight, long sleeves. This was cut in a form-fitting manner and reached to the lower hip.

Heavy gold embroidery was the legacy of Byzantium and left little room for jewelry. Some of this embroidery had jewels set into it. Three popular jewelry items, however, were brooches, crowns or circlets for the head, and rings. The wedding ring was a custom practiced by the nobility and the peasants copied it, although their rings were often of steel or iron.

1. 2. 3.

Figure 7–2. *Heraldic Crosses*

Another wedding custom that should be mentioned was the binding of the bride's hair. Evidently a woman's tresses were considered to produce lust in the male eye. After marriage a woman only let her hair down, literally, in the presence of her immediate family. Queens were excepted from this, but eventually they too bound and covered it. If a woman became a nun and married God, her hair was cut off as a sacrifice to her vows.

Best Sources

The Bayeux Tapestry
Tomb and church sculptures
The Visconti Book of the Hours

The Resurgence of the Dramatic Tale

This was the time of the troubadors, who traveled from castle to castle carrying the latest news and gossip, as well as time-honored stories, usually performed in songs called ballads. Often yesterday's news became today's story, and after a century or so, tomorrow's legend. A professor of mine once said, "For every pound of legend there is probably a grain of truth."

A priest by the name of Alan de la Hales wrote what amounted to the first musical in a playlette about Robin Hood. Is it mere coincidence that one of Robin's merry men, and a minstrel at that, was named Alan a Dale?

Middle Gothic—1300 to 1400

The Man—1340

The knight in Figure 7–4 wears a helmet of riveted plate armor with a hinged visor that has eye slits. He wears a coat of mail, tunic and stockings, and mail shoes. Over this he wears plate armored elbow guards, knee guards, and grieves to protect the lower leg. The chain mail has become much finer than in the days of the

Figure 7–4.   *Middle Gothic—1300 to 1400*

Norman conquest. His gauntlets are of plate armor. Underneath the chain mail he might wear a halbrick of heavily padded and quilted leather or canvas-like fabric.

Over the coat of mail is worn a tabbard emblazoned in the quartered colors of his coat of arms, as is his shield. This was for easy identification during battle, so one did not kill one's friend by accident. (It also made one's enemy easier to find.) He carries a broadsword. He also wears spurs. Spurs were won by knights for valor on the the field of battle, so they tended to be the identifying mark of the noblemen who acted as the "officer" class.

The Woman–1340

The lady in Figure 7–4 is about to bestow a handkerchief on her knight as a favor that he may wear into the lists or battle. She wears a cotehardie version of an undergown with quartered sleeves (the top half of each sleeve a different material than the bottom half), which come down and cover the back of the hands. These sleeves were very tight-fitting and required many buttons. Just above her elbow she has added "tippets," separate hanging sleevelets whose outside matches the upper quarter of the undergown and whose inside is still one more contrasting fabric.

Over the undergown is worn the female cyclas. It is sideless to the hip line. This one has been quartered with colors of the wearer's coat of arms. This heraldry mania was quite fashionable for a while.

Her hair is parted in the center, then braided and coiled into two elongated roll casings called "templettes" that are suspended from the jeweled headband and kept from flopping about by means of a short "barbette," a chin strap. She wears a veil only down her back, not over the top of her head. This either shows her unmarried condition or her rank.

General Description

If the knights were the officer class of their day then anyone below the rank of squire was the "enlisted man" of his day. The squires and pages acted as sergeants and corporals, or NCOs, of this time. Often the enlisted men wore a similarly-styled garment, made of padded and metal-studded leather with belled upper sleeves worn over a warm undertunic with long sleeves and gaitered woolen hosen. This padded and studded garment was called a gambeson.

Several important historical events had great influence on fashion. The continuation of the Crusades through 1272 helped keep the trade lanes to the Middle East open. Marco Polo went to China several times, returning for good in 1295. Besides bringing back gun powder (in the form of fireworks) and spaghetti (and pasta, in general), he also brought back new fabrics and new weaving and dyeing techniques. Silk was

used long before and called "Samite"; however, a type of heavy raw silk called "tartaire" (from the word Tartar) and a fine camel's hair woolen cloth called "camelot" were then introduced. It certainly was the beginning of the cut loop technique used to make velvet. Velvet had been imported at great expense as far back as Romanesque times. Many believe that the technique was not duplicated in Europe in great quantity until around 1290.

Heraldry had developed greatly since the days of the Norman Conquest. As families intermarried they combined their symbols and shields became quite complicated. Figure 7–5 shows the chevron, whose point could go up as well, and barred. The bar sinister at first usage meant bastardy. Animals, both real and mythical, became part of the shield and when space ran out on the shield itself, helmets and ribbons complete with mottos were added. The whole thing became knows as the family crest.

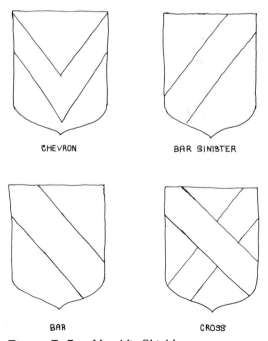

Figure 7–5. *Heraldic Shields*

To the list of identifying crosses of the Early Gothic must be added the Eleanor Cross. Edward I was married to Eleanor of Castile and was very much in love with her, an unusual state for royal marriages. When she died in 1290 he erected a stone cross at every place in which her body spent the night on its funeral journey. There were thirteen in all, only three of which are still standing. Geddington Cross is one of these. An excellent bronze effigy of Eleanor is on her tomb in Westminster Abbey.

When a man was not dressed for battle, he often wore a mid-calf length, sleeved tunic. Over that he wore either a surcoat or the male version of the cyclas. The surcoat was a belled-sleeved garment, which opened down the front and could be either mid-calf or floor length. The cyclas was cut something like a priests's scapula (see Ecclesiastical Garments), only not quite so narrow. The center hole was put over the head and then belted. Sometimes the sides were sewn up from hem to waist, leaving slit openings for the arms. Generally, if the tunic was mid-calf length the outer garment followed. There was even a fashion for adding a tubular piece of fabric to the neck hole and then letting it fall softly around the throat in a cowl-like effect.

In the middle of the 1300s the style for a short form-fitting garment called the cotehardie was made for men. Women had a version of this that was used as an undergown or by itself. In Figure 7–6, you will note that a chaperon is worn with the male cotehardie. It has a long lirepipe and castleated edge, but otherwise differs not at all from its Romanesque predecessor.

Another item that retained the name but changed the look was the peliçon. It was no longer the egg-shaped cape of the Romanesque, but a huge, three-quarter, circular, sleeveless garment worn by both men and women.

The underwear of the day should be mentioned. Women still wore the sleeveless, floor-length shift. Men wore a boxer short type of item called "slops" and a fitted sleeveless jacket to which they tied their stockings by means of "points." When the cotehardie became fashionable, this under jacket was often padded in the chest to give a better physique. Sometimes a corset of boned leather was worn to nip in the waist. Men even padded the calves of their legs. When the female cotehardie came into fashion, women returned to wearing a waist cincher type garment as well.

Head gear started to become fascinating. The close-fitting coif was standard for everyone from nobleman to peasant (see Fig. 7–7.1). They were made in many different ways (a helpful hint is to enlarge a baby bonnet pattern to fit the adult head.) A high-domed crown set within an extremely pointed visor brim was very fashionable from about 1250 on (Fig. 7–7.2). It could be worn with or without ties. Add a feather and voilà! You have Errol Flynn as Robin Hood, albeit several years too late for fact.

The married woman still bound and covered her hair. The style of a toque placed inside a crown was seen as early as the mid-1100s and continued in popularity until the late gothic (Fig. 7–7.3). Hair was first braided and then coiled over the ears in a style called "ramshorns." Special metal wire and often jeweled cauls were worn over these, called "crespines" (Fig. 7–7.4). The "porkpie" hat of Figure 7–7.5 was either worn by matrons as illustrated, or with a veil under it. The most peculiar fashion for men was the tall crowned hat of molded felt, called a "sugarloaf" (Fig. 7–7.6). Often both men and women wore one hat on top of another, as seen in Figure 7–7.7.

On the subject of hair one item should be noted. Phillip IV (le bell) of France decreed that all Parisian prostitutes be easily identifiable and dye their hair red with henna. As they were presumably unmarried, their heads were uncovered. This flaming-haired lady-of-the-evening concept has been with us in fiction from then until the twentieth century, when she was finally replaced by the peroxide blonde.

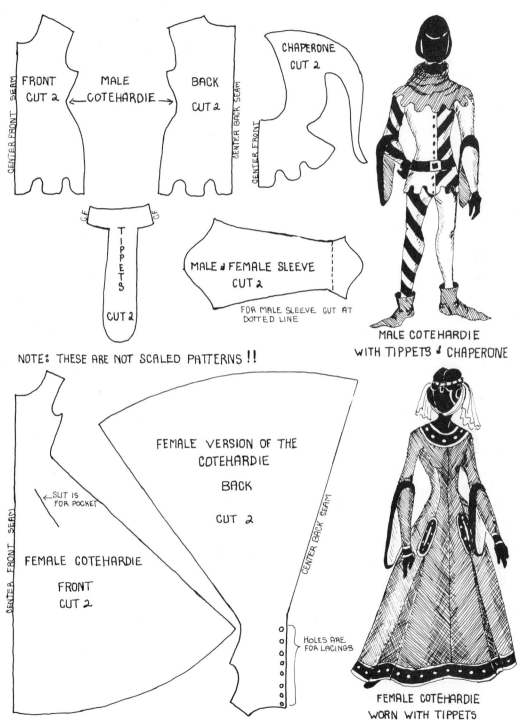

CHAPERONE
CUT 2

FRONT
CUT 2

MALE
COTEHARDIE

BACK
CUT 2

CENTER FRONT SEAM

CENTER BACK SEAM

CENTER FRONT

TIPPETS
CUT 2

C.F.   C.F.

MALE & FEMALE SLEEVE
CUT 2

FOR MALE SLEEVE CUT AT
DOTTED LINE

NOTE: THESE ARE NOT SCALED PATTERNS !!

MALE COTEHARDIE
WITH TIPPETS & CHAPERONE

FEMALE VERSION OF THE
COTEHARDIE

BACK

CUT 2

CENTER FRONT SEAM

CENTER BACK SEAM

←SLIT IS
FOR POCKET

FEMALE COTEHARDIE

FRONT
CUT 2

HOLES ARE
FOR LACINGS

FEMALE COTEHARDIE
WORN WITH TIPPETS

Figure 7–6. *Male and Female Cotehardie*

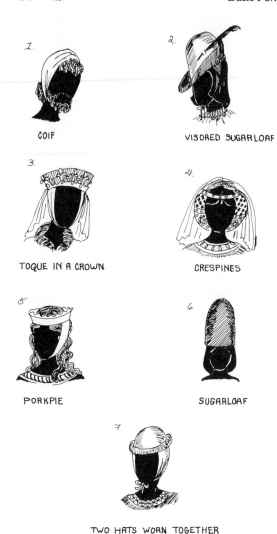

Figure 7–7. *Coif and Head Gear*

Best Sources

Pietro Cavallini
Cimbue
Duccio
Giotto
Ambrogio Lorenzetti
Pietro Lorenzetti
Simon Martini
Girard d'Orleans
Guido da Siena

One of the best sources of this period are sculptures, both tomb and church. Gothic churches took several hundred years to build and may encompass several styles. Another excellent source is the brass rubbings of tomb plates in the floors of these same churches. Any nobles who contributed large sums of money to the building of these churches had their remains laid in the foundations and these plates were used as markings.

The Resurgence of the Dramatic Tale

Alan de la Hale's musical playlette of Robin Hood (see Early Gothic) continued to be popular. So were the miracle and mystery plays produced by the Church in an effort to teach an illiterate population Bible stories and the lives of saints. An early form of the Punch and Judy show was popular at fairs. To the list of the troubadors' romances can be added two Scottish tales, *Lord Randell* and *Edgar* (sometimes called *Edward*). Both of these young men were done in by their sweethearts and died in their mother's arms. This is also the time of Geoffrey Chaucer and his *Canterbury Tales. The Travels of Marco Polo* is an excellent account of two worlds at this time.

Late (High) Gothic—1400 to 1485

The Man—1435

The dandy in Figure 7–8 wears a liripipe roundel, jupon (sometimes called pourpoint), hosen and turned-up, pointed shoes, all considered quite the mode in 1435 or there about. The roundel on his head is nothing more than an enormous stuffed doughnut and the liripipe is exaggeratedly long, up to approximately two yards. This particular roundel has a crown in it, but just as many were crownless. The liripipe is not merely as decorative as it looks. It gives balance when wrapped around the shoulders.

A fad for high, stand-up collars, seen on this jupon, started around 1400. They were stiffened to stand up and away from the bare neck. Often the jupon was gored and padded to give a ridged look between the seams. Sometimes they were cut very full and multi-darts were taken. Some were yoked in squares, Vs, or rounded, as this one is. His heavy gold chain covers that seam. This jupon has a semi-houppelande type of sleeve with scalloped dagging. The sleeve lining and the gore inserts are of the same fabric in a shade darker than the outer garment. He wears finely hand-knitted silk hosen in a color to match his roundel. His shoes have points so long that they have been turned up and undoubtedly stuffed at the ends to hold their shape.

Under this jupon he would wear a tunic of either fine wool (for cold weather) or linen. The sleeves of this tunic can be seen under his enormous jupon sleeve. His gold worked belt matches his neck chain in design.

The Woman—1435

The damsel in Figure 7–8 wears the high-belted, wide-collared houppelande so typical of this period. Worn by both women and mature men, it did not actually have a waist, but was cut like a tent dress that was then drawn in or belted under the breasts. The collar was sometimes cut into the dress and turned back. Often it was a separate piece added on. It has the typically ground-sweeping sleeves finished in deep scalloped dagging and lined with a contrasting fabric. The skirt of the houppelande became so long that this lady is forced to hold it up when walking. Because this allows the underside to show, it is faced with the same fabric as the sleeves. It also exposes the undergown of a pale colored silk embroidered with fleur de lis. The undergown has form-fitting sleeves with a cuff of contrasting fabric, which, as shown, can be turned down over the hand for added warmth in drafty castles.

She wears a high conical hennin with a hanging veil. The hennin is banded in the same velvet as the houppelande and is embroidered in the fleur de lis of the undergown. It is held on by a V-shaped wire over the center curve of the forehead and a barbette of fine white linen, which goes under the chin.

Around her neck is a fine gold chain with a pendent of precious stones in the newest fashion, which the wide bare neckline allows. Her forehead hairline has been plucked out, or shorn off, so that no hair shows beneath the headdress.

General Description

Probably the single most fascinating fashion item of the High Gothic period was the female desire for extreme headdresses, some of which are shown in Figure 7–9. Some of them became

Figure 7–8. *Late (High) Gothic—1400 to 1485*

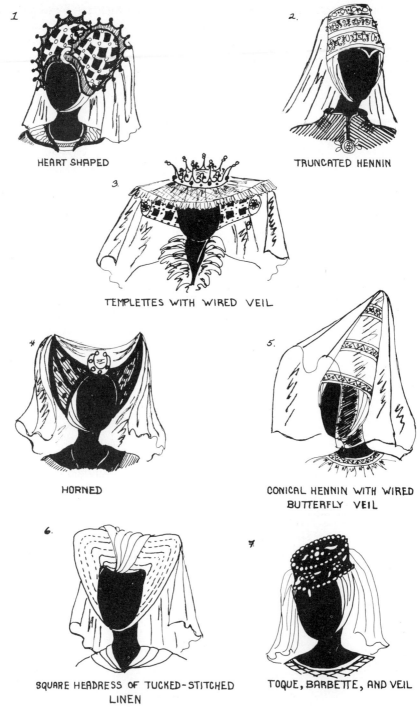

Figure 7–9. *Some Late Gothic Headdresses*

so high, wide, and handsome that the doors of the Chateau Blois had to be recut to accommodate them. The earliest of those illustrated (Fig. 7–9.3) was fashionable during the time of Jeanne D'Arc. It is nothing more than an exaggerated version of the templettes of the earlier century (see Mid-Gothic silhouette) with a wired veil and crown. The headdress shown in Figure 7–9.7 appears in simplified form in the Mid-Gothic times as well. This is a jeweled and beaded version and comes from a tomb carving in Spain. The squarish headdress (Fig. 7–9.6) seems to have been worn by middle class women. The French women called the veil head covering a "couvrechef," which was anglicized into "kerchief"; one carried in the hand became a "handkerchief."

The hairline was plucked back and the very long back hair was braided and coiled under the headdresses. The custom of only unmarried virgins showing their hair still persisted. Several different tales explain why the hairline was plucked back. Most agree that it was because the queen had suffered a hair loss and the Court did not want to embarrass her. Just which queen this was is a subject of question.

The male hair style was short, probably because of the excessively high collars. Beards and moustaches were pretty much a matter of choice, although the younger men seemed to prefer to be clean-shaven. Giles de Rais of France was known as "Bluebeard," because he dyed his beard and goatee a blue-black, leaving his own sandy color on his head.

The ideal blonde, blue-eyed heroine of the troubadors romances still persisted and women concocted all manner of recipes for bleaching their hair (only to cover it up). They also plucked their eyebrows to a pencil-thin line and in some cases plucked them out altogether to paint them on further up the forehead.

From Germany came the custom of wearing bells attached to belts, hats, shoes and sleeves. Is this where we get the idea of bells as part of the traditional court jester's costume?

The points on the shoes became so long that they were attached by gold or silver chains to garters around the leg. Pattens, thick wooden soles with instep straps, were worn over the slippered foot to keep the more delicate material of such slippers out of the mud. The peasants who did not have time for fancy points wore wooden shoes that looked just like our present day clogs.

Dagging was the name given to the cutting of edges into designs. The silhouette has illustrated the deep scallops. There were also foliated, daggered, and castellated. Often these edges were trimmed in braid or fur, or richly embroidered. This dagging appeared almost anywhere on the garments and for both men and women.

The same could be said for the hemline on male garments. Jupons stopped anywhere between crotch line and knee. The gown could be either mid-calf or floor length.

The headdresses and long sleeves precluded any use of bracelets or earrings, and the high collars cancelled out necklaces, until women started wearing them when the neckline was once more bared. Brooches were worn on both clothing and headdresses. Many things were hung from the belts of both men and women. The "misericorde" or short dagger, which was as important a utensil as the penknife is today, was one item. Pomanders and relicqueries were also suspended from the belt.

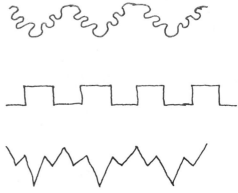

Figure 7–10. *Dagging*

Jeanne D'Arc was the first woman in history to rebel against skirts and don male attire for purely practical reasons. This also accounts for her hair cut. It caused more of a scandal than her voices did in the beginning. The female population at this time was truly outraged.

Favored furs were ermine, miniver (the belly fur of grey squirrels), and squirrel for the rich. The poor made do with fox, rabbit, or muskrat, and occasionally wolf. Sheepskin was used to line whole garments, as was astrakhan (young lamb pelts).

Favored colors were still the bright shades or red, gold, blue, and green, almost pure tones. Velvet had come into its own. Silks and fine cotton were worn by the rich. The poor made do with homespun, wool, linen, and homemade dyes. Purple was still the most expensive dye and only kings (or those very close to them) could afford it, so it continued to be associated with royalty, hence the expression "born to the purple."

Figure 7–11 shows the armor of the late 1400s. (This was proported to be what Richard III wore at Bothwell Field.) The rivetted plating encompasses almost the entire body, or certainly all that would allow for mobility. This was worn over a fine mesh mail. A complete suit of armor could weigh over one hundred pounds. The knight had to be hoisted onto his saddle by means of a block and tackle.

For me it has always been a source of amusement to have Richard III running around Bothwell Field screaming, "A horse! A horse! My kingdom for a horse!" If he had one, he could not possibly have mounted it. It is true that Richard III was so fond of his crown that not only did he wear it into battle, but contemporary accounts said he even wore it to bed.

Armor in the Renaissance was embellished with designs and worm more for ceremony than battle. Henry VIII had a suit of armor made of gold. Gradually, as will be seen, it lost out as being ineffective against guns.

Figure 7–11. *Armor of the Late 1400s*

There is an excellent museum of armor in Milan, Italy. In England, many castles display interesting suits of armor, but the old armory of Warwick Castle has some extraordinary pieces, including horse armor.

Best Sources—Artists

Henri Bellechase
Dieric Bouts
Robert Campin
Petrus Christus

Guillaume Dombet
Jean Fouquet
Nicolas Froment
Nuno Gonclaves
Simon Marmion
Quentin Massys
Hans Memlinc
Pisanello
Jan Van Eyck
Hugo Van Der Gaes
Rogier Van Der Weyden
Master of Werden
Conrad Witz

Several excellent sources of everyday Gothic life for rich and poor alike can be found in the minature illustrations in the Duc du Berry's *Tres Riches Heures* (Book of the Hours) painted by Pol de Timbourge, *The Book of the Hours of Etienne Chevalier* by Jean Fouquet, and the Lady and the Unicorn tapestries in the Musee du Cluny, Paris, France.

The Resurgence of the Dramatic Tale

The miracle and mystery plays continued, as did certain romances. Troubadors still went from castle to castle. The list of romances now included the tales of *Abelard and Helouise* and *Robert the Bruce,* as well as those mentioned in mid-Gothic. The court jester came into his own and several were written into history for their valiant deeds, including Genisius, who became a saint at approximately this time, although he lived in the dark ages of Christianity.

8

The Renaissance

While the rest of Europe was still in the throes of high Gothic philosophy, Italy had already entered the Renaissance—a revival or return to things classical in the Greco-Roman mode. This rediscovery stimulated a great bursting, first in the arts and then in philosophy. Perhaps it was philosophy that lead to changes in the arts. Either way, it did bring people's thoughts down from their lofty view of God to thoughts of their own power and capabilities of self-achievement in all aspects of life, science, and the arts.

This philosophy can be seen stirring the minds of Europe as its fashions move across the map, first Italy and then her immediate northern neighbors, Austria and Germany. Martin Luther's Reformation was one result. God was no longer for the hereafter but for the here and now. "How many angels could sit on the head of a pin?" was a question much discussed by Gothic clergy. Luther's answer was a cobweb-sweeping "Who cares?" The answer did not satisfy all, but it certainly let some air and energy into closed minds and even succeeded in establishing a reaffirmation of faith in the counter-reformation.

It has always seemed paradoxical that the Italians, who remained Catholic, painted lus-cious nudes of classical themes, while the Germans, who turned Protestant, painted tortured figures of hell and damnation, such as those of Bosch and Grunewald.

The most prevalent visual factor of the Rennaissance, which transcended all of the European nations, was what can be termed the "square look." Italy returned to the construction of symmetrical architecture of classic proportions. Spain gave the square headdress. A good quantity of the yokes and necklines were squared. The "Tudor" Arch was wide and squared off. Even the shoes had square toes.

Some people believe these shoes were created for Henry VIII to help his gout. He did develop this ailment in later life but square-toed shoes had been worn before that for a considerable time. If it was done for a monarch's vanity, it is far more likely to rest at the feet of Charles VIII of France. He did have a deformed foot.

My own private belief is that this was just an extension of the overall squarish fashion, which might have been a counter-reaction to the high V and upward thrust of the Gothic era. God indeed had been brought down from His heaven on high. Humanity was raised once again in its own self-esteem. People would never again be insects under the foot of God; they too were worthy of glorification. They had free will, the right to choose.

This glorification may account for the vast amount of money the rich spent on jewels with which to adorn themselves. The people of Gothic times liked jewels, but in comparison with Renaissance progeny they used jewels sparingly. In Renaissance fashions jewels were worn literally from head to toe. Pearls were number one on the hit parade, and were worn strung or as accents to other jewels. Rubies seemed to be the favorite gemstone, followed closely by emeralds and sapphires.

Early Italian Renaissance—1450 to 1500

The Woman—1465

The young lady in Figure 8–1 wears a high-waisted outer gown of silk and silver brocade that has been edged, belted, and bordered by cloth of silver onto which gem stones have been sewn. Her belt buckle is of silver, pearls, and gemstones, and a pair of matching brooches decorate her upper sleeves.

Her undergown is of a dark, but semi-sheer silk, also high-waisted, with many gathers across the breasts. Under this she wears a shift of fine linen lawn with full sleeves ending in wrist ruffles. The sleeves of her outer gown are really four separate pieces; two for the upper arm and two for the lower, all tied together by means of various ribbons and finally attached to the outer gown at the shoulders. She wears soft form-fitting slippers on her feet, not unlike modern ballet slippers. Her hair is parted in the middle and worn naturally. She wears a little brocade and beaded cap (with pearls and semi-precious stones), that has become known today as a "juliet cap" (after Shakespeare's youthful heroine). Around her forehead is a circlet of gold from which is suspended a drop pearl.

Figure 8–1. *Early Italian Renaissance—1450 to 1500*

The Man—1465

The young man in Figure 8–1 is dressed in the short doublet and parti-hosen typical of the young men of this period. Parti-hosen were not new; indeed they had been worn in the mid-Gothic period, but the variety of designs, not merely two different colors, was new. This gentleman's choice is modest. Some quartered their hosen; lower right and upper left legs might be striped, lower left a checkerboard, and upper right, plain. The man in Figure 8–1 wears one garter on his plain left leg. Two were frequently worn, one on each leg. His hosen also have a simple codpiece attached. His shirt has a striped body sewn to a square yoke and white full sleeves that end in a drawstringed ruffle. The doublet's sleeves are separate pieces, which are tied to the shoulder by means of ribbons, used as "points." Each sleeve has two slashes through which a little bit of the shirt sleeve has been puffed.

His hair is worn shoulder-length and the ends are combed under in a style that was called "page boy" in the 1940s. His hat is of a blocked felt with a turned-up brim that has been notched. It is adorned with a jewel and pearl brooch that holds a feather.

General Description

Even in Italy's Gothic period, clothing styles differed to the extent that a warmer climate demands. Because of the excessive heat, women wore little or no head covering, and the multilayered gown and houppelande sleeves were not popular for long. The sack sleeve gathered into a wrist band was worn, as was the open sleeve through which one put one's whole arm. There were two hats, however, that did seem popular for women though they were a bit extreme. The first is the inverted pumpkin (Fig. 8–2.1); the second was more reminiscent of a stuffed and jeweled arch (Fig. 8–2.2).

There were, nonetheless, certain universally observed standards of this time. The high-waisted dress was common to both, but the Italian version had little or no train. For men, the roundel was seen everywhere, but it was worn by the more mature man in Italy and often over another simple felt cap, minus lirepipe or drapery. Also the long gown for men of mature years and/or wisdom was fairly standard.

Certainly the love of jewelry was evident in both cultures, particularly among the ladies, who not only had them sewn onto their clothing, but wore additional pieces anywhere they could. Whereas the High Gothic woman might display her jewelry on her elaborate headdresses and hennins, the unhatted Italian lady took great pride in elaborate coiffures with ropes of pearls and jewel-studded chains wrapped or braided through their hair. The men of the time sometimes wore chains of office and jeweled belts and dagger sheaths, but for the most part were content with a single jeweled ornament on their hat.

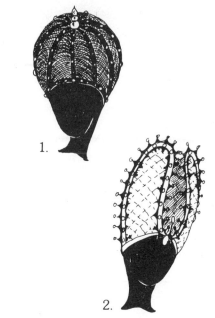

Figure 8–2.   *Two Italian Renaissance Hats*

The high-waisted dress gradually lost favor to one of a natural rounded look. What most characterizes the Italian Renaissance in comparison to either High Gothic or other European countries' Renaissance styles is its comparative freedom, particularly for women. They were not heavily corsetted and often did not wear double-layered skirts. Nor did they wear ruffs and constricting neck bands or heavy headdresses.

By 1560 the Italian man wore a modest pointed doublet and trunk hosen. His hair was often cut short, but his hats were modest and comfortable; his shoes, although slashed, were not squared. All in all, it was a very sensible mode, considering its time and place.

One style that seems odd was the platform shoe that Venetian women wore (see Fig. 8–3). Originally such shoes were worn to keep the feet dry in a city whose main thoroughfares were water. They were called choperines and they did go to extremes. They became so high that the lady of the house had to be supported by a servant on each side in order to walk.

Figure 8–3. *Venetian Platform Shoe*

Another oddity from Umbria was a very tall hat that looked like a water jug (without handle) turned upside down on the head. These can be seen in the frescoes of Piero Della Francesca, *The Story of the True Cross*.

The puffs seen in Figure 8–1 are the modest beginning of a Renaissance technique called "puffs and slashes," which went to extremes before dying out of style.

There is one trouble with the Italian Renaissance for the costume designer—namely, their pictures concerning the Virgin Mary and other holy females. The artists romanticized them and tended to draw them in mellifluous folds of overdrape. This was not a style. Actual women did not wear this anymore than they wore the gold gilt halos of Gothic paintings.

Best Sources—Artists

Botticelli
Ghirlandaio
Filippino Lippi
Fra Filippo Lippi
Raphael
Andrea del Sarto

Late Italian Renaissance—1500 to 1600

The Woman—1515

The lady in Figure 8–4 wears a natural waisted bodice of red velvet banded at neckline and waist with green silk in alternation with the red velvet. Her white shift is puffed through the neckline and shoulders. The enormously full sleeves and full skirt are of a golden silk, and the skirt is bordered on the bottom by alternating bands of the green silk and red velvet found on the bodice.

Turbans of various descriptions were very popular in the later Italian Renaissance. This version seems to be of a gold and red striped silk. She wears a fine gold chain around her neck. Her hair is probably worn in a bun, which has been covered by the turban.

The Man—1515

The man in Figure 8–4 wears the multi-gored and skirted doublet frequently painted by Raphael. This doublet is of a dark blue velvet,

Figure 8–4. *Late Italian Renaissance—1500 to 1600*

the enormously full sleeves are of a deep rose silk, and the bordering stripes are a gold satin. The doublet is worn over a chemise of fine white linen edged in a narrow lace around the neck.

His hosen are white, and his shoes are brown leather. His hat is of a molded felt, either dark blue or black. His leg garter, strictly a decorative item, is also dark blue.

General Description

The city-state of Florence gave birth to the Renaissance in the fifteenth century. By the sixteenth century the Renaissance encompassed all the Italian city-states with only certain native fashions interrupting the overall look—for example, a particular cap and cape worn by the Venetian Doge (Fig. 8–5).

As seen in Figure 8–4, the waistline in women's fashion has become a natural one and, unlike contemporary northern Europe, it remained this way, avoiding the pointed front altogether. Although the skirts were full and worn over several petticoats, there is also a lack of hoops, farthingales, and hip rolls. The hair remained uncovered. For a while (around the 1520s) very elaborately arranged coiffures were seen, but by the 1550s even these had again diminished. Jewels continued to be worn in the hair and

Figure 8–5.   *The Venetian Doge*

some small hats or scarves were worn as turbans.

For men the very short tunic top was gradually replaced by the skirted doublet pictured in Figure 8–4. The length of this skirt varied greatly. Young men wore them either to the upper thigh or sometimes to mid-thigh. Older men wore them from mid-calf to the floor.

Much of northern Italy was controlled by various Austrian conquerors; the various city-states changing hands two or three times within a period of a year. This situation might have been responsible for the rapid influx of Italian styles into Germanic fashions. Yet, when Germanic fashions went to extremes on their puffs and slashes (as will be seen in the section dealing with the German Renaissance) this in no way seemed to influence the Italian mode.

Best Sources—Artists

Angelo
Parmigianino
Raphael
Andrea del Sarto
Tintoretto
Titian

Raphael began painting in the late fifteenth century and continued well into the sixteenth so he is an excellent transitional source when not painting strictly religious subjects. The same is true of Andrea del Sarto.

Flemish-Burgundian—1485 to 1525

English—Gothic Transition—Henry VII
French—Gothic Transition—Louis XII

The Woman—1490

The woman in Figure 8–6 wears the earliest version of what was called in slightly later times a "French hood" (see English Renaissance—

Figure 8–6. *Flemish-Burgundian—1485 to 1525*

Tudor). This one has a head-hugging band of gold silk, only the top of which can be seen, plus a scalloped-edged black velvet band, narrow at the top of the head and getting progressively wider as it extends over the ears. Attached to this is a caul of gold threads that holds the hair.

Her overdress is of a dusty rose silk banded around the neckline, belled sleeves, belt, and hem by a rose and green on cream brocaded ribbon or braid. It is lined in a dark burgundy silk. The underskirt or petticoat is of a garnet velvet. Her inner sleeves (presumably part of her shift) are a cream color and made of soft fabric. The white scalloped edge insert around the neck is also of this color. This dress is cut in four pieces, not including the sleeves. For an unscaled illustration, see Figure 8–7.

The Man—1490

The gentleman in Figure 8–6 wears a long gown of silk, banded and belted in velvet. His surcoat is trimmed in lynx and has open hanging sleeves lined in a contrasting silk. The sleeves and hem have been bordered with gold braid. His chemise shows above the neckline of the gown and also has a velvet border at the neckline. The sleeves of the chemise are extra long and gathered up to fit the arm.

The hair style reflects a certain Italian influence. The hat is an elliptical padded roundel trimmed by a jeweled brooch. The shoes are already squarish, but made of soft leather and strapped across the instep.

This style of gown and surcoat, either floor-length or mid-calf length, was worn by young and old men alike. As the Renaissance gained its hold, the styles for shorter male garments became increasingly popular among the young. Clerics, ministers of the Crown, judges, and elderly men continued to wear the longer or floor-length garments.

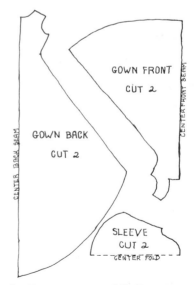

NOTE: THIS IS NOT A SCALED PATTERN

Figure 8–7. *Flemish-Burgundian Overdress Pattern*

General Description

This short period is best depicted by French and Flemish painters. There is a painting of Isabella and Ferdinand of Spain wearing not too unsimilar outfits. There is also a family portrait of Henry VII and Elizabeth of York and she particularly is dressed in a similar manner.

It is truly a transition look between the High Gothic and the various Renaissance looks. The high hats have gone, as has the high-waisted look, but the pointed bell sleeve, although modest in comparison to its Gothic predecessor, still retains a Gothic appearance, as does the train and the fact that the outer dress needs picking up. Sometimes women employed various belts and ropes to hold up the outer dress.

The man's gown and the hang-type sleeves hanker back to the Gothic period, but the roundel was still universally popular. Both men's and women's necklines reflect the new square look. Men continued the Gothic clean-shaven look. This period did not last very long, but like the Elizabethan Transition period nearly a century later, it shows that fashion had its feet in two worlds, one foot slightly behind the other.

Best Sources—Artists

Hieronymus Bosch
Jaume Huguet
The Master of Moulins
Martin Schongauer

German Renaissance—1490 to 1600

The Man—1510

This period is often called "German puffs and slashes," because it was from that area that the German mercenary came, and he wore outfits that carried this technique to the extreme, as can

Figure 8–8. *German Renaissance—1490 to 1600*

be seen from the gentleman in Figure 8–8. His upper "stocks" (stocks were divided hosen; upper covered from waist to knee and lower covered foot to knee) are divided into three sections for each leg plus the codpiece. These were puffed by means of three sets of drawstrings which tied on the inside. The puffs were pieces of an underlayer of fabric that were drawn through the outer layer and then held in place at the top and bottom of each slash by a little button or pearls. Sometimes the slashing was left alone so that just a hint of an undercolor appeared.

His sleeves are heavily padded, puffed, and slashed, and are sewn to a rather simple doublet laced across a shirt of fine white lawn gathered to a neckband of the doublet fabric and with a neck ruffle. Often the doublet would also be slashed.

His lower stocks match the color of his puffs. His shoes are the typical square-toed leather of this period. His hair is short. Moustaches and well-trimmed beards were fashionable.

His hat consists of a headband onto which is attached a roundel that has been quilted and stitched to give the desired effect, and then many plumes have been added. A birds-eye view of how this hat may have been constructed appears in Figure 8–9.

The Woman—1510

The women of the German Renaissance wore the high-waisted look akin to their Italian contemporaries. The dress was belted, as is the woman's in Figure 8–8, and a few puffs and slashes were worn over the breasts. A purse is suspended from the belt. A yoke-like bolero with stand-up collar was often worn over the shoulders and tied under the arm. This tended to cover the points with which the sleeves were attached to the bodice of the dress.

The hair was caught up into a caul of gold threads, then a stiffened roundel or crownless brim was worn over this. The woman in Figure 8–8 has jewels on her roundel and a long full ostrich plume. Her shoes would be flat slippers, but not as square-toed as the man's of this period.

General Description

The choice of fabrics in Germany was dictated partially by the climate. Fur, velvets, and woolens were used extensively because of the warmth they provided; soldiers made great use of leather. Young German women wore their hair loose, but matrons covered it with cauls, various hats, or coifs. The more mature women wore a veil attached to her coif. There seems to have been a brief period of long hair for men, as Albrecht Durer painted himself with it. In England there is also a picture of a young Henry VIII with long hair, but this vogue did not last.

A Germanic garment that became a very prevalent northern European Renaissance item was the square-yoked overcoat often worn over doublet, hosen, or stocks. It was often sleeveless, or with mere hanging sleeves reminiscent of a previous Gothic style. Just as often it had padded sleeves of its own, which came just to the elbow and allowed the doublet sleeves to show on the lower arm. It was often faced and collared in fur. Popular furs were squirrel, fox, lynx, muskrat, rabbit, and wolf. Ermine was reserved for royalty. The square-yoked overcoat in its furless state became the foundation for what we know today as the academic robe.

Best Sources—Artists

Albrecht Altdorfer
Hans Baldung
Bosch
Brueghel (the Elder and the Younger)
Lucas Cranach (the Elder)
Albrecht Durer
Matthias Grunewald

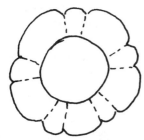

Figure 8–9. *Birds-eye View of German Renaissance Man's Hat*

English Renaissance (Tudor)—1485 to 1558

The Man—1533

The man in Figure 8–10 has seven separate pieces to his ensemble: slashed shoes, hosen, pearl studded codpiece, skirted doublet, surcoat, shirt, and hat. His shirt is of a fine white silk, gathered to a neck band and neck ruffle, and with full sleeves gathered to wrist ruffles. His hosen are of a fine knitted wool, and the codpiece is velvet and pearl studded. His doublet is of a heavy silk, padded, stiffened, and embroidered in gold thread down the center front, border, and sleeves. The sleeves are slashed to show the chemise (shirt) sleeve.

The neck and hem are bordered with bands of velvet and cloth of gold onto which have been sewn semi-precious jewels and pearls. This same treatment has been given to his belt. His surcoat has slashed sleeves with a collar and cuffs of white fox. The sleeves hang loose and his arms are put through the slashes. His velvet hat is trimmed with a series of matched brooches interspersed with two large pearls. White feathers of a downy texture trim the brim. His shoes are typically square-toed with slashes and fake puffs brought through. His hair is worn short and his beard and moustache are well-trimmed.

The Woman—1533

The woman in Figure 8–10 wears a headdress known as a "French hood." This style was popularized by both Ann Boleyn and Mary Tudor Brandon, Henry VIII's youngest sister. Both of these women spent time in France and brought the fashion back with them.

The overgown is of velvet with an enormous sleeve cuff of white fox. The inner sleeve is of velvet slashed and held together over another sleeve of creamy silk. A series of jeweled brooches act as fastenings. This inner sleeve was really a false sleeve, held to the elbow by means of a

Figure 8–10.   *English Renaissance (Tudor)— 1485 to 1558*

drawstring. It served to warm the lower arms. The neckline of the overgown is the square typical of the period. It is bordered by bands of silk and gold embroidery. The gown is slit down the center front to reveal an underskirt of heavy silk also banded and embroidered in gold. A corset was worn, which flattened the breasts, but a brooch and pearls looped from the center to the points of the border emphasize the bosom.

On a pearl studded chain suspended from her waist this lady wears a pomander, a jeweled ball containing certain sweet-smelling herbs and spices that supposedly prevented contagious diseases from spreading.

General Description

The Tudor period extends through the brief reigns of Edward VI, and Mary I (Bloody Mary), as well as Henry VIII. Henry VII was really the last of the Gothic kings in England. The English were expanding their horizons in the field of international politics, something they could turn to after the one-hundred years of the War of the Roses were finally laid to rest by Henry VII and his Tudor dynasty. The fashions reflected the international politics. The English quickly adopted the Italian codpiece, exaggerating it in size and jeweled adornment. They adopted the kennel or gable headdress of Katherine of Aragon and later the French hood. Although they adopted the German puffs and slashes, they never went to the extremes that the Germans and the Swiss did.

In the fabric line, brocades and carved velvets were very fashionable, as well as heavy silk. Wool was one of England's best home industries and with the reconquest of Ireland during the mid-Renaissance, linen was added to that.

All colors were worn by both men and women, but jewel tones such as garnet, topaz, and amethyst were favored. Embroidery of gold and silver threads was also used extensively.

The Renaissance philosophy of self-glorification may also have influenced the exaggeration of the codpiece. The original Italian purpose was one of modesty when wearing very tight hosen and short doublet (see Fig. 8–1), but the larger English codpieces served no purpose, except to call attention to the anatomical representation of masculinity. Although this seems absurd to us today, is it any different than Lana Turner's tight sweater look of the forties or Raquel Welsh's decolletage that extends practically to her navel? The only difference seems to be that in Tudor England it was the male who preened; today it is the female.

Best Sources—Artists

Jean Clouet
Jan Gassaert
Holbein the Elder
Hans Holbein the Younger
Lucas Van Leyden
Bernard Van Orley

English Renaissance (Elizabethan)— 1558 to 1603

The Woman—1575

The square look of the Tudor period is still in evidence in the neckline of the woman in Figure 8–11 and in the broad shoulders of her male companion, but it is gradually giving way to a more rounded look. The belled cone of the Spanish farthingale was still worn by some, but the bolster or 'bum roll' padding for the hips had replaced it to a great degree. That is what this lady is wearing under her double skirts. Her outer skirt is of a silk-bordered velvet; her underskirt has been quilted in a diamond pattern and then the outline corded with a gold colored cord held in place by a pearl at each junction.

Figure 8–11. *English Renaissance (Elizabethan)—1558 to 1603*

A similar treatment has been given to the lower sleeve. The neckline shows an under chemise of the same colored silk gathered to a plain band at the neck. The neck ruff and wrist ruffs are separate pieces, colored to match the silk of the chemise and underskirt.

This lady's bodice comes to a point in the front behind her hand, and is also velvet. The border of the neckline matches the border of the overskirt. The upper sleeves are puffed bias-cut velvet strips alternated with silk strips and gathered into an upper arm band. Pearls have been sewn to the velvet.

Her hair is caught up into a chignon. She wears the hard crowned and vastly decorated hat, which gradually replaced the softer cloth cap of Elizabeth's brother's and sister's reigns. Both men and women wore soft leather shoes attached to cork soles, which were slightly higher under the heel, much like what is called a "wedgie" today, as well as a short-heeled version.

The Man—1575

The nobleman in Figure 8–11 wears a decoration suspended from a wide velvet ribbon around his neck. He also wears a doublet with shoulder rolls covering the points of his sleeve attachments. His doublet has the deep V waist and slim body, quite different from the previous square look. To achieve this, many men took to wearing corsets. The doublet has a tabularized peplum to allow for the great bulging-out of the trunk hose (short pumpkin hosen). His stocks are tied up to the trunk hose. He wears a neck ruff and matching wrist ruffs, as well as leather shoes with wedgie-like cork soles.

A "Spanish" cape (short cape with a square short collar) hangs from his shoulders. His hat is the male version of the Valois bonnet with a turned-down brim. It is velvet and is adorned with a plume. This was equally popular with ladies, as was the lady's chapeau with the gentle-men. Hat styles were generally asexual in connatation, as they are today. The man's hair is short; his moustache and goatee are well-trimmed.

General Description

Elizabeth I was well aware that she ruled, because she was popular with her people and courted them in a lifetime affair. Her reign saw great advances in the middle classes, a stable treasury due in part to the excellent "privateering" of her navy, and a stable foreign policy that brought peace at home. She loved learning for its own sake and there was a great flowering of art and literature, particularly dramatic literature.

Her world perspective encouraged the rapid adaptation of foreign styles into English fashion. The farthingale went from the Spanish version, through the bum roll, to the large cartwheel farthingale adopted from France at the end of her life. The short men's "Spanish cape" and the Spanish female surcoat were also adopted. From the French came the Valois bonnet and the masculine style of wearing both trunk hosen and canions simultaneously (see the section on French Renaissance).

Also, toward the end of the era, the heeled shoe became popular. At her death Queen Elizabeth was said to have had approximately two thousand dresses, a room full of wigs, and several caskets full of jewels. She was an exceedingly vain woman, very proud of her slender hands, and she popularized the wearing of gloves. Before her time gloves were worn in battle and for warmth. She wore them or carried them on everyday occasions.

Her two greatest rivals were Catherine de Medici, perennial regent of France, and her first cousin once removed, Mary Queen of Scots. Mary brought back from France several styles that were adopted in Scotland (filtering down to England). One was the heart-shaped headdress

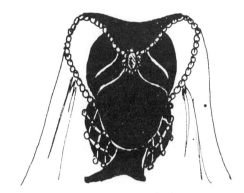

Figure 8–12. *Heart-shaped Headdress*

illustrated in Figure 8–12. It was usually accompanied by a long flowing veil down the back, made of some sheer fabric.

If contemporary paintings are to be believed, Catherine de Medici was the first to wear this cap and it designated widowhood. Mary was three times married and three times widowed herself.

Catherine de Medici was also known for wearing male trunk hosen and stockings under a frontally divided overskirt while riding, in the vain effort to recapture her husband's alienated affections from his mistress, Dianne de Poitier. This had not been done since Jeanne D'Arc in the High Gothic times. Catherine was Mary Stuart's first mother-in-law. Whether this gave Mary the idea or not is open to conjecture but Mary was known to lead her forces into battle wearing male attire. It certainly was a convention that Shakespeare used often enough, as in *As You Like It* (Roselind) and *Twelfth Night* (Viola).

Elizabeth I was active as a style setter. She suffered from a high fever and lost most of her hair, so she set a style of elaborate wigs which was quickly followed by the female court. It has been said she was left slightly pockmarked, so she began wearing great quantities of a whitish make-up and rouge in her later life; this style was also copied. Unfortunately, the make-up had a lead base and caused a certain degree of lead poisoning.

If anything, Elizabeth I loved jewels even more than her father. Her dress for her silver jubilee was of a heavy grey silk tufted with a sheer white silk in a diamond pattern and each point was held alternately with an emerald-cut ruby surrounded by pearls or an emerald. She wore a coronet and diadem of precious stones and teardrop pearls in her wig, multiple ropes of pearls around her neck, and both her high picadil collar and the heart-shaped stand-up collar of her mantle were edged in fine silver lace sewn with tiny pearls. As a rough guess, it probably weighed one hundred pounds and cost twenty-five times that.

But for the best sense of the dramatic as exemplified in fashion, the award would have gone to Mary Queen of Scots for what to wear to an execution. She appeared completely in black; a white organdy heart-shaped widows cap and white floor-length veil flowed from her neatly coiffured red head. She carried a black bound missal, a white handkerchief, and a rosary. She removed her headdress on the scaffold and gave it to one of her ladies-in-waiting. Then she removed her black dress and a startled murmur went through the crowd of witnesses. She was dressed in a scarlet low-cut underdress. She told the headsman she chose that color so the blood would not show. She gave her rosary to another lady-in-waiting, tied the handkerchief around her eyes, and calmly laid her head on the block. It took two whacks to sever her head from her neck. The headsman reached down to lift the head up by the hair, but the hair was a wig and the head fell out.

Best Sources—Well known Playwrights

John Lyly
Christopher Marlowe
William Shakespeare
John Webster

Note: Although there are many paintings of this period, no English artist stands out in particular, as Holbein did a generation earlier.

Spanish Renaissance—1506 to 1600

The Man—1570

The man in Figure 8–13 is a soldier, a conquistador, one of the many that explored the New World and gave to Spain riches and glory. He is dressed in doublet, pumpkin hosen, hosen, and thigh-high boots of leather. His armor consists of a razor-backed helmet, a steel gorget, and cuirass of convex mold. The crown of his helmet has strips of inlayed gold and chastened designs worked into it. The studding and rolled edge of his steel gorget are also gold. His cuirass is convex to deflect blows and it has two pep-

lum-like plates attached for the same reason. The front and back pieces of the cuirass are laced together with leather thongs.

His doublet has paned sleeves, which show off an undersleeve of rich brocade, much as the panes of his pumpkin hosen show off the same brocaded underfabric. His doublet also has the high neck and small ruff so typical in both male and female attire. His hair is short and he wears a small goatee and moustache.

The Woman—1570

The woman in Figure 8–13 wears an ensemble of five separate pieces: a doublet-like bodice, which has its own form-fitting sleeves, two separate hanging sleeves tied to the shoulder by tabs called picadils (see Spanish Baroque). The bodice has a high, tight neck topped by a small ruff. Similar ruffs trim the wrists of the narrow sleeves. In some instances the narrow sleeves as well as the hanging sleeves were separate. The overskirt is open in the front to display a richly banded and embroidered underskirt. A pomander ball hangs from a gold chain.

Her hair is caught up into a wire and pearl caul, and a small version of the Valois bonnet is perched on top of the head, held on by means of a jeweled hat pin and adorned with a short plume. The skirt is worn over the Spanish farthingale, a hooped petticoat of a bell shape.

General Description

The most distinctive look of the Spanish Renaissance was the high neck and short ruff worn by both men and women. The ladies in particular were extremely restricted and covered up. The hair was always bound up, the corset flattening the breasts, and sleeves went down to the wrist. If contemporary paintings are to be believed, black and gold were the favorite colors, with creams and reds coming in second. The brighter colors were worn by the younger generations.

Figure 8–13.   *Spanish Renaissance—1506 to 1600*

Figure 8–14. *The Spanish Ropa*

There is a look of quiet elegance to the portraits: the much-used lavish fabrics were worn in an offhand manner. Jewels adorned them, but they were matched sets with perhaps one type of stone and a few pearls judiciously used.

There was another version of the outer hanging sleeve, which was a gigantic semicircle, slashed on the radius and pinned to the wrist. It dragged the ground, much like the houppelande sleeves of the previous century. Another Spanish style that was adopted through much of Europe was the "ropa," a sort of surcoat, usually with short puffed sleeves and a somewhat form-fitting top, as illustrated in Figure 8–14.

Best Sources—Artists

Caravaggio
Alonso Sanchez Coello
El Greco
Antonio Moro

French Renaissance—1540 to 1600

The Woman—1590

The lady in Figure 8–15 wears a bodice and overskirt of velvet. Her underskirt and padded sleeves are quilted in a diamond pattern and each point is accented with a round and a drop pearl. Two chains of pearls with a large jeweled pendant each accents the waist and the neckline.

The padded sleeves are finished with a tucked-stitched cuff that has a small ruff attached, matching the standing ruff, which forms a high collar. The outer sleeves are of brocade-lined velvet, which, in this instance, just hang, but were often caught together over the padded sleeve at the elbow and/or wrist. Her shoes are of brocade. A little bit of a brocade underbodice peeks out above the very low neckline of the velvet one. Her hair has been dressed over a

Figure 8–15. *French Renaissance—1540 to 1600*

wire frame, which gives it that squarish look. It has been accented with a brooch and a feather.

The Man—1590

The gentleman in Figure 8–15 wears doublet, trunk hosen, canions, stocks, a short cape, a Valois bonnet, and plaited leather shoes. His hat and cape are velvet. The hat is trimmed with a string of pearls for a band and a jeweled brooch holds a small plume. His cape is banded in silk and decorated with a maltese cross.

His doublet is made of strips of silk sewn together in a herring-bone pattern and held by vertical stripes of velvet. The outer panes of his trunk hosen are horizontal stripes of the same fabric as the doublet. His canions and sleeves are of a matching brocade. His shoes are of intricately worked leather strips. The ruff is getting bigger. The hair style and beard are of a more constant style.

General Description

Ruffs were sometimes referred to as "bands" and were sent to professional ruff makers and starchers for laundering. The boxes were round and were referred to as "band" boxes, a term that remains with us even today. Later, around 1600 or so, when the softer collar came in, they were sometimes called falling bands. The variety of ruffs became greater and greater as the sixteenth century drew to a close, only to disappear in France and England not long into the new century.

The waistline point also became more and more elongated, particularly in France. Men developed a style called the peascod doublet, one whose waist reached a point far enough down to almost encompass the codpiece. It was padded well into protrusion. The point of the female waist began to reach down equally as far. When the cartwheel farthingale came into being, the point needed extra stretch so it was made of a piece separate from the bodice and that was the beginning of the style called the "stomacher," which would last almost two hundred

years. (This will be discussed further in the next section.)

Best Sources—Artists

François Clouet and the Clouet School
Marc Duval
Corneille de Lyon
François Quesnel

Elizabethan-James I Transition—1600 to 1620

The Man—1604

The gentleman in Figure 8–16 has adopted the French style of wearing canions under his trunk hosen, but the trunk hosen are both wider and longer than those of his French contemporary. His canions are gathered to their present knee length. Velvet garters hold them and his lower stocks in place. His doublet is of modest

Figure 8–16. *Elizabethan-James I Transition—1600 to 1620*

cut, although of a rich silk fabric. His falling band is of fine linen edged in lace, as are his cuffs. The short Spanish cape is still fashionable. Around his neck is a chain of office. His shoes are gold-studded velvet. His hair is a little longer, and now that his neck is not restrained by a ruff his beard a little fuller. The ruff was still worn frequently, however.

The Woman—1604

The woman in Figure 8–16 wears a nine-piece ensemble consisting of corset, cartwheel farthingale, underskirt of a richly embroidered silk, and a stomacher of the same fabric as the underskirt. Her overskirt, bodice, and heavily padded French-style sleeves are of gold embroidered velvet bordered in gold cord latticing and trimmed with pearls. This same gold and pearl trim accents the standing ruff and the mantle collar. Her sleeves end in fine lawn tucked-stitched cuffs with lace trim. She wears a diadem of teardrop pearls in her hair (which might be a wig), as well as two marshmallow-sized pearl ornaments. A rope of pearls is wound around her throat and hangs down her chest.

She carries embroidered and fringed white leather gloves in her right hand and a pearl-and-diamond encrusted lollipop fan in her left, the fan is attached by a ribbon to her stomacher. Her shoes are of a brocaded silk. The latest fashion at this time was for the skirts to be ankle-length.

General Description

Elizabeth I died in 1603. She believed that if she could remain on her feet she would not die, so she died standing up. Her successor was James VI of Scotland, who became James I of England, the first of the Stuart dynasty. He was the son of Elizabeth's old rival and cousin, Mary Queen of Scots.

He did practically nothing to change style in any way. Some historians venture to say he did practically nothing period. He did, however, support the invention of a stocking knitting machine, invented by William Lee, which revolutionized that market all over Europe. He also imprisoned and finally executed Sir Walter Raleigh on very shaky and highly unpopular grounds. His wife, Ann of Denmark, popularized the wearing of yellow ruffs, but only royalty was permitted the use of colored ruffs. James I was pleasure loving and suspicious by nature and allowed excessive witch hunting. All in all, the conservative Britisher stayed with the last of the Elizabethan styles.

As shown in Figure 8–16, the biggest style changes were the shortening of skirts for the women, the adoption of the cartwheel farthingale and the gradual lengthening and widening of the trunk hose, until they became the pantaloons or rhingraves of the later periods.

Best Sources

There are paintings, but the painter's names remain, for the most part, anonymous. A very good source for both late French Renaissance and this period is tapestries. This was a skill that was blossoming at that time, both in France and in the lowlands of Belgium and Holland. Well-known playwrights include Thomas Dekker, Ben Jonson, and Cyril Tourneur.

9

Baroque

When something is called Baroque, it usually means full of ornate curved lines and massiveness. Baroque music always contains ornamentation on a central theme and the interplay of thematic line in a rigorously structured circumstance.

In the Table of Periods at the beginning of Part II is included a period called Puritan. This was essentially an Americanism for a group of reactionaries against the prevailing fashions of their day. Once the Pilgrims landed in this country, they were isolated enough to establish their own fashions which held on much longer here than in Europe because of this very isolation. In England the Puritans were analogous to the Cromwellians, at least as far as their mode of dress was concerned and their outlook on the frivolities of life. Theatres were closed under Cromwell's protectorate (consult the Line of the English kings, Chapter 13).

One term of style does not appear in the Period Table for this era. That is "Jacobean." This seems to be more of an architectural term than a fashion one. Some of the Jacobean furniture examples are to Baroque as Puritan fashions are to Baroque fashions—the same basic lines greatly simplified.

In the fuss with the monarchy that absorbed England and her Stuart kings for most of this century a Jacobite political party developed, but this bears little relationship to the Jacobean style as it came at a much later time. (See Chapter 11, Romantique general description)

While England and France were being cavaliers, the Dutch seemed to harbor two worlds simultaneously, the late Renaissance and the Cavalier. This is particularly evident in the painting "The Amsterdam Burgomaster Dirck Jacobsy Bey and his Family" by Dirck Santvoort. It is a whole family together, painted in 1635. The younger members are dressed in the height of the Cavalier mode while the oldest partriarch and his wife sport the cartwheel ruffs and style of earlier times. This brings to mind a very important point about our fashionable continuum of time. Just because a particular style is in vogue does not mean that older styles were not worn at the same time.

Cavalier—1620 to 1650

The Woman—1640

The stiffness and starch left clothing with the demise of James I. As one can see from Figure 9–1, the corsetted stomacher remained a vestige of the former era, as did the deep square neckline. Our lady wears a linen collar trimmed in heavy V scalloped Venetian lace. Her cuffs are of the same material, but tuck-stitched, as is her undersleeve, which, along with the embroidered stomacher, is attached to the bodice. A jacket with a tabbed peplum is worn over this. The waist is accented with a ribbon belt tied in a bow. Bows also accent the overskirt where it has been ballooned by interior draw strings. Her underskirt is decorated with cordwork. Neither skirt was as full as the preceding Elizabethan ones, but the circumference is still about one hundred eight inches.

The multiple panes or slashes of the previous period sleeves are confined to one large slash, the sides of which are accented by embroidered ribbon. Ladies' hair styles are also softer, following the natural shape of the head with a coil in back and a few tendril curls. The egret feathers on one side are worn as a hair ornament. She carries a stationary "lollipop" fan of ostrich plumes. (Lollipop is my word.)

The great similarity between English and French fashions at this time is due to Henrietta Marie, a French princess, who married the future Charles I and brought French fashions to the English court.

The Man—1640

The lovely linen and lace collar that the gentleman in Figure 9–1 wears is called a "falling ruff." His cuffs are of the same fiber. He wears a tabbard jacket so popular with the "Three Musketeers." It is a jacket that flairs out over the hips and has slashed sleeves caught together midslash by a bow. The tabbard was a separate

Figure 9–1. *Cavalier—1620 to 1650*

piece, attached at one shoulder seam, that covered the jacket front lacings by hooking on the other shoulder and being held down at the waist by a ribbon that tied from the underjacket through buttonholes in the tabbard. This tabbard was sometimes padded if worn under a cuirass (see general description). In France the tabbard was embroidered with insignia to designate regiments. The thigh-high pumpkin hosen disappeared and were replaced by balloon breeches that extended to the knees and were softly pleated into a knee band. By 1640 the breeches had become much smaller, particularly in the thigh area. The lower leg was encased in either cotton or silk stockings. Long thigh-high boots were worn, but the tops were allowed to fall, making a large cuff-like top. These were called "slops." Our gentleman has lace even at his knee bands.

His hat is the circular, flat-brimmed, truncated conical crowned hat we associate with our Pilgrim fathers. The cavaliers trimmed theirs with vast quantities of ostrich plumes. Men's hair styles did an abrupt about face. Facial hair was limited to perhaps a moustache and a small pointed goatee now called a "Van Dyke." Hair did not need to be short to accommodate the stiff neck ruff, so it was worn long and flowing. Some young swains allowed one side forelock to grow very long and they adorned it with a bow in their lady love's favorite color, much as knights of old wore a lady's favor attached to their armor. The extreme use of buttons strictly as ornamentation was a very "cavalier" thing to do.

General Description

The word "cavalier" is defined in Webster's dictionary as: 1. an armed horseman; knight; 2. a gallant gentleman, especially a lady's escort; and 3. as an adjective meaning casual and arrogant. The Larousse French dictionary states that in old French it meant a knight in shining armor. In present French it means "off-hand." There is no better way to describe this period.

The Cavalier period saw the last of the old style hand-to-hand combat. The pikeman and hand-to-hand swordsman were more effective on horseback. They became the cavalryman and the lancer. Muskets and cannons were the order of the day and there is something very impersonal about a cannon ball. This could account for the off-handed manner in which gallantry was offered. It was offered for show, for ostentation. Simple everyday courtesies such as the bowing to a lady were done with extreme flourishing of hat and outward extension of right foot. If anything, the men's ostentation outdid the ladies'.

Although the basic lines of the fashions were simple, more casual, the extreme use of ribbon, lace, buttons, and bows belied that very simplicity. The heels on men's shoes became as high as those on the ladies'. Both sexes wore rich, bright colors, and heavy fabrics were favored, but generally unpatterned ones. An overlay of embroidery was used, however, as opposed to the brocades of the previous era.

Masks were worn in the evening, out of doors, by both men and women, as were muffs and capes; a woman's cape usually had a hood.

Women also wore the "pilgrim" hat decorated with plumes. A fashion borrowed from the Dutch of wearing a lace-trimmmed "coif" cap indoors gradually grew in England; the plumed hat was worn on top of this. When a matron went abroad in the daytime, a simplified version of this was particularly favored by the Puritans.

Armor consisted of a breastplate, backplate, helmet, and elbow guards. Phillippe de Champaigne's portrait of *Louis XIII Crowned by Victory* shows Louis XIII wearing black armor with riveted plates protecting his upper arms and thighs. His thigh-high buff leather boots are held up by points. This style gradually lost out and by the English Civil War (1650s) and Cromwellian Protectorate most of the armor had disappeared, leaving only the breastplate and backplate, called a cuirass and helmet. The baldrick was worn over the cuirass to hold the sword. Some of the noblemen wore fancy silk sashes instead of the formal baldrick. A sleeveless leather jerkin was sometimes worn over the jacket but under the cuirass, to prevent the metal from chafing the skin.

Best Sources

Artists:
Phillippe de Champaigne
Frans Hals
Louis Le Nain
Peter Paul Rubens
Georges de la Tour
Anthony Van Dyke

Frans Hals and Peter Paul Rubens were Dutch, and many portraits reflect this; but both, along with Van Dyke, seem to capture the true Cavalier feeling.

Playwrights:
Francis Beaumont
John Fletcher
Ben Jonson

Puritan—1610 to 1660

French Name: Cavalier
English Name: Cavalier-Commonwealth
American Name: Puritan

The Man—1640

The man in Figure 9–2 is a "roundhead." This name became synonymous with the Puritan movement and philosophy. It was due to the fact that Puritan men cut their hair short by means of the "bowl cut," in protest against the Cavalier fashion of long flowing locks. Puritan men were, for the most part, clean-shaven.

The man below wears knee-length breeches of a heavy homespun cloth, cotton stockings,

buckled black leather shoes, and an unbleached muslin shirt whose cuffs come out over the sleeves of his laced jerkin. He carries his hat, which looks exactly like his wife's.

The Woman—1640

The matron in Figure 9–2 wears the same corset and under petticoats as her female Cavalier contemporary. Her skirt and bodice are made of a heavy homespun. She wears an enormous square kerchief folded in an uneven diagonal around her neck and tucked into the front neckline (see Fig. 9–3). This is probably of unbleached muslin, the same material used for her apron, cuffs, and matron's coif. Her hat is either beaver or felt and is adorned with a buckled band. If we could see her feet, her shoes would also be buckled. The buckles of her costume, as well as those on her husband's shoes, would probably be plain pewter, as silver and gold were banned.

General Description

If you compare the basic lines of the Puritans and the Cavaliers you will find them to be the same. For both styles stem partly from the transition style of the Elizabethan-James I era. The Puritan costume also shows the Dutch influence. King James I made life so uncomfortable for the Puritans that early in the 1600s many of

Figure 9–2. *Puritan—1610 to 1660*

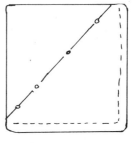

FOLD ON —○— TO - - - - - NECK BANDS

Figure 9–3. *Puritan Kerchief*

them moved to Holland. There they adopted many Dutch styles, which they took back to England and also to America. In America, the close proximity of the New England settlers and the Dutch settlers of New Amsterdam reinforced this style and made it last much longer than it did in the old world.

As an example, the previously mentioned matrons coif (see Cavalier general description) and the very full "pantaloons" (knee breeches of extreme width) stayed popular in the colonies long after they were out of style in Europe. Do not confuse this meaning with the long strapped trousers of the Romantique period. These derived their name from St. Pantalone, who was known for his baggy legs and poor clothing. (He is also a model for the commedia dell'arte character of the same name, who was famous for his long nose and baggy, patched hosen.) The Dutch were also fond of the color black (which is not technically a color; see Chapter 3). To dye a true, even black was difficult and expensive at this time. Therefore, it was worn by the rich and influential. This is best epitomized by Rembrandt's painting *The Night Watch*.

The Puritans were not adverse to color. They wore almost all colors, but in sober tones, bottle greens, dark blues, browns, garnet, and wine. They had a special reverence for bright scarlet. Oliver Cromwell wore a scarlet scarf over his cuirass. In New England scarlet was used to designate a town councilman or church elder, but was always used as an accent color for a sash or a sleeve lining. A red wool petticoat was standard equipment for women.

In the colonies where fabrics were homespun and home dyed, natural dyes and colors were persistent. Walnut juice made a good sort of nutmeg color. Berries could give soft blue greys and violets.

The wealthy wore fine woolens and linens; the less wealthy, wool, broadcloth, and muslin. Buttons as adornment, lace, and ribbons were banished by decrees. The only way to tell a wealthy Puritan was by his choice of cloth.

The Puritans frowned on frivolous entertainments and the London theaters closed—one reason for there being no playwrights. They also frowned on the excesses of the Catholic (and Anglican) church service and only permitted plainsong. Needless to say, this did not make for a great flowering of the arts.

Best Sources

See Cavalier and Dutch Baroque.

Dutch Baroque—1600 to 1700

The Father—1640

The father in the family portrait pictured in Figure 9–4 wears the wide "pantaloons" gathered into and ballooned over his knee bands,

Figure 9–4.   *Dutch Baroque—1600 to 1700*

which close in a bow. His stockings are black silk; his pantaloons and coat are of black heavy silk trimmed with stripes of black velvet. His knee bands and pantaloon waist band are also black velvet. His V-necked shirt is of fine snowy white linen embroidered with white silk floss and trimmed with lace.

His hair is shoulder-length, which indicates he is probably under thirty-five. The older gentlemen of this time and class often wore short hair and trimmed beards reminiscent of the late Renaissance. His hat is of beaver and similar to a "Puritan" hat, but the brim is not as wide and the crown is somewhat spherical on top. It is trimmed with a band of black silk, buckled by a silver buckle, and has one modest ostrich plume. His black leather shoes have red heels and a T-shaped tongue held by a leather "rosette."

The Mother—1640

The mother of this family group wears a matron's cap of fine snowy linen. It is actually almost two caps joined together and held close to the face and head by a band of flexible steel called a "hooftijsertgen." This band was often covered in white linen, so that it could be used with several caps and as the century wore on, it was decorated and worn alone (see Fig. 9–5). She also wears the millstone ruff that reached from neck to shoulders and was worn by the "regent class" women well into the 1660s.

Her bodice still retains the elongated, stiffened, and embroidered stomacher of Spanish influence. A bolster, known as a "fardegalijn," was used to hold out the skirts. She has turned back her overskirt to show an underskirt of silk. Her shoulders have the tabs of the previous period, but the sleeve is tight to the wrist, ending in elaborate cuffs. Her dress would be of a rich black woolen fabric with gold embroidery down the bodice front sides and turn back of the skirt. Her stomacher is worked in gold and red, as is her underskirt.

Figure 9–5. *Dutch Baroque Women's Cap*

Her hair would be worn in a bun under her cap and her shoes were almost the same as her husband's, but without red heels.

The Child—1640

The little boy in Figure 9–4 is dressed in almost an exact replica of his father's outfit. Only his collar line is different.

General Description

When Phillip, son of Maximilian of the Holy Roman Empire, and king of the lowlands (present day Holland and Belgium), married Juanna of Spain, daughter of their most Catholic majesties Isabella and Ferdinand, Juanna brought Spanish style, customs, and traditions with her. Her son, Charles, became the Holy Roman Emperor and king of Spain and the lowlands. This firmly entrenched the Spanish look—an extensive use of the sober color black, much rich gold embroidery, the Spanish farthingale, and the square headdress ("kennel" it was called in England, because its shape was basically that of a doghouse).

It is interesting to trace the shape of the "Dutch" cap through its stages back to this shape (Figures 9–6.1–3). Figure 9–6.4 illustrates a widow's "peak" or pointed cap popular in the lowlands and later in France. The centered point in a woman's hairline is named for this hat. In several Dutch paintings of churchgoing people, women are seen wearing the strange hat in Figure 9–7.

After several attempts, the Dutch ousted the Spanish in 1609, but the "regents" of the new "republic" (it was really a representative monarchy holding selective allegiance to the House of Orange) were the wealthy middle class, who were sober, Protestant, and industrious. They reestablished the textile industry and supported it by the use of luxurious fabrics, richly embellished with gold and silver, again a holdover from the sober, pious, and Catholic Spaniards. The Puritans in turn borrowed from them, but sim-

Figure 9–7. *The Question Mark Hat*

plified the line. (The Spanish did not officially recognize this separation until the Treaty of Munster in 1648.)

The court of William II of Orange spoke French and dressed in French fashions, but adopted several native styles. The breeches, instead of losing their fullness in the '30s and '40s, if anything, increased. These were called "rhingraves." The French breeches were also getting wider, looking eventually like skirts (see Mid-Baroque). The common people wore ensembles very much like the Puritans, but the colors tended to be a little more lively.

By the time William III of Orange became King of the Netherlands and through marriage King of England (William and Mary), Baroque fashions of courtly Europe had solidified into a generally accepted style and there were no longer regional differences in the haute-mode. Folk costumes were and have remained a different matter.

Children in Holland, like those elsewhere, generally wore miniature replicas of adult clothing. The little girls of Holland did not wear stomachers until about age eleven. Their bodices came just to the waist, but that was the only difference. Learning to eat and avoid ruining a millstone ruff must have been quite a job for a little child. The superstition that a boy dressed as a girl until age four would somehow fool God into

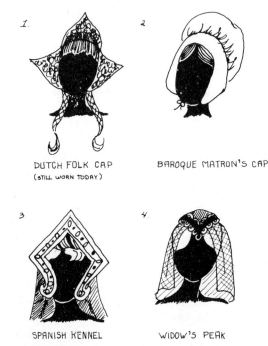

Figure 9–6. *Stages of the Dutch Cap*

letting him live (infant females have a better rate of survival even today) persisted. A boy celebrated his fourth birthday with a "breeching" ceremony. This was not a singularly Dutch custom, but had been practiced generally for several hundred years.

There was another Old World superstition concerning babies. If the newborn were wrapped in their mothers' dresses, they would magically become beautiful adults. This was one superstition that the Puritans approved, bringing it with them to America.

Best Sources—Artists

Frans Hals
Rembrandt
Peter Paul Rubens
Jan Steen
Cornelis de Vas
Jan Vermeer

Figure 9–8. *Spanish Baroque—1600 to 1700*

Spanish Baroque—1600 to 1700

The Man—1655

The man in Figure 9–8 is dressed in a V-waisted doublet and pumpkin-like knee breeches, cape, armored gorget, and boots. Like his Dutch contemporary, his breeches are very full, but the knee band lacks any sort of frills. His stockings are tucked under the bands and then an extra band is wound round both, as a sort of added protection. His boots have a roomy top, but are not the "slops" favored by the French and English.

The Spanish nobleman adopted certain military fashions into his everyday apparel. He was never without his sword and the steel gorget was merely protection against assassination. The doublet was almost exactly the same for over one hundred years. The length of the peplum may have varied, as did the epaulettes and sleeve width, but the basic garment remained.

This Spanish grandee chooses the typical black and gold.

The ruff, as a stiffened and throat-constricting chin rest, gradually lost out to the high linen turned down version pictured here. The wrist ruff lost ground to the softer linen version more universally worn, but some of the older gentlemen stuck to the previous styles. As in other countries, the demise of the ruff allowed for longer hair, but this grandee wears his hair as long as was thought proper and masculine.

The Woman—1655

The bell-shaped farthingale gradually lost out to a farthingale that went from side to side, as we see on the woman in Figure 9–8. When the House of Bourbon married into the Spanish throne in the latter half of the seventeenth century, this was taken to France and became the forerunner of the Rococo panniers.

Hair that had been swept up and away from the face during the late Renaissance was now also dressed side to side, often in a series of multiple braids done over a wire frame and always accented by an ornament of some sort, in this case a rosette and plume.

The high ruff went through a cartwheel stage and then a high "picadil" stand-up version, finally settling into any number of collars of which the silhouette in Figure 9–8 is but one example. It is of a pleated and then stiffened linen with a scalloped lace edge that perches on the shoulders and stands up a little around the collarbone. The Spanish continued to tie their sleeves onto their bodices (and doublets, too). A finely pleated linen epaulet covers the ties. The sleeves have been slashed down the front to expose an inner sleeve of pleated linen, whose cuff extends beyond the outer sleeve and is then turned back onto it. The corsets continued to flatten the breasts, but the bodice front came only to a modest point. This particular bodice is really more of a jacket, as it has a large peplum shirt made especially for the side-to-side farthingale.

General Description

Although black and gold were the most popular colors, red ran a close second, if paintings are to be believed. White and creams were very popular for young people. The somber shades of green and red were also very popular; blue was the most expensive dye of all, but somehow the wealthy considered it ostentatious and stuck with black. The fabric choices were rich, native merino wool, velvets, silks, taffetas, and brocades, woven with real gold and silver threads. The Spanish had a corner on the world's gold market at this time, because of her domination of the Americas.

In paintings of this period we begin to see women wearing a veil covering of lace. A widow's was black and reached the ground. A matron's was either black or white and merely touched

the shoulder, and some dispensed with it altogether. A young, unmarried girl was supposed to cover her face, all but the eyes, when abroad in daylight. It seems a very Moorish custom to have been adopted by people who only one hundred years before fought and ousted the Moors in a "holy" war. This was, however, the beginning of Spain's national trademark, the mantilla. The "fieltro," a mid-calf length cape complete with square collar that could be fastened into a type of hood, became very popular for a riding cloak.

A word should also be said about Spanish armor. The Spanish were the first to use a convex cuirass breast plate in the mid-Renaissance and this item was worn well into the Baroque era, along with the razor-backed helmet (refer to Fig. 8–13). The shape helped to deflect sword thrusts.

The word "picadil" comes from the Spanish word "pecadillo," which means spearhead or pike. Picadils to the Spanish were the tabs around the upper armhole and were pike-shaped and covered the sleeve ties. The high stand-up collars favored by the elderly Queen Elizabeth, Catherine de Medici, and even Mary Queen of Scots were also called picadil collars. Today the Spaniards have picadors, the men on horseback who spike the bull's hump in bull fighting. Otherwise the word has all but disappeared.

Best Sources

Artists:
Bartolome Esteban Murillo
Jose de Ribera (Lo Spagnoletto)
Diego Rodrigues de Silva Velasquez
Zurbaran

Well-known Playwrights:
Ruiz de Aiarcon
Pedro Calderon de la Barca
Guillen de Castro

Miguel de Cervantes (who wrote "Entre Messes" for the theater, the equivalent to our entr'actes or intermission vignettes)

Tirso de Molina

Felix Lope de Vega Carpio

Francisco de Rojas Zorilla

Middle (French) Baroque—1640 to 1685 (English) Restoration—1660 to 1720

The Man—1665

The gentleman in Figure 9–9 wears the short jacket and petticoat breeches typical of the French and English courts at this time. The petticoat breeches were a version of the Dutch "rhingraves" (see Dutch Baroque) with a skirt worn on top of it that reached almost to the knees. His shirt is of either linen or silk, and he wears an elaborate "falling band", or cravat of the same fabric trimmed in lace. His silk stockings are held up with white lace and ruffle trimmed gaiters that show beneath the kneeband. His leather shoes are trimmed with bows and have a high heel, probably painted red, although white heels were also popular, particularly among women.

His jacket and petticoat breeches are of a bright yellow silk; his stockings a pale yellow; and all the ribbons that appear on skirt hem and waist, kneebands, lovelock, and short jacket sleeves are a bright pink. His wig is auburn, parted in the center, and falls in flowing curls beyond his shoulders. His hat and shoes are black, but the multifarious plumes are shades of yellow and pink. All in all, he is quite the peacock.

Figure 9–9. *Middle (French) Baroque—1640 to 1685*

The Woman—1665

Although sumptuously attired, the woman in Figure 9–9 is no match for her male contemporary. She wears a chemise of fine linen over her corset, which, in contrast to its predecessors, was meant to push up and out, not flatten, the breasts. The female bosom was the focal point of fashion and the bodice neckline was cut very low. The neckline of this woman's chemise can be seen over the bodice and is tied to it in little puffs by tiny ribbons. The sleeve length most popular was to the elbow, with the ruffle made by pulling draw strings. This bodice is slightly pointed in front, laced closing in the back; and the slashed sleeves are elbow-length. It is of a bright red silk trimmed with bright pink ribbon. The red silk overskirt is divided up the front and held back to show an underskirt of yellow taffeta, which is banded at the hemline with the red and pink of the bodice. This underskirt is quilted to form a design. Her hair bows and the bows that hold back the overskirt are the same shade of pink as the bodice trim. Her hair is worn over the ears in coiled ringlets and a fanned coil in the back.

General Description

Charles II, son of the executed Charles I, was restored to the English throne in 1660. He had spent his formative years in France, living at the court of his uncle, Louis XIV. He brought French haute-mode with him in all things, style of dress, cuisine, architecture, and general life style. England, after twenty some years of sober piety, was indeed ready for the change and seemed to do an about face. The colors of clothing went from somber to brilliant, parrot colors and two or three colors at least on one outfit. There was also a profusion of all the things the Puritans had banned—ribbons, laces, and buttons. Charles was known as the Merry Monarch, and indeed he did seem to have a good time. He reopened and financially encouraged the theater in London. He found time to breed a particular type of spaniel dog, white with brown spots, that was named for him, and he invented a three-quarter length coat at the very end of the era that to a greater or lesser degree would remain in fashion for one hundred years (see Late Baroque).

Louis XIV was known as the "Sun King." He expressed his private philosophy in his famous saying "apres mois, le deluge" (after me, the flood). He indeed spent money like a drunken sailor, completing Fountainbleau and beginning Versailles. He discovered the principle of divide and conquer and created an honor system among the noble families of service to the King, no matter how small and insignificant, and allowed them to clamor for the scraps of his favors. One nobleman was assigned to help him on with his shoes; another, his stockings; another, his breeches; etc. It took ten men to dress him.

Men still wore red-heeled shoes. Tall walking staffs became popular. Gloves were reserved for soldiers and the working class. A gentleman kept his hands warm in winter with a muff, which was worn either on a belt around the waist or on a ribbon around the neck.

Hats for both men and women were still of felt or beaver and very much alike. The crown had become shortened, the brim wider, and the plumes even more abundant than what their Cavalier parents had worn. For a brief time women wore hats with an extremely wide circular brim that one hundred years later would be called a "Gainsborough" hat.

The women wore their hair long or sometimes in clusters of wired curls. The little linen caps of the previous decades was still worn for work and therefore by the working class. Under their wigs men usually had very short hair or shaven heads, so a wide variety of night caps became popular to keep the head warm.

The working class woman wore the same general style of garments, but her bodice often lacked the center front section and was laced up the front over a chemise. Some of these bodices were sleeveless and some had little short sleeves, which exposed a good deal more of the lady's chemise and breast. Certain actresses adopted and romanticized this.

Like the word "picadil" discussed in the general description of Spanish Baroque, the word "chemise" has a similar history of transformation. In Gothic France and Norman England it was originally a woman's shift, a full-length underdress usually of linen and worn for added warmth and to keep coarse fabric of outer garments from irritating the skin. In the Renaissance and Baroque eras it meant a fine linen shirt as well as a lady's underblouse. In the Victorian days it was either a man's or a lady's nightgown. In the roaring '20s it was a short straight slip of some exquisite fabric to be worn under a see-through dress. Today in France "en chemise" means rolled in a crepe and is something to eat.

One item of female apparel should be noted. At this time the first official riding habit for women became a style; it was adapted from the man's attire. This idea continues until the present day. Before this time a woman rode in any dress—except, perhaps women like Catherine de Medici, Mary Queen of Scots, and Joan of Arc (see French Renaissance, Elizabethan, and High Gothic, respectively). The process of printing fabric was brought to England from France by the Huguenot refugees.

Best Sources

Artists:
Charles Le Brun
Pierre Mignard
Hyacinthe Rigaud
Justus Suttermans
Joseph Vivian

Playwrights and Operatic Composers:
John Blow
Pierre Corneille
Moliere
Henry Purcell (opera)
Jean Racine

Late (French) Baroque—1685 to 1720
English Restoration

The Woman—1690

There is very little basic difference in the components of female attire between 1660 and 1690. As Figure 9–10 shows, it still consists of a bodice, an elaborate underskirt, but the silhouette has elongated. The point of the bodice has lengthened. The elbow sleeve has become form fitting. The underskirt is less full and more bell-shaped like the Elizabethan Spanish farthingale, but holds its shape by means of petticoats and not hoops. This lady's overskirt is lined in a quilted fabric of a contrasting color. It is pulled back all the way to the derriere and allowed to puff and fold in an almost bustle effect. The train of the overskirt is even longer than it was in the mid-Baroque. This woman wears a square lace-edged linen collar and linen double ruffles at her

Figure 9–10. *Late (French) Baroque—1685 to 1720*

elbows. Her underskirt and the stomacher section of her bodice are of a printed silk. Her hair is curled close to the head and pulled back into two or three large curls down her back neck. The pleated and beribboned headdress is called a fontage. It has two crinkled pieces of ribbon hanging down the back of it. Very little jewelry was worn during this time.

The Man—1690

The flowing male wigs of the 1660s had gradually developed into the series of studied curls called the "peruke" (perruque in French) that the gentleman in Figure 9–10 wears. He also wears the three-quarter-length coat that was originally designed by Charles II, but Charles's coat was of a straight line from shoulder to hem with fuller sleeves and smaller cuffs. This is the coat of William III (of Orange), form-fitting to the waist and then gently belled toward the hem. The sleeves of this version do the same, form-fitting to elbow and belling out into enormous cuffs. The breeches remain wide and are caught into kneebands of a contrasting fabric. His stockings are of a silk ribbed knit and his shoes are high-throated and accented with bows and oval buckles.

His shirt still has the full sleeves of its predecessor, but the body of the shirt is less full. The coat is completely collarless. The shirt is completed by a short falling band over which is tied a band of a contrasting fabric, which is tied in a big frontal bow, often red. Heels on shoes are still red. He wears a baldrick over his shoulders to hold his dress sword and carries a walking stick. His hat is the same wide-brimmed hat of the 1660s, but the brim has been rolled into three sections. This is the start of the extremely popular tri-cornered hat of the later Rococo periods. The enormous plumes gradually disappeared and were replaced by edgings of marabou,

fur, or lace. The coat hooks up the front and the buttons remain as decoration.

General Description

As for colors and textiles, what applies to the mid-Baroque also applies to the Late Baroque. The one exception is that printed fabric was seen more and more among the wealthy. Also, velvet made a dramatic comeback and was used particularly for gentlemen's coats. In general, men did not look quite as effeminate as in the previous two decades. Louis XIV did not like Charles's coat at first and called it a "Persian" coat, dressing his footmen in them as an insult. In a sort of reverse psychology it could be seen as the beginning of "livery," the servants' uniform for almost two hundred years.

Best Sources

Artists:
Gerard Ter Borch
Charles Le Brun
Pierre Mignard
Jacob Ochteruelt
Hyacinthe Rigaud
Justus Suttermans
Joseph Vivian
Antoine Watteau

Playwrights and Operatic Composers:
John Blow
William Congreve
John Gay (musical theatre)
George Frederick Handel (opera)
Henry Purcell (opera)

Note: the best look at England of this time (1660 to 1690 approximately) is through the writings of two men: 1. Samuel Pepys, his *Diary* and *Memories of the Royal Navy*; and 2. Jonathan Swift, for his satirical outlook in novels like *Gulliver's Travels*.

10

The Age of Enlightenment: Rococo through Empire

Louis XIV was nine years old when he inherited the throne. When he died, his nine-year-old grandson Louis XV became king, inheriting a great tradition but very little actual monetary wealth. Louis XIV had spent most of it. This perhaps accounted for the modifications in style. Both the Baroque and the Rococo shared a love of the ornate and curved line, but where the Baroque used solid woods, real gold, and massiveness, the Rococo used wood veneers and gold gilt and chose a more delicate appearance, thereby using less material.

By the time Louis XV came to the throne, neoclassicism had brought a return to the square and symmetrical, but this time overlayed with vestiges of Rococo ornateness.

This time in England was dominated by the New Hanoverian line and is called Georgian after Georges I, II, and III. People began to be concerned about "The rights of man," and revolutionary breezes began to blow, starting in American in 1776 and then in France in 1789. The United States borrowed red, white, and blue as its national colors from the British. The

borrowed it from America, so it is easy to see why for a while on both sides of the Atlantic it was a very fashionable color scheme.

Some fashion historians believe that the Directoire and Empire lines were an outgrowth of the neo-classicism epitomized by the works of the Adams brothers. Others believe it was a result of Napoleon's Italian and Egyptian campaigns. Whatever its cause the result was certainly a counterbalance to the curved lines of the previous century.

Early (French) Rococo—1720 to 1760
English Name: Georgian—1720 to 1790

The Man—1735

The man's ensemble in Figure 10–1 consists of five basic items. His shirt and stock are of either silk or fine linen. The sleeves are still full and end in ruffles at the wrist. The shirt is collarless. The stock, of the same fabric, is wrapped several times around the neck and knotted to

Figure 10–1.   *Early (French) Rococo—1720 to 1760*

form a jabot. His breeches, which fit much more snugly than previously, are of silk and are gathered into a velvet knee band that buckles on the outside of the leg. The same silk trims the coat's large cuffs and pocket flaps. The coat itself has a wide skirt, which comes just to the knee. Long coats were previously given flair to enable them to conveniently cover the former wide breeches, which held out the coat skirt. When the breeches became close fitting, the coat skirt was stiffened with an interfacing of horsehair to enable it to stand out on its own.

The coat sleeves also narrowed, making it necessary to button the enormous cuff up in order to keep them out of the soup. Cuffs often acted as extra pockets, which held a gentleman's accoutrements, such as handkerchief, snuff box, money pouch and, as powdered hair became increasingly popular, his powder box.

The coat is made of a figured silk. The waistcoat at this time also had a full skirt, which ex-

tended to the upper thigh. It too had pockets and generally buttoned from the upper chest to waist. The man wears silk "clocked" stockings, black leather shoes with a heel considerably lower than the previous era, but still adorned with buckles. His hair is worn in a basic "club" style tied with a large silk bow that also comes around the neck and ties in a bow in front. He carries a tri-cornered hat and a cane.

The Woman—1735

The woman in Figure 10–1 wears a morning dress and boudoir cap. This is an appropriate costume for an upper-class Rococo lady to wear while having her morning chocolate, seeing to the management of the household and tutoring the children. (For a pattern of this dress, see Fig. 10–2.) It has a watteau back that falls from a back yoke. It is not certain that the painter actually designed this, but he painted so many women wearing this style that it has been given his name. Actually, there were two versions of this and in their day they were called sac dresses. The dress in Figure 10–1 has a fitted bodice in front and the back yoke is also fitted, but the back is extra full and then box-pleated to the yoke. The sleeves are fitted to just above the elbow and end in a multi-layered ruffle, which is cut in such a way as to be almost egg-shaped, longer on the under elbow and shorter at the bend. This is banded by a velvet bow (see Figure 10–3).

Her hair is combed in a series of curls pinned close to the head. The boudoir cap is of a fine linen lawn and accented with a narrow velvet ribbon tied in a bow at center back and with a little flower cluster pinned to it. The flowers were often real.

Her dress is of a new fabric called "chintz." It is a cotton fabric, which has been "polished" (made to look shiny). "Chintz" also refers to a type of design, usually an evenly spaced floral design. This particular dress must be worn over the corset and panniers, a hoop that exagger-

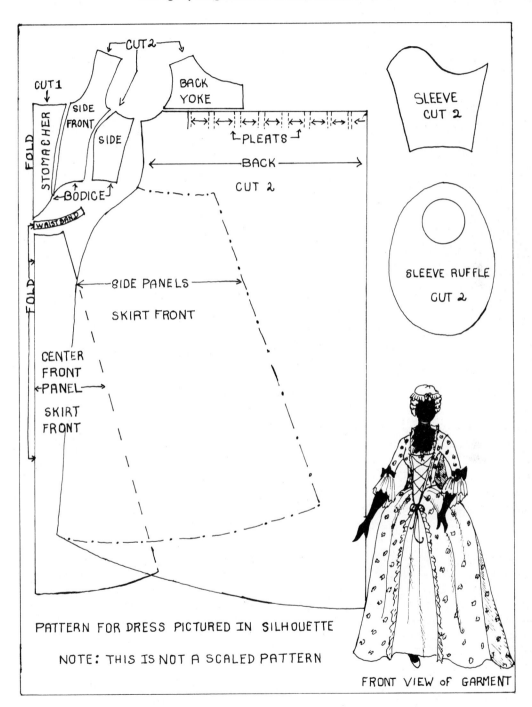

CUT 2

CUT 1

BACK
YOKE

FOLD

STOMACHER

SIDE
FRONT

SIDE

PLEATS

BODICE

WAISTBAND

BACK

CUT 2

SLEEVE
CUT 2

SLEEVE RUFFLE
CUT 2

FOLD

SIDE PANELS

SKIRT FRONT

CENTER
FRONT
PANEL

SKIRT
FRONT

PATTERN FOR DRESS PICTURED IN SILHOUETTE

NOTE: THIS IS NOT A SCALED PATTERN

FRONT VIEW of GARMENT

Figure 10–2. *Pattern for Dress Pictured in Figure 10–1*

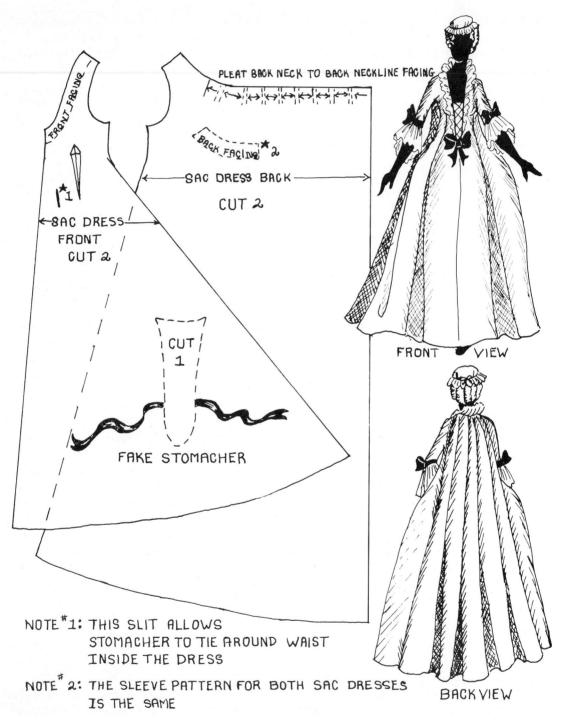

FRONT FACING

★1

◄— SAC DRESS —
FRONT
CUT 2

PLEAT BACK NECK TO BACK NECKLINE FACING

BACK FACING ★2

◄— SAC DRESS BACK —►
CUT 2

CUT 1

FAKE STOMACHER

FRONT VIEW

BACK VIEW

NOTE #1: THIS SLIT ALLOWS
STOMACHER TO TIE AROUND WAIST
INSIDE THE DRESS

NOTE #2: THE SLEEVE PATTERN FOR BOTH SAC DRESSES
IS THE SAME

Figure 10–3. *Second Version of the Rococo Sac Dress*

ates the width of the hips and supposedly minimizes the size of the female form from front to back. Also the sac back had a slight train effect. This version could be worn outdoors. Another version hung straight from the shoulders in the back, but was pleated at the neckline. The front hung from the shoulders also and was worn strictly at home form comfort, often without corset or panniers.

General Description

The return to simplicity can be seen in the styles of dress, particularly for men. The elaborately curled wig disappeared around 1720 and was replaced by either natural hair or a more simplified white wig with just two curls over each ear. Men of this period also remained clean-shaven. As the century wore on, the coat skirt lost more and more of its fullness, until it achieved a form fitting almost swallowtail cut (see late Rococo). For the first time military garb took on a uniformity, thus giving us the word uniform for a suit of military clothing. This uniformity only carried as far as a regiment and the various regiments took great pride in their different uniforms. The enormous skirt of the coat was found inconvenient for fighting, so it was cut down in size and then the corners were turned back and buttoned up, often showing a contrasting lining color.

All vestiges of metal armor disappeared. The sword was the thing. The saber was used in service. The rapier acted as dress sword and was worn by the general man about town. Baldricks became elaborate and fancy, sometimes even petite-point work. The coat continued to be vented down the center back to allow for the sword.

Ladies' dresses also became simplified during the early Rococo period. Certainly their coiffures were simple. Unfortunately this did not last and by 1740 the dresses were as elaborate as any dress of the previous century. By 1765 doors had to be cut bigger to accommodate the ladies and

"the ladies chair" was invented for the same reason. (A "ladies chair" is without side arms.)

For "at-home" wear the open-heeled "mule" was still popular, although the toe returned to pointed and briefly in the 1750s even turned up a little in an Oriental way. Many of the chintz prints of this period were also Oriental in design and I wonder if the word "chintz" is not derived from the French "chinoiserie" meaning Chinese-like. Although the cloth was made in several oriental countries, to the Europeans of this time chinoiserie was an all inclusive term.

The style setters of the period were Madame du Pompadour, Madame du Barry, and in the late Rococo, Marie Antoinette. Madame du Pompadour and Madame du Barry were both mistresses to Louis XV; Madame du Pompadour was a charmingly beautiful woman, who gathered around her the best artistic society that France had to offer. She also had the knack of seeming to stay well removed from the political world of her day. By confining her interests to matters artistic she shaped tastes to her own mode. She was fond of pastel colors, which became popular. She was petite and thin and of delicate health (she fought T.B. for years and finally succumbed to it). "Thin" was "in," as were lightweight fabrics. She loved flowers, particularly roses, wore them on her hats, starting a fashion that has lasted until the present day. The rose became the prevalent motif of her day. She loved the theater and from contemporary reports was an excellent amateur actress and an accomplished musician. The theater at Versailles was built for her. She financially encouraged the Comédie Français.

Unfortunately her successor, Madame du Barry, shared only one quality, that of physical beauty. The only thing with which this lady concerned herself was power. Her fondness for cupids as a sort of luck charm made them the prevalent motif for a brief period.

The painter Antoine Watteau was fascinated with the commedia dell'arte and has left us a rich source of these theatrical costumes.

Best Sources

Artists:
Francois Boucher
Jean Baptiste Chardin
Jean Honore Fragonard
Jean Baptiste Greuze
William Hogarth
Nicholas Lancret
Pietro Longhi
Jean-Marc Nattier
Maurice Quentin
Both Tiepolos
Antoine Watteau

Both Chardin and Hogarth were concerned with the everyday life of their times and consequently are our best sources for the fashions of the work-a-day person of this period.

Playwrights and Operatic Composers:
Carlo Goldoni
Oliver Goldsmith
Christoff Willebald von Gluck
George Frederick Handel
John Gay

Late (French) Rococo—1760 to 1789

English: Georgian—1720 to 1790
American: Federalist—1776 to 1820

The Nobleman—1775 to 1785

The nobleman in Figure 10–1 is dressed for court in a velvet suit, quilted silk waistcoat, powdered wig, and tricorn hat. His jacket cuffs are of the same quilted silk as his waistcoat. Both items are bordered with a stripped silk, and the coat has silk tabs, each buttoned with a velvet button. These buttons are strictly for decoration.

By the late Rococo era all pretense of having a jacket actually close was dispensed. Even the cord and velvet buttons on his waistcoat are merely decorative. The waistcoat actually fastens with a series of invisible hooks and eyes. Note how the waistcoat has shortened considerably by this date. The breeches fit quite snugly through the hips and thighs, but bell slightly to be gathered or softly pleated into a knee band that buckles on the outside of the leg. The man's white silk stockings are clocked on both the inside and out of the shin. His shoes have a flatter heel and the color red for heels has disappeared. Buckles could vary from plain to elaborate and from paste to gold. A snowy white cambric shirt and stock complete the outfit. The shirt is still full-sleeved, ending in wrist ruffles, and the stock is tied to form a puffed jabot. He wears the white wig with two curls on each side of the face and club behind held by a velvet bow, that was typical of court life. His hat trim matches his suit.

The Lady—1775 to 1785

This lady is dressed for a court ball in the extremely wide panniers of the late Rococo period. The pannier itself measures six or seven feet across and the hem could be another seven to eighteen inches bigger than that. Doors had to be recut to accommodate these skirts, and two women could not pass through the same door at the same time.

Her dress is of two parts, skirt and bodice, but made to look like one. This dress would be a winter ball gown of velvet. The underskirt and bodice stomacher are of a quilted and beaded silk, done in a fleur-de-lis motif. The side panels of the skirt and the fake cuffs of the sleeves are of a matching silk that has been latticed with gold cording, and at each juncture there is a pearl. A fine silk or organza is pleated into a ruffled trim called "frills"; these go around the neckline, down to the waist on either side of the stomacher, and edge the latticed panels of skirt

Figure 10–4. *Late (French) Rococo—1760 to 1789*

and cuff. The same fabric makes the sleeve ruffles and each sleeve has one velvet bow. A velvet bow and curled ostrich plume accent this woman's white powdered coiffure, which is moderate in its extremity. Some of the hair styles were so high that the women wore wire frames on their heads over which the hair was teased and combed. She carries a fan. Considering that this ensemble probably weighed thirty pounds, a fan was hardly an affectation; it was a necessity.

The Servant—1720 to 1790

The ordinary woman did not have the time or the money for the extremes of fashion. What

this girl is wearing could have been worn in any year from 1720 to almost 1800.

Our servant girl in Figure 10–4 wears her skirt hiked up by means of drawstrings on either side of her hips "panniers." This side to side arrangement also came to be called panniers. Her petticoat then acted as an underskirt. Her bodice has a low-cut square neckline and long muslin-lined sleeves, which are rolled up to the elbow for work. Her muslin fichu is tucked down the front of her bodice and held there with a brooch. Her apron is of a heavy serviceable cotton cloth, in this case striped and tucked. She wears a version of a mob (or mop) cap on her head to keep the dirt off her hair. Her stockings are cotton and she wears sabots (clogs) on her feet. These were used as overshoes. A thin leather slipper was worn with the sabots. Sabots were worn as protection against the muck and mud of rural life. The same girl would wear "louis," heeled shoes of black leather, and perhaps pewter buckles indoors or in the city. Her fabrics would be serviceable wools, linens, and cottons.

General Description

Paintings of this period seem very romantic and elegant, but beauty is only skin deep and even that smelled horribly if you believe contemporary reports. Because of a general belief that bathing in ordinary water was unhealthy, people did not do it very often. Also, it took so long to arrange a coiffure that great care was taken to keep it undisturbed for weeks; more powder was simply added to cover the grease. The poet Robert Burns dedicated one of his poems to a louse he watched eat a woman's scalp as he sat behind her in church. There were even tales of mice who made nests in coiffures. Perfume was poured on daily to cover body odor. Makeup of a whitish, lead-based paste became popular (to cover the dirt?) with much rouge added for color. It was worn by both men and women, as were patches, little pieces of velvet or metal cut in a variety of shapes (hearts, flowers, stars, and moons) and pasted on the cheek. In England certain male dandies wore their hair in extreme fashion with tiny tri-cornered hats perched on top. They also wore their clothing extremely tight with their coat tails cut off short, so that the derriere could show. They were called "macaroni," a term that will live forever in the song of our American Revolution, "Yankee Doodle"—"stuck a feather in his cap and called it Macaroni."

Patches were carried about in small boxes, as were powder and rouge. This necessitated a place to put them and the Macaroni took to carrying reticules. Ladies had secret pockets sewn into the folds of their dresses.

Both the servant and her mistress would have shared one item—the corset. It came just to the waist, except in the very front, where it extended down to a point about three inches below the waist. It made no provision for the breast and laced up the back. It cinched the waist and pushed up the breast, achieving the desired roundness. The corset succeeded in making something out of almost nothing and also supported the well-endowed.

Best Sources

Artists:
Jean-Honore Fragonard
Thomas Gainsborough
Jean-Baptiste Greuze
William Hogarth
Jean-Etienne Leotard
Joshua Reynolds
George Romney

Well-known Playwrights and Opera Composers:
Carlo Goldoni
Oliver Goldsmith
Wolfgang Amadeus Mozart (opera)

Republican—1789 to 1795

English Name: Regency—1790 to 1820
French Name: Republican
American Name: Federalist

The Woman—1790

The woman in Figure 10–5 wears an afternoon dress and jacket and a "Gainsborough" hat on her moderately extreme hair style. Her hair is unpowdered, teased, and puffed around the face with one gigantic curl down the back. Thomas Gainsborough did not invent the hat, but painted so many women wearing it that it

CARL A. RUDISILL LIBRARY
LENOIR-RHYNE COLLEGE

Figure 10–5.   *Republican—1789 to 1795*

took on his name. This particular one has a red, white, and blue cockade of the French national assembly.

Her dress is of an embroidered light-weight fabric (silk or lawn) worn over a bell-shaped hoop of whale bone stays and a little pillow worn on the derriere for a slight bustle effect. The jacket has a swallowtail cut to it, the tail extending just over the bustle in the back. It is of velvet with collar and cuffs of silk; the ruffled sleeve of the dress show below the jacket cuff. A wide tricolored belt is worn over both dress and jacket. A watch fob is attached to it.

The Man—1790

The gentleman in Figure 10–5 wears the new form-fitting coat of moire velvet fastened by dual directional tabs. Tabs accent the cuffs, and revers

are faced with a brocade of the same color. The waistcoat, buttons, and tail facings match and are of a darker shade of that color as well. The tails are of a square cut in the back. He wears long leather boots. His shirt is of white lawn or cambric (a very fine linen). His stock is of the same fabric as his shirt. He wears a tall, truncated, conical, crowned hat with flat brim and tricolor cockade. This hat is a modified version of the old Puritan hat or the hats that Welsh countrywomen wore for centuries. His hair is unpowdered and brushed back into a "club" that is bagged and bowed in black silk.

General Description

The return to a somewhat more modest silhouette for women than the extreme panniers of the '70s and early '80s had two causes. The English never adopted the extreme version for court. English tastes were more simple. This, and the beginning of neo-classicism, kept the silhouette modest for that country.

A breeze was stirring everywhere, a sort of "let's get back to basics" idea that many called the Age of Enlightenment. Even Marie Antoinette and the French court felt it. She was one of the first to endorse this new look. She built a model farm on the grounds of Versailles in her attempt to return to nature and had the court dress as milkmaids and peasants, if silk and satin can be called peasant.

Even fashionable women wore ankle-length skirts. One dress was called "Polonaise," which with the aid of interior drawstrings looped up the overskirt in the back and exposed an underskirt of a contrasting fabric. Only the hair remained elaborate, but the French queen enjoyed wearing her own natural blonde color and others followed.

The gentlemen were beginning to wear unpowdered hair as well, a fashion brought back to France by those who fought in the American Revolution. Gentlemen's clothes were more and

CARL A. RUDISILL LIBRARY
LENOIR RHYNE COLLEGE

more form-fitting until even the men began wearing corsets. The swallowtail cut-away front became most popular for evening. It was usually in dark blues, greens, and plums, with waistcoat of a pastel shade and often beautifully embroidered. The craze for "chinoiserie" earlier in the century had brought many Chinese arts and artisans to Europe and the technique of ribbon embroidery was being used more and more frequently.

For daytime wear a peculiar long waistcoat worn under a short-waisted double-breasted coat with square tails and tall beaver hat became popular. The ordinary male citizen began wearing dark stockings instead of white.

Note should be made of the fact that for the first time children began to be dressed somewhat differently from adults. Little girls were free of corsets. Little boys were put in ankle-length pants and ruffled shirts, which allowed freedom of movement. As would continue into the Directoire, the favorite colors were red, white, and blue.

Best Sources

Artists:
Thomas Gainsborough
Thomas Lawrence
Henry Raeburn
Joshua Reynolds
Hubert Robert
George Romney

Playwrights:
Pierre Augustas Caron de Beaumarchais
Richard Sheridan

Directoire—1795 to 1806

English Name: Regency, Neo-Classic
French Name: Directoire
American Name: Federalist

The Woman—1795

The woman of this time was called "une Merveilleuse"; she was the feminine counterpart of "un incroyable," the female hippie of the revolution, whose extreme fashion (of which Figure 10–6 is a mild example) was every bit as much a protest against the political thought of revolutionary Paris as that of the hippie was in the 1960s. Both were "drop-outs" of their respective times.

Her dress has a wide waistband adorned with not one, but two watch fobs. It is probably of muslin with the collar and cuffs of a slightly darker shade. Her shoes are perfectly flat leather slippers and she wears horizontally striped stockings. She carries a paisley bordered woolen shawl. Her hair is worn unpowdered, unteased, and in long curls. Her ribbon-trimmed turban is accented with jewels and egret feathers. She carries a small purse, as well.

She has neglected to wear petticoats and her dress falls naturally to the floor with a slight train. The only undergarment worn was a flesh-colored stocking knitted to a camisole-like top. The body stocking is not a new invention.

The Man—1795

The man in Figure 10–6 is a good example of "un incroyable," the male counterpart of "une Merveilleuse." His coat is long and merely touches closed at the waist, but versions of this coat were both single- and double-breasted in closure. The deep revers on his coat have a broad striped facing. His cuffs come over the back of the hand, but end in points. The collar of the coat is the double fold-over stand-up type so typical of this and the later Empire periods.

His shirt has a high collar that extends beyond his chin and his cravat, about eight feet long, is wound around his neck several times. It tended to lift the chin and put the nose in the air in an attitude that corresponds to the desired effect. His waistcoat comes just to the waist. His britches

Figure 10–6. *Directoire—1795 to 1806*

are festooned with ribbon garters and his gaily striped stockings have been rolled over the top of this boots. He wears his hair long and neither powered nor combed. A variety of extreme hats were worn, including the bicorn, which he carries, complete with its appropriate political cockade.

General Description

In France the styles were changed almost as rapidly as heads were rolling. The political leaders were different daily. Assassination was almost as frequent as the blade of the guillotine; first, Marat, next Danton, then Robespierre. The "muscadins" were out to make a profit from the downfall of anyone. They were upstarts who had all the vices and virtues of the nouveau riche of any time or place.

The "merveilleuse" and "incroyable" stood apart and laughed at fate and they were, in turn, ridiculed. They dressed the part. Extreme hats were as much in vogue as anything Marie Antoinette had ever fashioned. One feminine hat was a version of a jockey's cap, but the front peak extended out a foot or more, looking like a stork's beak.

The ordinary citizen's clothing changed very little. The lines of the republican decade were not generally accepted, but the wide waist band became standard as the stiffened petticoat disappeared, giving a softer fold to the dress. Muslin of a white or ecru color was very popular for these dresses. The working girl's fichu became adopted by even the wealthy and was tucked inside the low-necked afternoon dress. The "Gainsborough" hat remained popular.

One hair style, called the "hedgehog," became popular for both men and women. The hair around the face was cut short and teased, so that it stood almost straight out. The back hair for men was arranged in either a cue or club. Women let theirs just hang down the back. Powdered hair gradually began to decline.

Whether because of the English love of simplicity or the rise of the French middle classes, simplicity became the general order of the day. A style called a reddingcoat (from the words riding coat) was very popular among women. It was a single- or double-breasted coat that came just to the waist in front and to the floor on the sides and back. It was cut on exactly the same lines as a man's coat and was always worn with short waistcoat, shirt, and stock. English women had these made by their husband's tailors.

The variety of muslin fabric was fantastic. It could be "sprigged" (embroidered all over in evenly spaced little flowerettes or leaves), embroidered in borders, plain or cut out, and each cutout buttonhole stitched in a thread of the same color. This was the foundation of today's "eyelet" fabric.

The most popular colors remained those of the revolution: red, white, and blue. The citizens of France were not satisfied with just a sash or cockade to display their political sentiments, but now wore whole ensembles in these colors.

Note should be taken of the Adams brothers, English architects and interior designers, who during this period returned to the simplicity of the Greek line and gave impetus to styles yet to come.

Best Sources

Artists:
William Carpenter
Francisco Goya
Thomas Lawrence
Henry Raeburn
George Romney
Gilbert Stuart
Thomas Sully
Giandomenico Tiepolo
John Trumbull
Elisabeth Vigee-Lebrun

Playwright:
Richard Sheridan

Empire—1806 to 1820

English Name: Regency
French Name: Empire (Napoleonic)
American Name: Federalist

The Man—1810

The man in Figure 10–6 wears a summer silk suit with the knee breeches tight-fitting and buttoned on the outside. The knee band has become unpopular. His coat has the shortened waistcoat and square tails typical of the era. The turned-over stand-up collar and reveres are trimmed in velvet, as are the cuffs. The shirt has the high collar and heavy cravat of the "incroyables" of the previous decade. The waistcoat is of a figured silk, buttoned high and worn slightly below the waist, accentuated with a watch fob. His stockings would be white and his shoes would have silver buckles reminiscent of the Ro-

Figure 10–7. *Empire—1806 to 1820*

coco. The bicorn hat has become slightly rounded and standard fare for the man on the street. The man's hair is cut short á la Napoleon, whose hair was cut short during his southern campaigns in Italy and Egypt.

The Woman—1810

The woman in Figure 10–6 wears a dress and coat ensemble in the high-waisted vogue of the Empire. The dress is of muslin with an embroidered border. The bodice fits the bosom and the skirt is attached just under it. She wears a double ruffled collar with the dress. (It was probably a separate piece.) Her coat was called a "pelisse." This too fits the bosom and has the cutaway lines of the man's tailcoat. The sleeves are fitted from wrist to upper arm, going into a puff from there to the shoulder. Her shoes are the soft leather slippers of the Directoire Merveilleuse. Her stockings are white silk. She carries a "blinder" bonnet, which hugged the sides of the face much like the eye-hugging blinders of a horse's harness. Her hair is cut short in the "Grecian boy" fashion and she wears a headband of ribbon with a cameo. Cameos enjoyed a revival thanks to the passion for things "classical."

General Description

It is generally thought that Napoleon's Italian and Egyptian campaigns brought about a return to Classicism. This might be true for the French, but the English had begun this return, at least in architecture, as early as the 1700s. Napoleon did add certain motifs, however—e.g., the laurel leaf surrounding his letter N, although his personal symbol was the bee. He did model his empire on the old Roman lines. Josephine's symbol was the swan. Napoleon also brought back Egyptian motifs that were superimposed onto the classical lines of the furniture. Thus, one finds a lyre-backed chair with a pair of sphinxes on the arms. These same motifs were often either woven into or embroidered upon cloth. The fashion for diadems and tiaras came straight from the old Roman statues, as did the draped look. Early in the Empire era the little muslin dress was worn low-necked (without fichu), short-sleeved, and even dampened to make it cling to the body in a suggestive manner. The soft leather flat slipper had ribbons added to it for lacing up the leg á la the old Roman sandal.

Beautiful heavily embroidered satin dresses on much the same line were worn for evening, high-waisted and with short puffed sleeves. This was often worn with a velvet sleeveless "spencer" with train attached to the back. A spencer was a short jacket that just covered the breasts when worn by women. The male version was a tailless jacket that came just to the waist, usually double-breasted. It was later adapted into children's garments.

The picadil collar returned for evening and court wear. The short sleeve ushered in a fashion for extremely long kid gloves, which extended to the upper arm. Whereas the Rococo woman had not worn great amounts of jewelry, the bareness of the Empire fashions displayed jewelry to great effect. The "parvu" of jewels became fashionable. A parvu was a matching set, usually consisting of necklace, earrings, and a bracelet or two, all designed to match. Sometimes it also included a tiara and brooch. Cameos were worn and, of course, the various precious stones of diamonds, rubies, emeralds, and sapphires; also onyx, lapis lazuli, malachite, coral, and turquoise became popular.

As previously mentioned, Napoleon set a style for short hair. His sister, Caroline of Naples, also cut her hair into short ringlets (much like the Poodle Cut of the '50s.) For the first time short hair for women became fashionable, but was considered "fast." Many more conservative ladies cut the hair around the face short and wore their longer back hair twisted into various knots and chignons.

Napoleon set the pace for male fashion in France, Beau Brummel in England. George "Beau" Brummel was the style setter of the Regency and he revolutionized men's fashions, giving us the well-tailored gentleman. He was a friend of George IV, who was "portly" to say the least. Some believe that Brummel devised certain fashions to make George IV look better. He was very wealthy in his own right, but died a penniless and broken man, out of favor with his king. Nevertheless, it was he who introduced the long trousers and reintroduced the extremely high collar and enormous cravat. The long trousers were worn for daytime as early as 1815, but were not accepted generally until 1840. Even in the '30s breeches were considered proper for evening wear and court functions. He made England the center of men's fashion, which it has retained, albeit somewhat conservatively, ever since.

For evening a gentleman still wore knee breeches and white stockings with buckled shoes. The waistcoat was shortened to the waist with a pocketed three-inch peplum only in the front. The evening coat was the swallow-tailed cutaway line with a high, stiffened collar. Heavy metallic embroidery was used around the collar and down the front. The coat could fasten at the neck but did not fasten elsewhere. The shirt was worn with a white stock and jabot and wrist ruffles.

The prevalent colors were buff, scarlet, and bottle green for Napoleon. Pastels were worn in summer and for evening; dark jewel tones were for winter wear. Embroidery, bead work, and much use of gold and silver threads were often employed. Cut velvet and brocade enjoyed a vogue once again, particularly in Napoleon's attempt to reestablish the French silk industry.

Best Sources—Artists

Marie Giulhelmine Benoist
Jacques Louis David
Theodore Gericault
Francisco Goya
Jean Antoine Gros
Jean Dominique Ingres
Francais, Pascal; le Baron Grand
Pierre-Paul Prod'hon
Elisabeth Vigee-LeBrun

11

Romanticism:
Romantique through Victorian

The fall of Napoleon in 1814 was the last trumpet of European autocratic rule. Most European monarchs ruled with some form of parlimentary assistance; the one exception was Russia. It was also the sounding trumpet for nationalism, the pride of each individual nation for things of its own. Within this feeling of nationalism there seemed to be romantic notions concerning this very patriotism.

We call someone a "romantic" who sees life not as it is but how he wishes it to be and accepts the desire for the fact. This desire lead to a great flowering of artistic achievement, particularly in music and literature, somewhat less so in dramaturgy. We often associate certain countries with their composers who romanticized their folk melodies and rhythms into classical music: Poland—Chopin, Hungary—Liszt, and Norway—Grieg.

In much of the art of this time one can see this almost golden halo of heightened reality, particularly in the works of Millet, Corot, and Courbet, and in the landscapes of Constable and Turner. In England this seemed to reach its apex with a group of painters who called themselves the Pre-Raphaelite Brotherhood, which included Dante Gabriel Rosetti, William Holman Hunt, John Everett Millais, and Ford Maddox Brown. Edward Burne-Jones seemed cut from the same cloth. In Germany this Romanticism was epitomized by Johan Heinrich Wilhelm Tichbein and Caspar David Friedrich.

Mention should be made here of a German style called "Biedermeier." It began with the elegant and simple lines of the neo-classic, a contemporary of the Regency and Empire mode, but during the 1820s and '30s it began to change, to become overstuffed, tufted, tassled, and fringed. As architecture and furniture changed, so did fashion, exchanging the elongated draped look to one of exaggeration of sleeve, shoulder line, skirt, and bonnet brim. The Hanoverians were, after all, Germanic and then Victoria married German Prince Albert, which probably helped to reinforce the English taste for this sort of look.

Each country is said to have its golden age—Alexandrian Greece, Imperial Rome, Seventeenth Century Spain, France under Louis XIV. England had two such times. The first was under Elizabeth I and the second under Victoria. A dissertation could be written comparing the two women and their times. Both ruled a long time, were blessed with extremely capable ministers, and took advantage of exploration and colonization, Elizabeth the New World, and Victoria India and China. Both were stubborn, strong-willed women who set the tone for their times. The paradox is that Elizabeth, the virgin queen, was as lusty, zestful, quick-witted (and quick-tempered) as her age. Queen Victoria, the matron with many children, remained prudish, plodding, and after Albert's demise, preoccupied with death; so was her age. This prudish plodding quality certainly characterized the lower and middle levels of society, but the aristocracy found its champion and leader in Prince Edward Albert, the Prince of Wales. He led society a merry dance.

Figure 11–1. *Romantique—1820 to 1840*

Romantique—1820 to 1840

The Woman—1830

By 1830 the waistline had definitely dropped to its natural place. The young lady in Figure 11–1 wears an afternoon ensemble and carries a wide-brimmed sun bonnet of Italian straw trimmed in a striped ribbon and red poppy to match the belt and skirt trim of her costume. The ensemble is actually two pieces: a bodice of fine linen lawn with the highly exaggerated dropped shoulder and enormous leg-of-mutton sleeves, which were typical of this look. The skirt is of a pale green silk with a border of bright red poppies embroidered on it and set off with bands of dark green velvet ribbons. The embroidered leaves are a matching dark green. This skirt reaches the ankles and is worn over a series of stiffly starched petticoats called crinolines, a style brought back in the 1950s. Her belt is a wide red and white striped grosgrain ribbon that has been stitched

to a stiffened backing. Her hat and hair ribbons match. The cuffs and fluted yoke collar are striped in thin red cord. She wears a cameo on a dark green velvet ribbon around the bodice neckline. Her stockings are white; her shoes are soft black kid and heelless, with black ribbons criss-crossed across foot and around the ankle.

Long hair was back in fashion, parted in the center and worn in a trio of knots, one over each ear and one on the very top of the head. This center part and ear puff look would be in fashion to a greater or lesser degree until 1870. The top knot went out by 1840, only to return in 1890 but in a less flamboyant mode.

The Man—1830

The gentleman in Figure 11–1 wears a high collar and enormous cravat, a popular holdover from "incroyable" days. By this time the collar was less stiffly starched, an idea introduced by Beau Brummel. He also started the fashion for long trousers as illustrated in Figure 11–1. Originally such pantaloons were more often called "Beau Brummels." The pantaloon was extremely full in the front and gathered to a waistband. The front had a squared flap opening, much like sailor pants, but with hidden buttons. This balloon-like top tapered toward the ankle and was held under the foot with a strap. To accentuate their size even further they were usually of a light color, dove grey, faun or buff.

This gentleman's frock coat is of a bold plaid jokingly referred to as a "horse blanket" plaid. It sports velvet lapels and cuffs and was considered just right for the viewing of sporting events. This could be considered the first sports coat. A man who wore such an ensemble was called a "sport."

A high-belled topper and faun kid gloves complete the ensemble. Sideburns were worn down to the chin with a great variety of moustaches and an occasional very small goatee.

General Description

The frock coat derived its name from its full skirt resembling a woman's "frock" (another name for dress). In the 1830s its skirt was at its fullest. The width of men's coattails from the "Persian" coat invented by Charles II of England varies as much as a woman's hemline. Both seem to measure the centuries by the minuteness of the centimeter.

The top hat was originally introduced in 1795 by a group of French dandies called "les muscadins," who were profiteers of the revolution, an early French version of a carpetbagger. At the time it had a crown of approximately eight inches and a brim with a four-inch width. By 1830 it was a belled-top stovepipe of twelve to fourteen inches with a rolled two-and-one-half-inch brim. It would continue to go up and down and in and out, until it became the opera hat, which is still worn today with white tie and tails at ultra formal occasions.

The English exploration of the Far East and the French exploration of the Near East brought many new fabrics into common use, particularly in the silk line. Raw silk and silk shantung were commonly used, as were the irridescent silks achieved by weaving one color for the warp thread and another for the woof, such as an emerald green and peacock blue together. The English colonialization of India gave the Romantic and Victorian Age madras cotton in soft plaids and stripes and the paisley design, which became a rage in the Regency and Romantic decades for shawls. By 1840 the English copied the design in wool, silk, and even calico. All colors were used by both men and women.

Women wore completely off-the-shoulder dresses for evening and a strange puffed and feathered headdress called a turban. This turban looked more like an enormous stuffed bowl. The huge sleeve, worn for evening, stopped just above the elbow and was worn with elbow-length white kid gloves or crochetted mitts. The mitt was a glove that covered only the hand and fingers to the first knuckle, leaving the fingertips free.

The fabric called taffeta was extremely popular for evening wear, particularly in stripes and plaids. Plaid had been previously relegated to wool. After 90 years of legal banishment, the wearing of Scotch tartans was again permitted. One need no longer be a clan member to do so, although in England the various Stuart tartans were reserved for the Royal Family.

The political insurrectionist party known as the "Jacobites" favored the restoration of the direct Stuart line after the abdication of James II and caused such havoc in the early eighteenth century that the wearing of clan tartans was strictly forbidden in 1745.

In America no such taboos were imposed and the three Stuart tartans were the ones most commonly used for all occasions. The plaid pattern is the same for all three tartans, only the background color changes. Red is ceremonial, white is dress, and green is for hunting.

What is the difference between the words "tartan" and "plaid"? In today's American usage they are interchangeable but to our grandparents' generation the word "plaid" meant a pattern of stripes crossing at right angles, and the word "tartan" signified the cloth composed in that pattern. To the English both the pattern and the cloth are called "tartan." A "plaid" is a long shawl used by Highlanders instead of an overcoat.

Best Sources

Artists:
John James Audubon
Eugene Delacroix
Rembrandt Peale
J. A. Dominique Ingres

Operatic Composers:
Gaetano Donizetti
Gioacchino Rossini

Early Victorian (Crinoline)—1840 to 1850

English Name: Victorian
French Name: July Monarchy—1840 to 1848
American Name: Ante-bellum—1840 to 1861

The Woman—1840

As we can see from Figure 11–2, quite a few changes have occurred since 1830. The hemline is back to the ground. The waistline has a slight point in the front as well as the back. Shoulders follow the natural slope but there are still vestiges of the former extension in the dropped look. The upper arm of this particular sleeve is form-fitting while the lower sleeve is puffed. One was just as likely to see the reverse as long as some part of the sleeve conformed to natural anatomy. The bodice and upper sleeves are of a mint green silk faille. This fabric was also known as corded silk

because the woof threads were of a heavier weight than the warp, causing a tiny ridged look. The puff of her sleeves and her skirt are an embroidered cotton dimity. The dress is trimmed in fine lace ruffing and dark green velvet ribbon. It is worn over several layers of crinolines.

Her hair, like her predecessor's, is still divided into three sections but the high center top knot is gone. The side hair is curled into long banana curls over each ear. The back hair is worn in a bun. She wears an "at home" cap of lace, symmetrically decorated with pink roses and mint green ribbons. This same item when tied under the chin was called a "babette." This ensemble is well suited to an afternoon at home receiving visitors.

The Man—1840

Although at first glance the gentleman's attire in Figure 11–2 seems about the same as his 1830 predecessor, differences can be seen in small details. The belled topper is a little lower

Figure 11–2. *Early Victorian (Crinoline)— 1840 to 1850*

and its brim has more of a roll. His mutton chops are less grandiose. He is corseted to achieve the desired wasp-waisted look and the body of his coat is extremely form-fitting, as are his trousers.

The front waist of this coat has a bit more "cut-away" to it than previously. Note the notched collar and puffed sleeves, as well as a somewhat fuller skirt. His cravat is the flamboyant bow á la Byron (Lord Byron started this style in the late teens and 1820s). This cravat suggests that this gentleman was a dandy or perhaps a Bohemian.

His trousers continue to be held down by means of a strap under the still popular short boot. His coat is a deep burgundy wool with matching silk lapels, collar, and lining; contrast was achieved by texture. Note that the cuff of his sleeve goes over the bottom of the hand "gothically." He carries a walking stick and a bouquet of flowers for his companion.

General Description

Queen Victoria came to the throne at age 18 in 1835. Her youth set a new tone for the court. Of her immediate predecessors, her uncle William (IV) had been an elderly bachelor and her uncle George (IV) had been a very easygoing monarch who preferred life with his morganatic wife to official fuss and bother. At the start of her reign Victoria blew away court cobwebs and at the same time her youthful innocence kept everyone on their best behavior. During her lifetime this youthful innocence would become downright prudishness, turning "merry olde England" into moral old England. When this attitude reached America, it only reinforced the Puritan ethic.

She married her German cousin Prince Albert of Saxe-Coburg and together they brought England into the full flower of the industrial revolution. Fortunes were to be made and the middle class grew in astonishing proportions. The agrarian aristocracy began intermarrying with the wealthy middle class and there began an ebb and flow in the social strata. Style and taste were often dictated by the nouveau riche.

Prince Albert was intensely interested in the industrial revolution. He sponsored the Great Exhibition which opened in 1851, inviting manufacturers and artisans from all over the world to display their products. During the 1840s great numbers of English artisans and craftsmen were employed creating the Crystal Palace as the showcase for this momentous event. (This paved the way for the Chicago World's Columbian Exposition of 1893 and all subsequent World's Fairs.) The Crystal Palace was itself a marvel of architecture and engineering in lacy ironwork and glass.

With the industrial revolution easing people's work-a-day life, the middle class had more leisure time. There was a great resurgence of home arts and crafts. An accomplished Victorian matron was expected to do all forms of needlework, needlepoint, petit point, crewel, cross stitch, tatting, faggoting, lace work, bead work, applique, and quilting. The social graces demanded that the female be able to sing or play a musical instrument, dabble a little in painting, and keep up the voluminous social correspondence that life without a telephone required.

Throughtout the long Victorian Age there would be many changes in style and fashion. Even within the 1840s there were small changes. The pointed waist, both front and back, of our silhouette lady's dress would go back to being completely rounded, only to return to a deeper point in the front with a rounded back. The long curls over the ears would disappear by 1855. Only elderly women would cling to side curls and the babette after that time. These same minute fashion changes would hold true for the men as well.

Yet there is an overall taste to Victorianna which lasted the entire era and extended to all forms of decor whether furniture design, fashion, jewelry, or architecture. That seems to be a general busyness; pattern upon pattern, layer upon layer, fringe over ruffles over swags, and a taste for massiveness—heavy, sturdy, solid, and comfortable (but not necessarily beautiful).

Strict rules of etiquette governed everyone's life and prescribed some fashions as well. A man could choose any color of glove for daytime, but weddings required lavender and dances strictly required white. He was required to wear them while dancing so that the perspiration from his hands did not cause water spots on the lady's dress.

Both men and women were required to remove hats in the theater or at the opera. Women stopped wearing hats to these occasions and this gave rise to elaborate coiffures once again adorned with flowers, jewels, ribbons, and laces. Eventually men's fashion would develop the collapsible opera hat. Through the era there was a love of rich jewel tones, bold patterns, and heavy fabrics such as velvet, wool, satin, and much use of fur.

One invention of this time is very important to us. That is the sewing machine, originally invented by Elias Howe. By 1851 Isaac Singer had made some improvements and was selling them for the home. Between 1851 and 1871 he had sold over 230,000 home models throughout the world. At about this same time Ebenezer Butterick (a Massachusetts tailor) began selling paper patterns. By the middle Victorian period he had a nationwide business. A rival published a magazine of patterns called *Smith's Illustrated Pattern Bazaar*. In 1873 Butterick began publishing his *Delineator* magazine. Butterick's original paper used for his patterns was brown and about the weight of today's posterboard. Because of this several of them have lasted and you may come across them from time to time. If you do, hang on to them. They are worth their weight in gold!

Best Sources

Magazines:
Gazette of Fashion
Godey's Ladies Book

Artists:
J. A. Dominique Ingres
Hugo Winterhalter

Well-Known Playwrights

Although Alexander Dumas' (the son) play *The Lady of the Camellias* did not open until 1851, it is set in the 1840s.

Early Victorian (Hoopskirt)—1850 to 1860

English Name: Victorian
French Name: Second Empire (1848 to 1870)
American Name: Ante-bellum

The Man—1855

The gentleman in Figure 11–3 is dressed in the manner typical of an American southern gentleman, whose daily routine included several hours on horseback, either inspecting the agricultural work of his own fields or riding considerable distances to vist his neighbors. (The women generally went by carriage.) His coat is a cross between the lines of the evening tailcoat and the frock coat and was called a "broadtail." It was vented in back for riding, so that the tails could be pulled sideways over the upper thigh for added protection and at the same time not pick up the sweat from the back of the horse. It was made of a serviceable cloth called "broadcloth" (a wool that was woven in wide squares, hence its name). This particular version is for summer and is not meant to be buttoned. The winter versions did button, was either single- or double-breasted, and sometimes had a detachable cape.

The upper collar and cuffs are either velvet or suede. The tails are lined in broadcloth as well, but in a color to match the collar. The waist is always a natural one. The waistcoat is double-breasted and a striped silk, cut on the bias. The pantaloons are not as full at the top and have the

Figure 11–3. *Early Victorian—1850 to 1860 (Hoopskirt)*

square four-buttoned fly opening. These legs are unstrapped, but strapped ones were just as popular. Sometimes breeches were worn with high boots, particularly for riding through high crops. This gentleman's hat is unique to America. It was an adaptation of the Spanish caballero's hat with a low, flat crown and broad brim, but the southern gentleman rolled his brim slightly to control the spill of rain. It was called a planter's hat. This gentleman wears a turned-down collared shirt of popular daytime usage and a wide knotted cravat held by a stickpin.

The Woman—1855

The woman's skirt line in Figure 11–3 could be achieved by multiple crinolines and by a "Dr. Thompson," a hoop skirt of spring steel hoops. The ensemble pictured is in three pieces: a skirt,

a blouse, and a bolero jacket. The blouse is of a fine linen lawn with a tucked front, little rounded collar, and belled sleeves gathered to a wristband. The jacket has the dropped shoulder reminiscent of the extreme shoulders of the '30s and an open bell-shaped sleeve. This type of sleeve was called a pagoda sleeve. It is made of a heavy silk faille trimmed in looped brail and ball fringe. The top portion of the skirt is the same silk faille, decorated by a crisscross of looped braid and ball fringe. The bottom of the skirt is velvet, as is the waistband. The bonnet is of matching materials. The brim is getting a little smaller than that of the '30s and not as close to the face as the 1848 version.

The prevalent hair style, as shown, was parted in the middle and worn over the ears in puffs and curls. The hair was gathered into a little bun at the back of the head. These side curls were often false and went out of vogue by 1850. The woman's parasol is of a polka-dotted and fringed silk.

General Description

The men's high, stiff collar of the 1830s and early 1840s no longer extended beyond the chin line, but confined itself to just under the chin. By 1850 it was worn turned down as often as turned up for the daytime. Evening attire was rigorously maintained. The wrap-around cravat was not as long or full-flowing as the century progressed. The frock coat retained its full skirt through the 1840s, gradually losing fullness until it established itself in the 1870s with almost nothing more than a flared princess line. The cut-back tailcoat popular from the Directoire era gradually lost out to the cutaway for daytime use, but was retained for evening attire.

The most popular summer colors were buff, pale blue, and bright red. Winter colors were hunter green, brown, and black. Black or very dark blue was always worn for evening. The man showed his pride in the gorgeous brocade of his waistcoat, which was done in silks, satins, and even petit point.

The top hat was standard for just about everything. Even women adopted it for riding, but added to it a long flowing veil. The female riding habit, as in the previous century, was an adaptation of the man's tailored suit, complete with high collar, cravat, and tailed coat. The skirt was full, worn over leather pantaloons. Leather was necessary for grip. In later years of the century men learned from the women and added leather pads at the inside knee of their riding trousers or britches. In England britches were called "small clothes" of just plain "smalls." Women, of course, rode sidesaddle. Both legs being on one side of the horse knocked their center of gravity cockeyed. Many women became far better at the sport than their male contemporaries, because they had to depend more on their own sense of balance and the rhythm of the horse's gait; however, for the timid and inexperienced rider, weights were sewn into the hem of the riding habit's jacket back, peplum, or tail. This gave an added sense of balance. These same weights were often sewn into the hems of skirts, which had been made of lightweight fabrics to prevent an accident of wind showing an ankle. These weights varied from buckshot pellets to fishing line sinkers. Even lead washers were used. (The crinoline of the 1830s, or starched-over petticoat, was worn to the floor by 1840 and "limbs" disappeared completely.)

Several items of this lady's apparel cannot be seen, but were absolutely essential. The hoop created a distinct draft underneath, so a proper lady wore "drawers" (fancy knickers) and woolen or silk stockings. A camisole was worn over the chest. Then the corset of whale bone or steel stays that cinched the waist to the desired eighteen inches was added. A petticoat was worn under the hoop as a sort of protection from it. Hoops tended to show their ridges in outer garments unless another petticoat was worn above it.

To a Victorian lady the sun was the arch enemy. She therefore always carried a parasol and wore gloves. Fine doe skin gloves in black and white were favored. Buff was the color favored for riding, and for the woman who might drive her own buggy there were fine gloves with ridges stitched in them for the purpose of better grip on the reins. In the evening the little lace "mitt" in white (for summer) or black (for winter) was very popular.

For warmth various new "coat-type" garments were devised. The mantle was the most widely used. It was somewhat fitted in front and like a cape in back, with enormous cape sleeves. There was a jacket called a "pelerine" that buttoned to the waist and had an enormous peplum that extended one-third of the way down the skirt in the front and scooped down even farther in the center back. In the late '50s and '60s a style came back from the Middle East (thanks to the Crimean War) of wearing a "burnoose," which was an enormous circular cape often with hood attached.

Best Sources

Godey's Ladies Book

Artists:
George Caleb Bingham
J. B. Camille Corot
Robert Havell
J. A. Dominique Ingres
William Mount
Jerome Thompson
Hugo Winterhalter

Well-known Playwrights and Operatic Composers:
Alexander Dumas, father and son
Gioacchino Rossini (opera)

Note should be made that this was the time of Charles Dickens, the Brontes, and Thomas Hardy in England; George Sand, Gustav Flaubert, Alexander Dumas (father), and Victor Hugo in France; Edgar Allan Poe in America. There was a great flowering of literature, but not necessarily of a theatrical nature.

Middle Victorian (Fishtail Hoop)—1860 to 1870

English Name: Victorian
French Name: Second Empire

The Man—1860

The waltzing gentleman in Figure 11–4 wears a set of evening tails not too unlike the white tie and tails of today. In 1860 a man could choose between a white or black cravat and also how to tie it, although the narrow bow was used. His ruffle-fronted shirt is a fine cotton or linen and his low, collared waistcoat is a white brocaded silk. His black tails have black silk lapels, cuffs, and side stripe. He wears leather dancing slippers called "pumps." The tailcoat was tailored

Figure 11–4. *Middle Victorian—1860 to 1870 (Fishtail Hoop)*

not to button; the four buttons are mere decorations. Note that the waist of the coat is about one inch short of the natural waist, just as the waist of the waistcoat extends about two inches below the natural waist in front. This allowed the watch chain and fob to show from the waistcoat pockets.

The Woman—1860

The waltzing young lady in Figure 11–6 is wearing a ball gown typical of the hoopskirt at its most extreme. It has reached six feet in diameter and is no longer completely rounded, but slightly egg-shaped, so that a train was suggested in the back. This knocked the center of gravity slightly askew, so a little padded pillow was worn at the back of the waist and just under the hoop to help support it. The bodice is pointed over the waist in front, completely off the shoulder, with little puff sleeves and a "bertha" of lace around the neckline. It is made of the same satin as the skirt. The skirt itself has three flounces of wide scalloped lace, and little nosegays of artificial flowers are tucked randomly between the flounces.

Her hair is held in a snood of crocheted velvet ribbon with bunches of similar artificial flowers and ribbons at either side.

General Description

If you compare Figure 11–4 with Figure 11–3, you will see why the hoopskirt became the favorite object of ridicule for the cartoonists of the day. It had gone completely out of proportion. What was started by a few starched petticoats in 1830 had become ludicrous. A Japanese painting in Tokyo shows several Japanese women and children giggling behind their hands at an American naval officer and his hoop-skirted wife. One little child is seen crawling under the skirt. The painting was dated 1866. Young ladies were made to walk balancing books on their heads. This was to learn the particular glide necessary to not move the hoops enough to show an ankle.

This was the era of the waltz, a dance which enhanced the sway and glide of the hoops. As a matter of fact, it was considered a scandalous dance because the hoop belled up when the lady twirled and the ankles were briefly exposed. The hoop was made of flexible steel and was somewhat pliable. As with other periods of hip exaggeration (Elizabethan England and Rococo Europe) the armless "ladies chair" became a necessity once more. Once again a lady's arm movements radiated from the elbow curve, because it was impossible to put them "down."

Unlike the Rococo period in which only the wealthy could afford the extremes of fashion, the industrial revolution put the mass produced hoopskirt within the economic range of even the shopgirls and servant class.

Aprons and little white frilled "morning" caps were worn by matrons, servant, and shopgirls alike, while residing indoors. Young unmarried girls were exempted from this. Shopgirls usually wore large black aprons and sometimes black "cuff covers" which actually reached the elbows. Matrons wore very fancy silk and lace aprons, more as an affectation than a necessity.

Hair was still parted in the middle and arranged fully over the ears, but many more interesting rolls and knots appeared at the back of the head than in the simple bun of the 1850s.

A desire for more jewelry brought about three new forms. The first item was the use of jet, which was a fossilized coal that could be facetted and polished to give off a reflected sparkle. The second item was called marquesite—facetted pieces of steel set in silver, which gave off a brilliance akin to diamonds, although the brilliance faded with the tarnishing of its neighboring silver. The third was a process of alloying a gold-like metal called pinchback after its creator, Dr. Pinchback, a dentist, who originally was looking for a stronger alloy for false teeth. Using his formula for jewelry, he made a fortune and when he died in the late 1870s he took his formula with him. (Oddly enough the stuff is scarce today and worth as much as gold on the antique market.)

The bonnet was still the most frequently worn hat, but it was often completely brimless. A little ruffle was added to the bottom as sort of a protection for the back of the neck. By the middle of the '60s straw "sailor" hats with long veils tied around the hat band were popular for summer seaside wear. The parasol became smaller until it protected nothing more than the nose.

Men's styles changed very little between 1840 and 1870. The passing years were marked more by the minute detail, such as the changes in the length of the waistcoat or the width of the frock coat than by anything major. The pantaloons of the 1830s and 1840s were replaced by the trousers. Trousers were no longer strapped beneath the boot by 1850–52. The first version of the stovepipe hat belled out slightly on top. By the 1860s it was absolutely cylindrical.

The English version of the bowler hat is the one we associate with the word, but the French had a version with an equally rounded crown, but a flat brim. Men wore somber colors. Women wore pastels for evening and summer daytime, jewel tones for winter evenings, and neutrals for daytime. Note should be taken here that although Victoria may have set the moral tone for the age, the two reigning beauties of this age were the Empress Eugenie (married to Louis Napoleon of the second French empire) and the Empress Elizabeth (sometimes called Zizi), who was married to Franz Joseph of Austria. They were the style setters.

Best Sources

Godey's Ladies Book

Artists:
Theodore Chasseriau
Jean-Baptiste Corot
Gustave Courbet
Nathaniel Currier and James Merritt Ives
Honore Daumier
Edward Lamson Henry
Winslow Homer
Jean Francois Millet
Hugo Winterhalter

Well-known Operatic Composers:
Jacques Offenbach (opera, ballet, operetta)
Giuseppe Verdi (opera)

Middle Victorian (Bustle)—1870 to 1878

English Name: Victorian
French Name: Second Empire
American Name: American Gothic—1870 to
1885

The Woman—1870

The lady in Figure 11–5 is dressed for taking
the air in a white wool walking ensemble trimmed
in black velvet scalloped edging and ribbon with
crochetted pointed black fringe accented by jet
drops at the apex of each point. Her ensemble
consists of three pieces: a blouse, a skirt, and a
shawl-collared cutaway jacket. The blouse is of
a fine white linen with a low ruffle above the velvet neckband and long sleeves, ending in a wrist
ruffle. It is trimmed in tiny jet buttons down the
center front. The skirt shape is the first of the bustled hoop. The enormous dome of the previous
decade has narrowed around the bottom. The
little cushion used to support the weight of the
dome has enlarged to a wire cage on the back of
the hoop. The skirt is of three basic pieces: an
underskirt trimmed in velvet at the hem and finished in a pleated ruffle. The front has an apron-
like drape, which is gathered up in the back over
not only the underskirt, but the back overdrape,
as well. The back overdrape has a modest train
and is prevented from flapping by two large velvet bows, which weight it and attach it to the underskirt at each side. A wide velvet belt covers all
three pieces at the natural waistline and is tied in
a bow at the back.

In contrast to the more rounded hairstyles of
the previous decades, this lady's hair is pulled
more severely back from the face, but piled high
on the top of the head and arranged so that it
came well down the back in braids, curls, or coils.

Figure 11–5. *Middle Victorian—1870 to
1878 (Bustle)*

Her small straw, rolled-brim hat is decorated with
white roses, black velvet leaves, and several
black crows feathers. Black gloves and a black
lace parasol complete the outfit.

The Man—1870

Although the lines of this gentleman's ensemble in Figure 11–5 were standard for the 1870s,
his choice of fabric would lead one to believe he
was a carpetbagger out for a stroll. (What was
called carpetbagger in the south after the American Civil War was called "city slicker" in the
north; both terms referred to an opportunist.) It
was, perhaps, the last flicker of flair among men's
tailored clothes. His coat is a buff-colored wool
with coffee-colored silk faille lapels and cuffs,
both of which are trimmed in brown velvet. His

shirt has a stand-up collar and stitch-tucked front. His brown cravat is square knotted. His vest is a buff and coffee plaid double-breasted with a rounded collar and dropped waist in the front. His pants are a brown and cream check. He wears his hair brushed back from his face with muttonchops (a brief dandy affectation in the '70s) and a belled topper of brown felt. The topper was not as high as the stovepipe and the top of the crown was slightly larger than the headband dimensions.

Note should be taken that although this coat may resemble its predecessor of the 1830s ('40s and '50s) it was not as full-skirted. The trousers were straight-legged and approximately thirteen inches in diameter at the bottom. The jodhpur boot was the popular walking boot.

General Description

The 'seventies was a time of recovery from wars. America was recovering from the disastrous Civil War in the north and south, and in the west the constant and shameful war against the Indians was waged on and off through the '50s, '60s, and '70s. Much of Europe had suffered in the Crimean and Franco-Prussian conflicts. One visitor to America shortly after the Civil War called it "a nation of women in black."

The Victorian mourning code was complicated and strict. Victoria herself was the archangel of widowhood. After her husband's death she changed to black and wore that color the rest of her considerably long life. Although the rules varied from country to country, the code was approximately this: A woman mourned three years for a husband or son; two years for a father, brother or fiancé; six months to one year for other close relatives. Black was worn by all who attended a funeral. Both women and men wore mourning veils; the man's tied around his high silk hat; the woman's was draped over her bonnet, face, and shoulders. Black armbands were worn by the men and black-bordered handkerchiefs were carried. Women

carried black handkerchiefs. The peasant woman wore her shawl over her head in place of hat and veil.

The first year of mourning a woman wore "unrelieved" black. That meant lusterless fabrics, such as serge, flannel, or cotton, untrimmed and with no jewelry, except a wedding band and small jet earrings. (Earrings were permitted, because in three years the pierced hole might grow back.) All sleeves were long and necklines high, even for evening wear. A woman was not seen socially at all for six months, except for such necessities as shopping and church. After six months she might be seen at female gatherings, but not out in the evening or in mixed company.

The second year a widow need not be excluded from normal social intercourse; however, attending dances or the opera was considered in questionable taste. She was permitted finer fabrics, such as velvet and silk, and even satin, as long as the color remained black. She was also permitted simple jewelry of jet, onyx, and gold. Cameos, made by carving the conch shell, were extremely popular. Diamonds and pearls were still déclasseé as was the decollete. Hats were trimmed with black ostrich and crow feathers.

The third year the black could be augmented with touches of dark colors, a bottle green, purple, or perhaps garnet. White collar and cuffs were allowed, as were diamonds and pearls. Low necklines were permissible, as was attending a theater or dance, as long as one was escorted by a married couple or was acting as chaperon to younger members of her family. Is it any wonder that Aunt Pitty-Pat fainted when Scarlett danced with Rhett Butler at the charity ball?

Best Sources

Godey's Ladies Book

Artists:
Edgar Degas

Thomas Eakins
Jean-Jacques Henner
Winslow Homer
Edouard Manet
Jean-Francois Millet
James Whistler

Composers:
W. S. Gilbert and Sir Arthur Sullivan (comic opera)
Jacques Offenbach (opera, ballet, operetta)
Peter Ilich Tchaikovsky (opera, ballet)

Late Victorian (Sheath)—1878 to 1882

English Name: Victorian
French Name: Second Republic 1878 to 1914

The Woman—1878

The lady in Figure 11–6 wears a sheath skirted ensemble with train and "back interest," but no bustle. The skirt is quite narrow to the knees and then bells out in a gradual line to the floor. This is an at-home dress and therefore the train is somewhat modest. Evening dresses had trains that sometimes trailed four feet behind. This required a long loop that could be worn over the wrist to facilitate dancing. By 1882 the sheath was extended to mid-calf and, like its sister, the hobble skirt of a later period, greatly inhibited movement.

The "basque" has the form fit to the upper hip line, extending downward a little over the abdomen in front and well down to the derriere in the back. The buttons down the back are merely for added interest, as it actually hooks down the front in a closure hidden in the center front seam. The material of the basque (a basque was a combination bodice-jacket that closely hugged the upper hips) is velvet, as are the stand-up collar, cuff bands, and sash. The stripe is a wool and silk combination as is the plain fabric used for yoke insert and ruffles. Note how the striped fabric has

Figure 11–6. *Late Victorian—1878 to 1882 (Sheath)*

been cut. The basque front and back yoke are cut on the bias; the sleeves, underskirt, and gathered "apron" front overskirt are cut vertically, but are bound in a wide bias border. The train is cut so that the stripes run horizontally. Standard fabric width was twenty-eight inches in this day for fancy dress goods, particularly oriental silks. Cotton and calico and some wools were as wide as one meter (thirty-nine inches). This lady wears her hair in three rolls held by large tortoiseshell hair pins and a Spanish comb.

The Man—1878

The gentleman in Figure 11–6 is wearing a typical double-breasted frock coat, which enjoyed a long vogue. This particular one is black serge with black faille collar and cuffs. The white shirt has a stand-up collar and the cravat is black and grey striped. His trousers are black and grey striped also and he carries a black top hat. In Paris the stovepipe hat of the 1860s came back "in," but with an exceptionally wide silk band (up to six inches). This man wears high top boots of two textures; the bottom is black polished leather, while the top and throat are black suede. He also wears a high buttoned black vest and sports a well-trimmed beard and moustache.

Figure 11–6 demonstrates transitional styles and should be viewed in relation to the bustle styles of 1870 and 1882–86.

Late Victorian (Bustle)—1882 to 1890

English Name: Victorian
French Name: Second Republic
American Name: American Gingerbread—1885 to 1900

The Man—1886 to 1900

The gentleman in Figure 11–7 wears a "lounge suit," a cross between the sac coat and the cutaway (or morning tailcoat). This is worn for less formal business transactions. It retains the lines of the cutaway, but the tail, although longer than the sac coat, is not as long as the cut-away and is more squarish in rear bottom line. The bottom chest button is about one inch above the waist, so that a contrasting waistcoat might show. This one is of a printed silk. Although this gentleman wears a knotted cravat, the upright collar could be worn with either an ascot or a cravat tied in a bow. One could also choose a top hat or a derby. This type of suit grew greatly in popularity in the late '80s and '90s and was completely replaced by the sac coated suit in the twentieth century, although morning tails survived. This gentleman also wears two-toned, high-buttoned shoes.

The Woman—1886

This lady wears a bustled walking ensemble of velvet and wool plaid. The bustle of 1870, which went out in 1878, came back again very

Figure 11–7. *Late Victorian—1882 to 1890 (Bustle)*

modestly in 1883. By 1886 it was definite and by 1888 demanded full attention. It was gone by 1891. This particular version has no train, because it was an ensemble for walking. In frontier towns of the American West and Australian outback, these skirts only came to the ankles, because sidewalks did not exist and roads were either dust or mud.

The lady also wears a tiny crowned, peaked-brimmed version of the bonnet. It perches on the back of the head and needs both its chin bow and a hat pin to keep it secure. It also disappeared by 1888 never to return, except for children's wear. She wears the popular hair style of curled or crimped forehead curls, á la the infamous actress Lillie Langtry. The rest of the hair was pulled away from the face and arranged in elaborate rolls or twisted braids at the nape of the neck.

General Description

The silk-collared, velvet-piped frock coat of the '70s, though still worn, was on its way out, to be replaced by what we think of today as the traditional frock coat—black, silk-lapelled, either double- or single-breasted. It could be worn with either black or striped trousers. The Prince Albert suit was similar, but buttoned very high on the chest. The top hat was worn with it. Morning tails of black or grey were gaining acceptance. Workers favored rough linen open-collared shirts and hard wearing fabric, such as corduroy or duck for their trousers and jackets. In America the Levi Company made an extremely servicable cotton fabric called denim and fashioned durable ready-to-wear pants that became standard items to the western male. Also, the pioneer American had long made use of deerhide for clothing, copying the native Indian. By this time a fringed suit of all leather was well known as "buckskins." Men kept their hair short, but the muttonchops of the '70s became well-trimmed beards in the '80s, particularly fancied by the older gentleman as a mark of distinction. Young men wore sideburns and moustaches. The frontier men, because of a lack of barbers, grew long hair and shaggy beards. Some men kept long hair as a mark of self-esteem. General George Custer and Buffalo Bill Cody were high on that list.

The female bustle of the '80s, unlike its wire cage predecessor in the '70s, was more of a padded cushion worn on the derriere. In 1882 it was merely a fake overskirt drawn up on the sides and bunched in the back, tied by many ribbons and "frou-frou," a term meaning an abundance of trim. The cushion came in by 1884 and got progressively more pronounced. Most dresses were not dresses at all, but separate skirts and bodices. By 1886 the front waist had dropped to a point between four and five inches below the natural waist. Most of the bodices were a varia-

tion of the five- or seven-piece variety with the peplum cut with it. Figure 11–8 shows a rough version (unscaled) of the silhouette; not including sleeves, ruffles, and facings, there are fourteen pieces.

The high neck was popular, but the open neck was permissible. Even the high neck had not reached the rigidity it would at a later time. Evening wear was very daring and by 1886 the sleeveless dress was back, worn with long white kid gloves that extended to the upper arm. Because they were extremely hard to put on, a three-button slit was invented so that the wearer could slip her hand out and tuck the finger part under at the wrist to partake of refreshments. Fans were back as standard paraphernalia.

Women used all manner of flora and fauna as trimmings for their hair, hats, and dresses. There was an enormous craze for whole stuffed birds (some of the rarest varieties, such as South

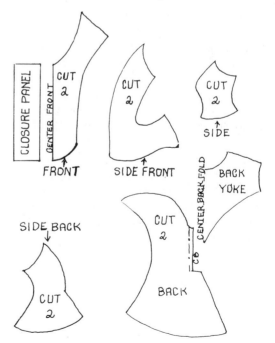

Figure 11–8. *Late Victorian Bodice*

American purple-throated hummingbirds) as adornment. Fox heads and even domestic cat heads adorned hats. Animals too perishable in reality (butterflies and bees) were copied in silk. Even human hair was woven into artificial flowers. The byword for the era was indeed "frou-frou."

"Ladies" did not have legs yet. To see an ankle was shocking, so the high-button shoe was standard for daytime. The evening slipper of kid or satin was often quite elaborately festooned with bows, beads, and brilliants.

In Montmartre, a village just east of Paris, a shocking dance was being done by a group of laundresses, who showed not only their "limbs," but practically everything else. It was called the Can-Can. By the last of the '80s and early '90s the owner of a dance hall called the Red Mill (Moulin Rouge) had organized these women into a troop of professionals and gave them a standard costume consisting of an elbow-length sleeved bodice with a décolleté neckline and a calf length skirt that was actually a 360° circle lined with concentric rows of ruffles that showed when the skirt was picked or kicked upwards. Bloomers and stockings were required by the police. High button shoes and a broad brimmed bonnet, much like the bonnet of the 1850s, completed the outfit.

With minor variations this look also became the standard outfit for the dancehall girl of our American West. These variations included a sleeveless bodice and a knee-length skirt. Occasionally a corset was substituted for the bodice and a feather boa was added. Anna Held, Florenz Ziegfeld's star in his early reviews (and his first wife), wore a similar costume as late as the nineteen teens.

Colors favored for daily use ran the rainbow of hues, tints, and shades but the mature person preferred the more somber tones. Men began their final descent into "the great neutrality" which would last until the liberation forces of the hippie movement almost 100 years later.

Fabrics were worn in combination as to texture and pattern; a wool with a velvet, and a stripe with a plaid. Even fibers were blended in the weaving process resulting in new types of cloth, such as camelshair. This is a blend of the hair from the mane of the male camel and other standard wools. At this time a giant step was taken in what would become the world of synthetics. A Frenchman, M. Chardonnet, invented a process of using waste fibers and created artificial silk.

Best Sources

Mary Cassatt
Edgar Degas
Vincent van Gogh
Henri de Toulouse-Lautrec
Edouard Manet
Berthe Morisot
Frederick Remington
Pierre Auguste Renoir
William Russell
James McNeill Whistler

Playwrights and Composers:
Anton Chekhov
W. S. Gilbert and Arthur Sullivan (comic opera)
Henrik Ibsen
Jacques Offenbach (opera, ballet, operetta)
Peter Ilich Tchaikovsky (opera and ballet)
Giuseppe Verdi (opera)
Richard Wagner (opera)
Oscar Wilde

Late Victorian—1890 to 1900

English name: Victorian
French name: Fin de Siecle—1890 to 1900
American name: The Gay '90s

The Man—1875 to 1910

The gentleman in Figure 11–9 wears a Norfolk jacket nicker suit, which was a popular sporting outfit of the Late Victorian age. This particular Norfolk is a herringbone tweed with leather trim

Figure 11–9. *Late Victorian—1890 to 1900*

to shoulder welts, belt, collar, and buttons. It even has leather elbow patches. There was a hunting variation with a leather shoulder pad. The matching tweed nickers are worn with heavy woolen kneesocks and hook-up-the-front, two-toned walking shoes. It is worn with a turned-down collar, but could be worn with an upright one as well. The deerstalker cap was designed for hunting, the brims front and back shading the eyes and the back of the neck; the side flaps can be lowered to keep the ears warm.

The Woman—1895

The woman in Figure 11–9 is dressed for walking in a bell-skirted ensemble of a worsted silk and wool combination fabric in green. The braided trim has a jet beaded edging to it. The collar, cuffs, hem, and hat brim are black Persian lamb. The hat is Tyrolean, complete with feather brush on the side. Her hair style is called by some a "French knot," a less grandiose version of the later Gibson Girl. She wears black leather gloves and high-buttoned shoes. Her muff is a combination muff and purse and is also black Persian lamb.

General Description

For the man the suit style remained about the same; the frock coat or cut away for the professional man, the sac coat and cloth cap for the worker. The lounge suit gained in popularity. Sometimes the waistcoat matched the coat and trousers as an ensemble; sometimes the coat and trousers matched and the waistcoat was of a contrasting fabric. Very sporty types might have a plain coat, striped pants, and flowered waistcoat all together. Spats were worn. Pocket watches were grandly displayed. The upright collar was considered businesslike. The cravat was broad and was held in place by a stickpin. The derby could be worn with the lounge suit. The topper was worn with the more formal attire.

The bustle suffered its final demise, as did any vestige of the bonnet-type hat. Women adapted many men's styles to their own use—particularly the boater, which they decorated with fancy bows, birds, and flowers. The shape known as a "sailor," much the same as the Venetian gondoliers hat, was often used, as was a strange thing called a "pancake," which was almost all flat brim with hardly any crown; it perched precariously on top of the head, held on by several hat pins or tied under the chin.

The waistline went back to the natural place and was rounded, although a slight point began to appear in 1898. Collars were high and often boned for daytime, very low for evening. The two-layered evening cape was most popular, made of satin with many pleated ruffles for summer and velvet and fur for winter. A lady's winter overcoat of heavy wool with the two-layered cape top became popular for daytime travel and warmth.

The boa of either feathers (for summer) or fur was an important accessory. Women wore watches or chains around their necks and tucked into their belts or pinned on the shoulder. The wristwatch became popular around 1900.

If there was a byword for this age, it would be hypocrisy. While Victoria still upheld moral virtue, the Prince of Wales and his Marborough House set lived lasciviously. To paraphrase Shaw, they didn't care what they did as long as they pronounced it correctly. It was a time when the industrial revolution was putting great creature comforts at everyone's doorstep, yet in all the big cities the slums were in a shocking state.

The invention of the zipper in the late 1880s and the advent of ready-made clothes literally changed the world of fashion overnight. What the designers originated one year was copied en masse the next. This called for a more rapid change of style. The princess line dress came in in 1892 and had vanished by 1895. Zippers were used in ready-made clothing to such an extent that it became the trademark of the dressmaker to have often hidden and exquisite closures, hand crocheted eyes and thread-covered hooks, fabric-covered snaps, hand-made frogs, and beautifully tailored buttonholes. Zippers were considered too dangerous for men's flies, which remained buttoned, but they were used on jackets, boots, and a rubberized overboot called "golashes." The Victorian mourning code remained intact, so black was a much worn color. Neutrals and jewel tones were favored for daytime; whites and pastels for evening.

Around the late '90s and well into 1910 the "ice cream" dress became popular. Ice cream parlours or emporiums came into being, somewhat replacing the tearoom as a respectable place where women and children could congregate and refresh themselves. (This was particularly true in small-town America.) The "ice cream" dress was made of a white or ecru eyelet (or lace) worn over a pastel petticoat and camisole, which thus tinted the outer garment to an even paler pastel. Pink, blue, yellow, peach, and mint green were the favored shades. They were often augmented with beautiful hand-worked trim, such as tatted lace, drawn work, and faggotting. As these were worn almost exclusively in the summer, a parasol of an accompanying pastel shade was considered a necessity to maintain the proper peaches and cream complexion.

Best Sources

The fashionplates of Worth and Paquin; the Impressionist movement in painting still held forth. The best-known painters for this decade were John Singer Sargent and Henri de Toulouse-Lautrec. Others still painting in the '90s were Cezanne, Degas, Renoir, van Gogh, Mary Cassatt, and James McNeill Whistler.

Playwrights and Composers:
La Bis
Anton Chekhov
Henrik Ibsen
Giacomo Puccini (opera)
George Bernard Shaw
Richard Wagner (opera)
Oscar Wilde

12

The Twentieth Century

The first breath of things to come can be seen in the Impressionist art movement which began in the last several decades of the nineteenth century. This was a conscious movement away from realism and into the perception of its memory. Composers began a similar search, using the sound of things as the springboard for their compositions. Claude Debussy particularly seems to achieve this, and in turn his compositions were adapted to the ballet.

In those same latter decades trade between Japan and the west opened up, giving a great impetus to artifacts of an Oriental mode; to quote W. S. Gilbert's chorus lyrics from *The Mikado,* "If you want to know who we are, we are gentlemen of Japan: on many a vase and jar, on many a screen and fan."

These two stimuli seemed to lead to the flowering of another stylistic movement called Art Nouveau. Art Nouveau was a conscious intention to superimpose nature and the continuous flow of the natural curve on the static form. Flowers, particularly lilies, snakes, butterflies, dragonflies, and the peacock were its most important motifs. They were found on everything—jewelry, furniture, architecture, and even

the entrances to the Paris Metro stations. This movement continued until World War I, which brought things to a halt and ended the ridiculous as well as the sublime. Never again would the world see the truly "idle" rich and the fashions they created. Never again would people be able to change their clothes for every small occasion throughout the day.

While the male population fought the war, young women left the home fires burning under someone else's watchful eye and entered the work force in great numbers. New freedoms brought new changes particularly in feminine dress. The first thing to be liberated were a lady's legs. Then they cut their hair as short as a man's. In the 'twenties they even attempted to look like little boys.

The next stylistic movement to follow the war was Art Deco, linear, geometric, and functional. This could be viewed as the reverse swing of the Art Nouveau pendulum. The Depression of the 'thirties did not really inhibit fashion (but it did make it less obtainable). Hollywood saw to that. It showed a glamorous fantasy that anyone could share for the price of a ticket. Then along came World War II and once again women left the home for an ever widening circle of endeavor in the work force. This ushered in the wearing of slacks for practicality. Women stayed in the work force, and slacks have stayed in fashion ever since.

Now with inflation it takes both partners in the family to be able to financially achieve the standard of living a child of the '40s or '50s was accustomed to. At least from the 1950s on, the fashions have followed the dictates of functionalism.

The Turn of the Century—1900 to 1914

English name: Edwardian Era—1900 to 1914
French name: La Belle Epoch—1900 to 1914
American name: Turn of the century
                    Art Nouveau 1890 to 1914

The Man—1906

The gentleman in Figure 12–1 wears the three-button, semi-circular cut sac coat typical of the time. It is a piped-edged plaid and the piping matches the trousers and vest. His shirt is striped with alternating bands of white and one other color and has a white, detachable, rounded collar and white cuffs. He also wears a straw boater, a style of hat popular with both men and women. His shoes are a daring new invention called "spectators," a two-tone shoe that imitated shoes worn with spats. This costume is appropriate for strolling through the park on a summer evening. Note that the breast pocket is put on the slant.

The Woman—1906

The woman in Figure 12–1 is corsetted into the typical hourglass silhouette of the period. The skirt is a gored bell; the jacket a form-fitting princess line; the blouse has a high, boned neck and a jabot of circular ruffles. Her hair style is the "Gibson Girl," natural hair combed over

Figure 12–1. *The Turn of the Century—1900 to 1914*

artificial hair called "rats." Hats were quite large, this particular one being a version of the "tray" hat. These were secured on the head by fourteen-inch-long hat pins. She carries a beaded and fringed purse.

This typical walking suit was of a monochromatic color scheme, shades of blue, from pale blue to navy. Her shoes are of the high-buttoned variety.

General Description

Queen Victoria died in 1901 and took with her the last of the wasp waists. Some doctors finally persuaded women that pulling the waist into the desired eighteen inches (or a more realistic twenty-one to twenty-three inches) was very unhealthful. A new garment came out, which smoothed the figure into an hourglass curve; it was called a "corsellette." For the flat-chested, ruffles were added called "improvers." The dresses of the early 1900s had a bloused front, which gave them a pouter pigeon look. By 1909 the actress Lillian Russell had smoothed out all the gathers and the true hourglass figure was born. The illustrator Charles Dana Gibson gave his name to a certain look of the period as well as to the puffed hair style previously mentioned.

For daytime, necks were high and boned; evening dresses were extremely décolleté, but a "dog collar," a necklace that became the rage, was worn. This could be a three-inch-wide velvet ribbon tied around the throat with a real or silk flower attached at the side, a large oval pin (a cameo was still popular) in the center, or pearls arranged like a dog collar.

Women's fashions began to adapt themselves to the change in their social status as more and more women became employed in the working world. The shirtwaist, dark skirt, and simple straw boater became the working girl's stock in trade. The shirtwaist came with detachable collar and cuffs, just like the men's shirts. Women became accepted as bookkeepers, typists, clerks, garment workers, teachers, and nurses. Nursing outfits were white ankle-length versions of the working woman's outfit, with the additions of large aprons and the nurse's cap. The cap was originally invented to cover the head but became a note of distinction, for each nursing school adopted its own particular design, much like monastic orders had done for centuries.

"Sports clothes" came into being. Some were outrageous, considering the sports involved, but at least modesty was preserved. It's a wonder all women didn't drown, considering that a woman's bathing outfit consisted of bloomers, tunic top, stockings, canvas shoes, a belt, and a bathing cap that was useless.

Bloomers and jacket were considered acceptable for cycling and golf. A mid-calf length skirt with high boots was permissible for shooting, as was a feminine version of the deerstalker cap. There were even certain white sharkskin dresses that were designed strictly for yachting, with the appropriate red, white, and blue trim.

The rich went through their daily dressing and undressing ritual—a morning robe, an at-home dress, a walking suit, a tea dress, an evening gown and nightgown for sleeping. For the man, the dressing ritual was much the same—morning robe, business suit, a leisure jacket of some kind, evening tuxedo (for all male informals), or the usual white tie and tails, and lastly a nightshirt. Pajamas for night wear were becoming more popular.

The sac suit was becoming standard for business/daytime wear, although professional men like bankers, doctors, lawyers, etc., still wore the more formal cut-away frock coats. The most popular hats were boaters and the derby or bowler, with the high silk hat for evening. The "opera hat" was invented; it was a high silk hat that collapsed so it could be sat on at the theater. Women were requested to remove theirs. The "four-in-hand" tie (just called "tie" today) was a name given to a particular type of cravat that could be tied in a number of ways; the most popular style became known as the windsor knot.

A rubberizing process brought the raincoat into being for both men and women. It was not perfected, and the rubber tended to chip and peel off its cloth base. There was a variety of overcoats for men: chesterfields with velvet collars, ulsters (coats with a cape over the shoulders), invernesses (two-layered capes) and raglans (coats with not only raglan sleeves, but a very full back, the back seam having been cut on the bias).

The colors were neutral and subdued for daytime, lovely pastels for evening. The fabrics were all variations of natural fibers. Imitation jet—a black glass bead from France—became popular. There was also a resurgence of marquesite jewelry.

The automobile brought out several fashions for men and women. Both wore "dusters," linen coats that covered them from head to foot to keep the dust off. Both wore eye goggles. Men wore soft caps, some of which had flaps that completely covered the ears, back of head, and neck. Women held on their hats by throwing a large net over the entire hat, head and face; the net was then tied under the chin.

Franz Lehar's musical play *The Merry Widow* gave Europe its craze for big hats with mounds of feathers. Called Merry Widow hats, they were really nothing more than a return to the Gainsborough hat of the eighteenth century.

Best Sources

Magazines: The Butterick Delineator, Marshall Field Catalog, Sears and Roebuck Catalog, The Tailors' Review

Artists: Aubrey Beardsley, Charles Dana Gibson, Alphonse Mucha, Pablo Picasso, John Singer Sargent

Well-known Playwrights, Composers, and Theatrical Trend Setters

David Belasco (playwright, director, and innovator of scenic realism)
Georges Bizet (opera)
Claude Debussy (ballet and opera)
Sergei Diaghilev (impressario of the Ballet Russe whose Russian-Oriental motifs took Europe by storm in 1911)
Georges Feydeau
Victor Herbert (operettas)
Franz Lehar (operettas)

Giacomo Puccini (opera)
George Bernard Shaw
Konstantine Stanislavsky (innovator of the realistic school of "method" acting)

World War I and the 'Teens—1914 to 1920

The Man—1912 to 1914

The couple in Figure 12–2 is dressed for the races at Ascot, Longschamps, etc. The man wears the dove grey morning tails, vest, and striped trousers still considered proper for Ascot. His striped cravat is even called an ascot. He wears a dark grey top hat, but a dove grey hat with dark band and binding on brim was considered equally permissible. He also wears dark grey spats and a white wing-collared shirt. The cravat would be held in place with a pearl-headed stickpin. A boutonniere of a white carnation or white rose is sported on the lapel.

The Woman—1912 to 1914

The woman's costume in Figure 12–2 would also be appropriate for the Queen's garden party or high tea. Her skirt is almost a hobble skirt, being no more than fifteen inches around the knee, but its overlapping drape allows for a slightly more generous stride. The dress is made of several layers—a taffeta underslip of coral pink, an overdress of several layers of voile in shades of peach to pale banana yellow on top. The sleeves are unlined, as is the attached cape. The waist is slightly raised to exaggerate the length of the skirt. It was further emphasized by being done in pleated deep coral pink satin. The ruffles of the muff are of banana voile.

Large hats of proportions not seen since Marie Antoinette's time made a brief comeback. This one is made of banana satin in the same shade as the voile of the dress. The feathers match the

Figure 12–2.   *World War I and the 'Teens—
1914 to 1920*

deep coral of the dress's waistband. The pleated ruffle is of the same fabric as the coral pink underslip. Fancy net "clocked" stockings and beaded leather pumps complete the ensemble.

General Description

Just before World War I there was a brief flowering of fantastic fashion. The powder pigeon look of the Edwardian Age disappeared, to be replaced by the slim silhouette, the hobble skirt, and the enormous hat. Some hats were three feet wide when flattened out. There was one Paris creation, a literal mound of ostrich plumes, that was small but two and one-half feet high. How a woman moved was a complete mystery when their skirts allowed for a stride of no more than fifteen inches. There was a peculiar dress, called a "lampshade," which consisted of a hobble skirt

with a short, stiffened overskirt that came to the knees, but hung out from the body. A woman still had "limbs," but the naked ankle was permissible to view and the high-buttoned shoe, although still worn for warmth and inclement weather, was no longer necessary for modesty. Silk stockings in many colors and sometimes with fancy designs known as "clocks" were an accepted standard.

During the war style came to a standstill, although the Paris fashion houses still catered to some, including the famous spy Mata Hari. The most daring new designer was a young teenager named Erté, who started as an illustrator and went into high fashion. (By the 1930s he was by far Paris's most famous theatrical designer.) He introduced soft, flowing fabrics and beadwork, which stopped during the war years, only to return in the '20s. He and Leon Bakst of the Ballet Russe were responsible for the lavish use of color introduced from 1912 to 1914. The Edwardian Age had favored neutrals and pastels. The War colors were tans, browns, khaki, and navy.

The Art Nouveau movement that had started as early as 1890 reached its zenith by 1914. It is my private opinion that the Art Nouveau emphasis on the superimposed curved line brought about the hobble and lampshade skirts and exaggerated hats.

Best Sources

Magazines:
Harper's Bazaar, Vogue

Art Nouveau Artists:
Leon Bakst
Aubrey Beardsley
Erté
Joseph Mierhoffer
Mucha
Thiriet

Artists:
Modigliani
Pierre Bonnard

*Well-known Playwrights, Composers,
    and Theatrical Trend Setters*

Claude Debussy (ballet)
Isadora Duncan (freed dance from traditional
    ballet)
Rudolph Frimmel (operetta)
Luigi Pirandello
Sigmund Romberg (operetta)
George Bernard Shaw
Igor Stravinsky (ballet)
Florenz Ziegfeld (musical revue)

The Roaring Twenties (The Jazz Age)— 1920 to 1930

The Young Man—1927

The young man in Figure 12–3 is dressed as a typical college freshman of 1927. He has on his freshman beanie, generally worn in the school colors, and is carrying a fraternity "hazing" paddle. He wears white, very wide, cuffed flannel trousers known as "oxford bags," a white shirt left open at the neck and a sweater vest with an argyle pattern around the chest. He sports white canvas shoes with crepe soles, a forerunner of today's tennis shoes.

The Young Woman—1927

The young woman in Figure 12–3 is a typical "Betty Coed" with her bobbed hair and big pearl drop earrings, her rolled down hose, Mary Jane strapped shoes, and her "clutch" purse. Hems were just to the knee in 1927. In 1928 some daring girls hiked skirts up to two inches above the knee, but the stock market crash in October of 1929 lowered everything, including skirt hems. Her dress has a "jumper" top and pleated skirt. (A jumper was another name for a low-necked and sleeveless dress.) The flat-chested look was in and this young woman was probably as braless as her granddaughter is to-

Figure 12–3. *The Roaring Twenties—1920 to 1930*

day. Her hat is the soft-brimmed Italian straw that was used as a summer sunshade.

General Description

When we think of the Jazz Age, we automatically envision short skirts and long strings of beads. Actually, the World War I mid-calf length stayed in fashion well into 1925 and only the young wore their skirts really short, and then not for very long. By 1928 long dresses, or at least uneven hemlines, were back for evening wear. The handkerchief skirt was made of fabric squares joined on the bias to come to several points, and the fish tail was short in front and longer in back. The breast and waist disappeared and the emphasis was on the "boyish" figure. The hipline was the main place a dress needed to fit.

The invention of good imitation pearls put those long ropes within everyone's budget. Tissue chiffon dresses heavily beaded in glass beads and worn over an interesting chemise slip were very popular, as was long fringe, which accentuated the movement of the Charleston and shimmy dance steps.

The cloche hat (cloche is French for bell, and the hat was bell-shaped) was worn down to the eyebrows and then if desired, the front brim was turned up. It was the most popular hat of the decade. More and more women bobbed their hair in short blunt cut until the shingle came in. The shingle was done with a razor and cropped close to the head in back. A bandeau worn around the forehead for tennis became popular as a sort of evening hat, usually with a feather or jewel at the side.

All colors were worn, but beige came into its own as a neutral for both sexes. Fabrics were mostly pure fibers. The French came out with a thing called tissue velvet, a very thin, shiny, and lusciously movable silk velvet. Sometimes it would be a silk chiffon with a velvet pattern woven into it.

Men's styles, except for the previously mentioned collegiate fashions, changed very little. The frock coat was still worn by the diplomatic corps and some old-fashioned gentlemen, but the charcoal grey or black morning tailcoat was replacing it. The arrow shirt, with a pointed, permanently attached collar became standard. Knickers were still worn for sport, but not as baggy as the "plus fores" yet to come. Argyle socks were popular, as were argyle sweaters. The vest was worn less and less.

The byword for the decade was "freedom." World War I had brought an end to the old social order everywhere. Thrones had tumbled. The world saw the rise of the bourgoise class and with it new hopes and dreams took shape. For the veterans returning from the trenches there was also a "live for today" philosophy. In America, women finally got to vote (for Warren G. Harding). "Limbs" were "out" forever and "legs" were back permanently. Makeup, previously the prerogative of the actress and whore, was now used by everyone.

Best Sources

Magazines:
Harper's Bazaar, Vogue

Designers:
Coco Chanel, Erté, Marcel (who invented the permanent wave in the late '20s, which became standard in the '30s)

Artists:
George Bellows
Thomas Hart Benson
James Chapen
Gari Melchers

Well-known Playwrights, Composers, and Theatrical Trend Setters
Busby Berkley (innovator of the element of spectacle in the musical revue)
Irving Berlin (musicals)
Buddy De Silva, Lew Brown, and Ray Henderson (musicals)
Rudolph Frimmel (operetta)
Frederico Garcia Lorca
Sigmund Romberg (operetta)
George Bernard Shaw
Florenz Ziegfeld (musical revue)

Art Deco (The Depression)—1930 to 1945

The Woman—1935

The woman in Figure 12–4 is wearing a bias cut satin evening gown. She carries a long white fox stole. Her hair is cut short and done in mar-

Figure 12–4. *Art Deco—1930 to 1945*

celled waves and she wears long drop pearl earrings. This outfit was more typical of what America fantacized, á la Jean Harlow and Carol Lombard, than what was actually worn in the Depression. Still, the bias cut line was typical. Jean Harlow as the platinum "blonde bombshell" started a craze for peroxide blonde hair.

The Man—1935

The gentleman in Figure 12–4 is wearing a tuxedo with a shawl collar and cuffs of silk faille, a black silk vest front, black tie, and white wing-collared tucked-front evening shirt. His shoes are a return to the typical evening "pump" of the late Victorian Age, often made of black patten leather with silk faille bows. Thanks to the Duke of Windsor (then Prince of Wales) the tuxedo gained social acceptance in mixed com-

pany as a substitute for the more formal white tie and tails. The tuxedo first came into prominence in the early 1900s, but only for all male gatherings. By the 1930s the same jacket lines adapted into jewel tone velvets were called "smoking jackets" and could be used for at home wear in the evening.

General Description

Men's clothing changed very little, although the oxford bag trousers went "out" (to return in the late '60s-early '70s), as did the frock coat, which never returned. The morning tail outfit was standard for weddings and ushers at church. The dove grey version was still worn at the races with a grey felt top hat. The sportsman wore "plus fores" and knee socks for golf, hunting, and hiking. The sports coat of tweed, stripe, or plaid, often trimmed in suede, was popular with contrasting plain trousers, usually of off-white, tan, or soft grey.

The bias cut dress that hugged the female silhouette called for a smooth line and the corset came back, this time as an "all-in-one" garment of elasticized fabric (sometimes called a "combination"). It was a bra, girdle, and garter belt all together. The hem line returned to the mid-calf of the late 'teens, and early 'twenties, and gradually the square shoulder came into effect, so that is was standard by 1939.

In the area of sports wear women were at long last liberated. They adapted regular riding breeches and the newly popular jodhpurs with vest and "hack" coat (a man's jacket with back vent) for horseback riding. The habit was still worn at the hunt, however. The side saddle went into permanent decline. The one-piece low-backed swim suit of wool knit became standard. Slacks were also standard beach and yachting wear. Tennis dresses came to the knee, but legs were bare. Shoes had a high throat and "baby Louis" heels. The two-tone "spectator" masculine style of previous decades was adapted for women, either black and white, navy and white, or brown and tan.

The machine-knit or hand-knit dress became very popular, as did the gored skirt with godet inserts. Most of the hats were small; the cloche stayed popular, but not covering the forehead as it had done in the '20s. In 1935 the large floppy brimmed, stiffened organdy hat became popular, particularly for summer teas and garden parties, but a sudden shower turned them into a soggy mess.

The byword for the decade was "phantom elegance." European designers turned out stunning creations and had to cut their costs. They were copied, but the average individual homemaker was lost if she did not know how to sew. Hollywood turned out movies not of life as it was, but life as was wanted and desired; it was truly the dream machine. The period combined Bauhaus functionalism with geometric cubism and the Art Deco movement flowered, at least on the silver screen. Very little of it is left. It is most evident in jewelry design and architecture.

The popularity of colors depended on their usage: red, white, and blue for beaching and boating; black and tan for riding; white for tennis; neutral tweeds and plaids for golf and hunting. Everyday wear consisted primarily of muted pastels for summer, and wine, hunter green, navy and dark neutrals for winter. One color deserves special mention and that is a particular hot pink brought out by the designer Elsa Schiaparelli and named for her. The fabrics were mostly pure fibers but rayon, previously known as artifical silk, was improved and found great favor in all strata of society.

Best Sources

Magazines: (high fashion)—*Harper's Bazaar, Vanity Fair, Vogue* (realistic view)—*Colliers, Ladies Home Journal, Life, The Saturday Evening Post*

Well-known Playwrights and Composers

Maxwell Anderson
Irving Berlin (musicals)

Bertolt Brecht
Noel Coward
George and Ira Gershwin (musicals)
Lillian Hellman
George S. Kaufman and Moss Hart
Jerome Kern (musicals)
Eugene O'Neill
Cole Porter (musicals)
Richard Rodgers and Lorenz Hart (musicals)
Jean-Paul Sartre
Kurt Weill (musicals and opera)

The World War II '40s—1940 to 1950

The Woman—1945

The woman in Figure 12–5 wears a "man-tailored" pinstripe suit; the shoulders are padded. The material is the same as a man's suit, wool gabardine or flannel. The sleeves have a pointed cuff detail and the jacket is fitted. The hemline is one inch below the knee to conserve material. Even the silk blouse is man-tailored and the hat is merely a feminine version of the man's fedora with a veil attached. Shoes have "Cuban" heels, are "sling-backed" and have a V opening for the big toe. Her hair is worn in a page boy.

The Man—1945

The gentleman wears a padded-shouldered, double-breasted, pinstripe suit. The lapels are wide and deeply notched. The pants are baggy. The tie is wide, up to three inches, and of exceedingly bold designs, generally geometric in nature. The handkerchief is folded into two or three points and shows above the breast pocket. The soft fedora is back with a very broad brim.

General Description

The Second World War brought about some permanent style changes, particularly to women, who left the home in droves to work in all types of previously male-dominated professions, in-

Figure 12–5. *The World War II '40s—1940 to 1950*

cluding heavy labor. It ushered in masculine styles for feminine wear, because of its practicality. Blue collar women wore pants and tied up their hair in scarves, babooshka fashion borrowed from their Russian counterparts, Aunt Jemmima fashion borrowed from the slave days, or snood fashion borrowed from Lana Turner in the Hollywood film, *The Postman Always Rings Twice.*

Hair was worn in a page boy, á la Veronica Lake and her peek-a-boo style, until it became dangerous in the factories and she cut her hair short for the war effort. The "upsweep" hair style with the pompadour became popular.

Women found the freedom slacks afforded and immediately adopted them for work as well as sport wear. Fabric shortages caused the hemlines to rise. Parachutes used up all the silk, so stockings were precious items. Pancake leg makeup was used and fake seam was drawn on with an eyebrow pencil. Toenails, fingernails and lips were all bright red, and eyebrows were plucked pencil thin.

Men's styles were fairly consistent with those of the '30s, mainly because it was '30s clothing to which they returned after military service. The military itself brought about certain style changes, foremost of which was the Eisenhower jacket— a jacket bloused onto a waistband, adopted permanently by the Army Air Corps, because of the convenience of no coat tails in the cockpit. The navy picked up a zippered front version known as a "windbreaker." Both versions were adapted to civilian use.

The second trendsetter was the navy's P coat, a short double-breasted, large-collared wool coat. The army had a longer version in khaki called the duffle coat. After the War they were still worn as standard equipment for both male and female undergraduates. The German S.S. had a similar garment of black leather, which became standard for all the villains in spy pictures from '42 to '56.

The typical female undergraduate had a pleated plaid skirt, a cardigan sweater buttoned down the back, a string of graduated pearls around her neck, bobby socks, and either saddle shoes or penny loafers.

The one-piece latex bathingsuit came out in 1948, thanks to Hollywood and Esther Williams. The brightly flowered, short-sleeved, open-necked "Hawaiian" shirt was standard for a man's summer leisure wardrobe, as were short thigh-length pants for women, *ever* after known simply as shorts.

The byword for the '40s is "practicality." Everything was rationed and hard to get, so one made the most of what one had; for example, pieces of a relative's uniform. There were tales of brides literally being married in their fiance's white silk parachute made over.

The colors of the period were the service colors—khaki, army brown, navy blue, Sea Bee blue and white. Also, neutral shades were popular, because of their serviceability, and black, because everyone seemed to be in mourning for someone.

The new fabric was nylon, made from petroleum. Nylon was far more successful than rayon, particularly in a knitted form.

Best Sources

Magazines: *Life, Look, Vogue, Colliers, The Saturday Evening Post.*

Norman Rockwell was technically an illustrator, but no artist better captured 20th Century America, particularly the '40s and '50s.

Well-known Playwrights, Composers, and Theatrical Trend Setters

Maxwell Anderson
George Balanchine (the perpetrator of classical ballet in the U.S.A.)
Irving Berlin
Bertolt Brecht
Christopher Frye
Jean Giraudoux
Martha Graham (mother of modern dance)
Lillian Hellman
George S. Kaufman and Moss Hart
Alan Jay Lerner and Frederick Loewe (musicals)
Arthur Miller
Cole Porter (musicals)
Richard Rodgers and Oscar Hammerstein III (musicals)
Jean-Paul Sartre
Robert Sherwood
Kurt Weill
Tennessee Williams

The "New Look"—1950 to 1960

Woman on the Left—1958

In Figure 12–6 the woman on the left wears a sack dress of grey wool that has been hobbled to a bandeau from knee to mid-calf. Her hat is a bouffant version of the Rococo mop cap, made of a sheer stiffened net. The neck of the dress has a stand-up collar and the sleeves are raglan. Her shoes have three-inch stiletto heels and the entire toe area is cut away, not just a V for the big toe, as in the '40s sling back shoes.

Woman on the Right—1954

The woman on the right wears a typical summer's day dress of a lightweight polka-dotted

Figure 12–6. *The "New Look"—1950 to 1960*

fabric, cotton or rayon, with a décolletté shawl collar and full sleeves caught into long cuffs. The waistline is natural and the full skirt is worn over several crinoline petticoats. Her hat was known as "the little nothing" hat, created by Mr. John. It was a stiffened circular net with three silk flowers on the very top and held in place by a comb sewn to the underside of the flowers. Her shoes have the needle-pointed toes and the stiletto heels typical of the period.

General Description

A man was not included in Fig. 12–6 because men's clothing styles changed very imperceptibly from the previous decade. The trousers became less full, until by 1957 they were pencil slim. The sack suitcoat retained its box look, but without the padded shoulders. Lapels narrowed and ties went to as narrow as two inches. The Brooks Brothers Company in New York set the fashion for the businessman with their grey flannel suit, white buttoned-down-collar shirt, and narrow black tie. A narrow, brimmed grey straw or felt hat with a miniature Tyrolean brush on the side became the order of the day for the young businessman. Hombergs, popularized by President Eisenhower, became standard for the more mature.

For the ladies, however, there was a dual style of fashion. On the one hand there was the very full "bouffant" skirt, and a very narrow sheath on the other. The sac dress seemed to be the worst of both styles. Hem lines dropped dramatically in Paris in 1947. This style did not catch on in the U.S. until '49 or '50. By 1959 it was just two inches below the knee. Balenciaga, who had created the sac dress, brought out the Trapeze dress in 1958. It was gone by 1962, but that very trapeze gave birth to the A line of the '60s.

Sheath skirts were pencil slim to the hip and straight down from there, with either a slit or a pleat to allow ease of walking. The shirtwaist dress became standard daytime wear, having either a full or a sheath skirt and button-down collar, and was often worn with a small open circular pin nicknamed the "virgin pin." Shoes all had pointed toes, but heels varied from the popular "flats" (a ballet type) to the previously mentioned stiletto heels, which were very inconvenient and caught in sidewalk cracks, gratings, and escalator steps.

The young people wore heavy cotton socks and "white bucks" made popular by singer Pat Boone. There were also two looks for youth—the Ivy League look and the "greaser" look. Mr. Boone represented the Ivy Leaguers; Mr. Elvis Presley, the greasers, but the greased look really started with Marlon Brando in the 1954 film *The Wild One.*

Men's hair styles were either the "butch," the "flat top" (a longer version of the teddybear haircut of the World War II soldiers), or the pompadour and D.A. of Elvis Presley. (D.A. is an abbreviation for Duck's Ass.) Women's hair styles were many and varied, with everything from the poodle cut to the ponytail.

There was a fad for circular skirts made of felt and decorated with poodle dogs, and girls wore dog collars around their ankles. They also carried Korean War Army-issued surplus ammunition bags (bullet bags) as purses.

The byword for the '50s would be "prosperity." It was a reflection of our belief in our own invincibility and a reaching out to try many new things; thus, many rapid changes in styles.

The newest fabric on the market was the synthetic called dacron, a combination of synthetic and cotton, with the breathability of cotton and the easy care and cool iron possibilities of synthetics. Nylon also came completely into its own. All colors were used, but for men the one outstanding color was charcoal grey.

Best Sources

Photos and magazines, particularly *Vogue* and *Life.*

Well-known Playwrights, Composers, and Theatrical Trend Setters

Jean Anouilh
Leonard Bernstein (musicals and opera)
Benjamin Britten (opera)
Betty Comden and Adolph Green (musicals)
Agatha Christie
Christopher Frye
Martha Graham (mother of modern dance)
Lorraine Hansbury
William Inge
LeRoi Jones
Alan Jay Lerner and Frederick Loewe (musicals)
Gian-Carlo Menotti (opera)
Arthur Miller
John Osborne
Richard Rodgers and Oscar Hammerstein III (musicals)
Jerome Robbins (director and choreographer who completely intertwined dance to the story line in musical theater)
Stephen Sondheim (musicals)
Jule Styne (musicals)
Tennessee Williams

The Hip '60s—1960 to 1970

The Man—1965

The man in Figure 12–7 represents the younger adult male of the "hippie" type. His hair is long and worn with a headband. Jewelry, particularly pendent necklaces for men, was quite the "in" thing. Even older men wore them with turtle-necked sweaters and jackets instead of ties. The jeans were hip-huggers and had belled legs from the knees down. The open-front shirt had a long cuff and very full sleeves and was made in everything from cotton to satin. Boots of all types were popular and the jodhpur boot was sometimes worn for everyday. His belt is wide and the buckle ostentatious.

Figure 12–7. *The Hip '60s—1960 to 1970*

The Woman—1966

Women wore their hair long, often straight, but sometimes teased around the face and on the crown of the head. The woman in Figure 12–7 wears a biased cut mini-skirt, a sweater, and wide leather belt. The shoulder bag once again became as popular as it was in the '40s. The bag often came down further than the skirt. High boots were very popular and colored tights were worn on the legs for warmth. This style was fun for the young, but was unfortunately also worn by matrons, who should have known better.

General Description

This decade started with the bang of the Kennedy election, the election of "youth" to the

White House, particularly in Jackie as First Lady. She set the style. Hemlines went to two inches above the knee. Dresses were A line in cut and often had no waist. A short princess line coat was popular and was worn with either a pill box or a brenton large brimmed hat. Evening dresses were princess line and pencil slim. Hair was medium length and "bouffant" (teased away from the head). Shoes went to rounded toes and sensible one and one-half inch heels. In Paris, Coco Chanel's "little boy" suit with braid trim and silk shirt to match the silk jacket lining was the rage.

Men still wore the grey flannel suit of the '50s, but ties went to three inches in width. Jack Kennedy did not like hats, so hats were worn less than before.

The dissatisfaction with the war in Vietnam brought about civil protest among the young. Mary Quant, an English designer, created the first mini-skirt, and a flat-chested model named Twiggy, along with the Beatles (men's clothes), brought these fashions to America. The youth used clothing as a form of protest, or to show what side they were on, much as Heraldry did for the feudal knights. Long hair for men of draftable age was as much a protest against the military as it was against the older generation, who supported the war effort, but did not have to fight it.

With both men and women wearing long hair, shirts, and hip hugger pants it was often very hard to tell the girls from the boys, particularly from a rear view. The boys started growing beards and by the end of the '60s a well trimmed beard was socially acceptable. Long hair for men went "out" gradually, starting in '68, with the close of the war and the lowering of the voting age from twenty-one to eighteen.

The women's liberation movement ushered in a unisex look and with it the jumpsuit—a name applied to an all-in-one pants outfit, a holdover from the paratrooper outfit of World War II.

If I were to pick one word for the '60s it would be HAIR. There was a very popular Broadway show by that name (now very dated), which sums up the '60s very well. Its most memorable song was *The Age of Aquarius*. The musical discussed the war, the Kennedy years of unfulfilled promise, the drug cult and the occult, and introduced nudity on stage.

The colors of the '60s were "psychedelic"; every color was bright in tone and intense in pigment with harsh colors used in combination. A dress might have hot pink, bright orange, magenta, and bright red altogether.

The new fabric was the synthetic polyester, made from a petroleum base and undyable for home dyeing. It can be knitted or woven but lacking breathability, it is often hot in summer and cold in winter. When it first came out, the colors were either psychedelic or muted and greyish in tone. It can be washed and needs practically no ironing. It works extremely well when combined with a natural fiber.

Best Sources

Magazines and photographs, particularly *Vogue, McCalls, Ladies Home Journal,* and *Women's Wear Daily.*

Well-known Playwrights and Composers

Edward Albee
Jean Anouilh
Jerry Bock (musicals)
Ossie Davis
Jerry Herman (musicals)
LeRoi Jones
Arthur Miller
Harold Pinter
Neil Simon
Stephen Sondheim (musicals)
Jule Styne (musicals)
Tom Stoppard
Peter Weiss
Tennessee Williams

The Eclectic '70s—1970 to 1980

Man—1978

The man in Figure 12–8 wears the three-piece white suit made popular by John Travolta in the movie *Saturday Night Fever*. It is often worn with a colored shirt and a three and one-half- to four and one-half-inch wide tie. It can also be worn tieless, with the neck of the shirt open and showing a necklace or fine gold chain. The hair is worn short and covers the ear in a full fashion achieved by a "hot comb" or "blow-drying." This suit has the wide lapels and French-fashioned waist popularized in this country by Bill Blass.

Figure 12–8. *The Eclectic '70s—1970 to 1980*

The Woman—1978

The woman in Figure 12–8 wears what Paris termed in 1977 the "Gypsy" look, which in 1978 *Women's Wear Daily* would call the layered look. Although this looks like a skirt and blouse, it is really a one-piece dress made of five different fabrics, but all lightweight cottons. The camisole bodice is made of a black background flowered print lined and laced with a plain fabric, matching the flowers. The sleeves and flounce boarder are of a striped fabric edged in a black cotton, while the flounces themselves are a polka-dot. She wears a matching polka-dot scarf tied "gypsy" fashion and large plastic hooped earrings. She wears mid-calf high boots and is braless.

General Description

I have named this decade Eclectic because it has no style of its own. We have seen a rehash of the '30s, '40s, and '50s, the "gypsy look," the "romantique look," and the underwear look. In actuality very little underwear is worn and those who do wear it try to look as if they don't. It has given birth to "underalls," a pantie top knitted right onto a stocking base and the rounded, no-seam bra.

Then someone decided that since underwear was "out" for its own purpose, it should be romanticized and brought back as daytime outerwear, giving a resurgence to cotton eyelet, lace, and ribbons. This is also seen in the "romantique" and "gypsy" looks, layers, flounces, and ruffles.

Hemlines are wherever you want them, except that the mini-skirt is as dead as the Dodo. The smock top or loose fitting overblouse is popular when over slacks for casual and sport wear. With the advent of birth control pills, maternity clothing suffered a sharp decline, but with the "smock top" everyone looks pregnant.

A key-word for today's fashions is "functionalism." One wears what is comfortable for whatever one is doing. Women and men still dress for certain occasions (weddings, church, the theater) and long dresses of a casual type (the patio dress) can be worn in the daytime as well as evening. Slack suits can be worn for all occasions as well, depending upon their fabric and cut. Men still wear tuxedos, but a good dark suit or velvet jacket is equally acceptable. In the summertime, or in the tropics, men often wear the "leisure suit," an adaptation of the safari jacket of the '30s, with matching pants and in colors other than khaki.

The '70s represented an "anything goes" decade. I make no predictions. I think, however, that our reestablishing relations with China will bring a resurgence of the mandarin look; as "detente" with Russia brought in a brief Russian look. All colors were used. Some of the new fabrics include fantastic synthetic knits, gorgeous and washable, the reappearance of panee velvet, nylon, instead of silk, and fake, washable leather.

Best Sources

Magazines and photographs, particularly *Vogue, McCalls, Ladies Home Journal, L'Official, Elegance,* and the trade paper, *Women's Wear Daily.*

Well-known Playwrights, Composers, and Theatrical Trend Setters

Edward Albee
Jean Anouilh
Ossie Davis
Bob Fosse (director, choreographer, who is bringing dance into theater for itself)
Geoffrey Holder (director, writer, designer, and actor of extravaganza musicals)
Harold Pinter
Neil Simon
Stephen Sondheim (musicals)
Tom Stoppard
Stephen Schwartz
Peter Weiss

THREE

Research and Organization

This section attempts to give you a wide spectrum of knowledge. It is not intended to prevent trips to the library; it is merely to give you a basis from which to do your research in the hope that it may save you time. Time is the essence of all organizational games. By expending a little time in the early stages one hopes to save great amounts of both time and effort at the latter stage. This is where the word "practical" comes into play. A practical person sees choices clearly, chooses wisely, and acts economically upon that decision. Research shows you the available choices; organization allows you to act upon them economically.

13

A Springboard to Research

Helping Hand Information

This chapter provides a jumping-off place into accurate historical research. Part II contained a Table of Costume Periods and their approximate dates and also gave elementary period detail. In this chapter will be found the lines of emperors and kings, including ancient Rome, England, France, The Hapsburg-Holy Roman Emperors, Spain, and Romanov Russia. There are also tables for the dynasties of China and Japan. One could go on forever with this, so the selection has been narrowed to those countries and kings that most affect dramatic literature.

Oddly enough, there seems to be a direct correlation between stability of government and the flowering of artistic events. In England the stability of Edward III's reign produced Chaucer. One hundred years of fighting—nothing. Elizabethan stability produced Shakespeare, Jonson,

Webster, Marlowe, and Tourneur; the Civil War—nothing. The Restoration produced Sheridan, Congreve, Swift, and Samuel Johnson. In France the stability of Louis XIV produced Moliere, Racine, and Corneille. The Rococo produced Beaumarchais, but he lost his head to the Revolution. When the Italian citystates fought among themselves little was produced, yet Florence, under strong Medici leadership, started an artistic movement that revolutionized Western civilization.

For this reason the saga of citystates and principalities has been excluded. The Holy Roman Emperors of Byzantium are also excluded because of a singular lack of innovative dramatic literature at that time. I have included a family tree of the de Medicis, because of their relationship to the other ruling houses. Through their marriages, their blood flows through the veins of the House of Windsor (Hanover) and Bourbon Spain, as well as France.

The lines of the English and French kings help immeasurably in untangling Shakespearean histories. For this reason I have also included the family trees of those main protagonists and antagonists of the War of the Roses. The whole problem started with the fact that Edward III had seven sons, two of whom died in infancy. The remaining five were all ambitious. Unfortunately, the direct line of eldest to eldest stopped with Richard II, who had no children. He was deposed by his cousin, and so forth.

It is very necessary that the costume designer understand this particular part of history. It is covered extensively in dramatic literature. If *you* do not understand who is who, your audience never will. They may never catch on to your color code (the Yorks in whites, the Lancasters in reds, the Nevilles in greens, the Mortimers in black, the Percys in blue), but unconsciously it will help to keep the "teams'" straight. It may also help cut costs.

Also included in this chapter are tables of artists, designers, and composers classified by period, nationality, and style. Obviously, one cannot name them all. Once again, I have tried to select a representative group. I hereby apologize if, through ignorance or forgetfulness, I have inadvertently left out your favorites. Artists who painted only still lifes, landscapes, or seascapes were not named because these are not necessary for the costume designer. There are many artists whose work is primarily illustrative. Therefore there is a separate table cataloging them.

Another thing one is constantly running into in dramatic literature are references to gods and goddesses. They take time to look up and compare, so I have included some of the most frequently used of Egyptian, Norse, Greek, and Roman mythologies. For this information I am indebted to *The Larousse Encyclopedia of Mythology,* which is not only loaded with facts, but has excellent photographs, making it an excellent source book.

Why include a table of musicians? There is no quicker way to get into the mood of a particular period than by listening to its music. You can understand the movements and rhythms necessary for period action. Then too, as costume designers we are called upon to design for opera and the ballet as well as the theater. In this century and country, half of our theatrical output is musicals.

Please remember this chapter is only the springboard, the means of giving more lift to the diver. Don't be afraid of research. The effect is cumulative. The more you dig, the more you learn and the less you have to do in the future. As a practical research suggestion, keep an ongoing card file, index, or notebook of some sort with reference and period data. Eventually it saves hours in the library.

Useful Books for Your Private Library

If you like your information at your fingertips, you should begin thinking about building up a library of your own. It should include books on the following general categories: A good and up-to-date general encyclopedia; several survey books on the history of art, architecture, music and general history; several specific books on the history of fashion. For a broader perspective, it pays to have one or two from countries other than the United States.

You should include books on armor, heraldry, and uniforms. You must include a good book on sewing techniques and various types of needlework, fabrics, and fabric designing. There are also several good books, which include period patterns in scale. You might want to include books on painting and drawing techniques, jewelry design, makeup and wig making, theatrical scenery, props, and a good history of interiors. A comprehensive bibliography can be found at the end of this book.

Table 13–1. The Royal Line of Kings

The Roman Caesars from Julius to Constantine[1]

Julius Caesar	47–44 B.C.	
Augustus Caesar (Octavian)	44 B.C.–14 A.D.	Technically he ruled jointly with Marc Antony until Antony's defeat at Artium in 31 B.C.
Tiberius Caesar	14 A.D.–37	
Caius Germanicus Caesar (Caligula)	37–41	"Caligula" is a nickname meaning "little boots," because as a child he was fond of parading around in his father's boots; his father was the general Germanicus.
Claudius I	41–54	
Nero	54–68	
Vespasian	69–79	
Titus	79–81	
Domitian	81–96	
Nerva	96–98	
Trajan	98–117	
Hadrian	117–138	
Antonius Pius	138–161	
Marcus Aurelius	161–180	
Commodus	180–192	
Septimus Severus	193–211	
Caracalla	211–217	
Macrimus	217–218	
Heliogabalus (Elagabalus)	218–222	
Alexander Severus	222–235	
Maximus Throx	235–238	Maxinim I
Gordian I (father)		
Gordian II (son)	238	Ruled jointly
Gordian III	239–244	Second son of Gordian I
Philippus	244–249	
Decius	249–251	
Gallus	251–253	
Aemilianus	253	

[1]The lines of the kings, Roman Caesars through the Romanovs, was compiled from *The Columbia-Viking Desk Encyclopedia*, Bridgewater, William (Editor-in-chief), New York: Viking Press, 1953, 1959.

Table 13–1. *(Continued)*

Valerian (father)	253–260	
Gallienus (son)	253–268	Ruled jointly
Cladius II	268–270	
Aurelena	270–275	
Piobus	276–282	
Carinus	283–285	
Diocletian (East)	284–305	Ruled jointly until 286
Maximus (West)	286–305	Ruled jointly
		Diocletian believed the empire too big to be ruled successfully by one man, so he divided it in two parts, East (which he kept), and West (which was ruled by Maximus). This worked well for a while, but led eventually to total partition between the Romanesque and Byzantine Empires.
Galerius (East)	305–310	
Severus (West)	305–307	
Constantius I (West)	307–310	
Constantine I (West)	310–337	Ruled jointly until Licinius' death in 324, then reunited the Empire in one person; moved capital from Rome to Constantinople.
Licinius (East)	310–324	

Table 13–2. Line of English Kings and Queens

House of Wessex	
Egbert	802–839
Ethelwulf	839–858
Ethelbald	858–860
Ethelbert	860–866
Ethelred I	866–871
Alfred	871–900
Edward I	900–924
Athetstan	924–939
Edmund I	939–946
Edred	946–955
Edwig	955–959

Table 13–2.   *(Continued)*

Edgar	957(?)–975	
Edward II (the martyr)	975–978	
Ethelred II	978–1016	
Edmund II	1016	Died and line usurped by Canute
Canute	1016–1035	
Harold I	1035–1040	
Hardicanute	1040–1043	
Edward III (the confessor)	1042–1066	
Harold II	1066	Died from wounds at Battle of Hastings

House of Normandy   (later Plantagenets)

William I	1066–1087	
William II (Rufus)	1087–1100	
Henry I	1100–1135	
Stephen	1135–1154	
Henry II	1154–1189	Beginning of Plantagenets
Richard I	1189–1199	
John	1199–1216	
Henry III	1216–1272	
Edward I (4th)	1272–1307	
Edward II	1307–1327	
Edward III	1327–1377	
Richard II	1377–1399	
Henry IV	1399–1413	Usurpation by House of Lancaster
Henry V	1413–1422	King at time of Jeanne d'Arc
Henry VI	1422–1461	Died 1471
Edward IV	1461–1483	
Edward V		Usurpation by House of York. Edward V never ruled; killed with brother in tower
Richard III	1483–1485	Edward IV's brother-usurper and reputed to be murderer of two sons of Edward IV

Table 13–2. *(Continued)*

House of Tudor		
Henry VII	1485–1509	
Henry VIII	1509–1547	
Edward VI	1547–1553	
Mary I	1553–1558	
Elizabeth I	1558–1603	
House of Stuart		
James I	1603–1625	
Charles I	1625–1649	Beheaded
Oliver Cromwell	(Lord Protector)	1649–1658
Richard Cromwell	(Lord Protector)	1658–1660
Charles II	1660–1685	
James II	1685–1688	
William III and Mary II	1689–1702	
Ann	1702–1714	
House of Hanover (later Windsor)		
George I	1714–1727	
George II	1727–1760	
George III	1760–1820	
George IV	1820–1830	
William IV	1830–1837	
Victoria	1837–1901	
Edward VII	1901–1910	
George V	1910–1936	
Edward VIII	1936	
George VI	1936–1953	
Elizabeth II	1953–	

Table 13–3.   Line of French Kings

Carolingians

Charlemagne[1] (Charles I) note: "King of the West," including all of France, Germany, Italy, Spain and Portugal

	768–814	Ruled France
	800–814	Ruled everything
Louis I ("the Pious")	814–840	
Charles II	840–877	Both sons of Charlemagne
Louis II ("the Stammerer")	877–879	
Louis III	879–882	
Charles III ("the fat or the simple")	882–929	
Robert I	929–936	
Louis IV ("from across the sea")	929–954	Robert ruled in fact until 936, but was not the legitimate heir. Louis IV lived in England in exile until Robert's death, at which time he was crowned.
Hugh the Great	954–967	Never officially crowned king, but ruled in fact and passed throne to son and the Capetian line.
Louis V ("the sluggard")	967–987	

Capets

Hugh	987–996	Son of Hugh the Great
Robert II ("the pious")	996–1031	Grandfather to William the Conqueror
Henri I	1031–1060	
Phillip I	1060–1108	
Louis VI ("the fat")	1108–1137	
Louis VII ("the young")	1137–1180	Divorced Eleanor of Aquitaine
Phillip II	1180–1223	
Louis VIII	1223–1226	
Louis IX (St. Louis)	1226–1270	
Phillip III	1270–1285	
Phillip IV ("the fair")	1285–1314	

[1]Charlemagne divided his kingdom between his sons. Pepin I received the Aquitaine and Spain; Louis "the German" received Bavaria and Italy; and Charles received northern France and the Low Countries. When Charlemagne died, the sons fought and Charles won supremacy, but the area was too vast and therefore he had to return the major portion to his brothers; he retained the title of Holy Roman Emperor, starting the line of Kings of the Holy Roman Empire, which will be found in Table 13–4.

Table 13–3.   *(Continued)*

Louis X[2]	1314–1316	
Jean I	1316	Born posthumously to Louis X and lived only four months
Phillip V ("the tall")[2]	1316–1322	
Charles IV[2]	1322–1328	

Valois

Phillip VI	1328–1350	
Jean II	1350–1364	
Charles V ("the wise")	1364–1380	
Charles VI ("the mad or the well-beloved")	1380–1422	
Charles VII ("the victorious")	1422–1461	This is St. Joan's "Charlie."
Louis XI ("the spider king")	1461–1483	
Charles VIII	1483–1498	
Louis XII	1498–1515	Was married briefly to Henry VIII's sister, Mary Tudor (later Mary Brandon)
Francis I	1515–1547	
Henri II	1547–1559	Married to Catherine de Medici; Diane de Poitiers was his mistress
Francis II[3]	1559–1560	Married to Mary Queen of Scots
Charles IX[3]	1560–1574	Became insane over the St. Bartholomew's Day Massacre
Henry III[3]	1574–1589	

Bourbons

Henri IV	1589–1610	
Louis XIII	1610–1643	King to the Three Musketeers
Louis XIV ("the sun king")	1643–1715	
Louis XV	1715–1774	
Louis XVI	1774–1793	
Louis XVII ("the lost dauphin")	Never crowned	
Napoleon I	1801–1814 1815–1816	
Louis XVIII[4]	1814–1815 1816–1824	

[2]All sons of Phillip IV
[3]All sons of Henri II and Catherine de Medici
[4]Louis XVIII was a brother of Louis XVI.

Table 13–3. *(Continued)*

Napoleon II	Never crowned	Napoleon's son by Maria Josepha of Austria
Charles X	1824–1830	Deposed, exiled to England
Louis Phillippe	1830–1848	
Louis Napoleon	1852–1870	

Table 13–4. Line of the Hapsburgs of the Holy Roman Empire and the Austro-Hungarian Empire[1]

Albert II	1438–1439	
Fredrick III	1440–1493	
Maximilian I	1493–1519	
Charles V	1519–1528	He added Spain and the Lowlands.
Ferdinand I	1521–1564	
Maximilian II	1564–1576	
Rudolf II	1576–1606	
Mathias	1606–1619	
Ferdinand II	1619–1637	
Ferdinand III	1637–1657	
Leopold I	1658–1705	
Joseph I	1705–1711	
Charles VI	1711–1740	
Maria Theresa	1740–1780	She ruled jointly, first with her husband Francis I, and then with her son Joseph II
Joseph II	1765–1790	
Leopold II	1790–1792	Brother of Joseph II and Marie Antoinette
Francis II	1792–1806 1806–1835	He dissolved the Holy Roman Empire, but remained emperor of the Austro-Hungarian Empire.
Ferdinand IV	1835–1848	
Francis Joseph	1848–1916	
Charles I	1916–1918	End of monarchy

[1]Please note that the Hapsburgs can trace their line back to Tandolt I, who died in 991. They were emperors of all or part of the Holy Roman Empire since Rudolf I, who ruled it from 1273 to 1291. When he died, he divided the empire between his two sons, Albert I and Rudolf II. This practice of crowning sons king of parts existed until Albert II, who reunited the Holy Roman Empire in his own hands in 1438.

Table 13–5.   Spanish Kings from Ferdinand and Isabella[1]

Ferdinand V	1469–1516	
Carlos (Charles) I	1516–1556	
Philip II	1556–1598	
Philip III	1598–1621	
Philip IV	1621–1665	
Carlos (Charles) II	1665–1700	Last of Hapsburg kings on Spanish throne
Philip V	1700–1746	First Bourbon Spanish king
Ferdinand VI	1746–1759	
Carlos (Charles) III	1759–1788	
Carlos (Charles) IV	1788–1819	
Ferdinand VII	1819–1833	Deposed his father Charles IV in 1808, but Napoleonic Wars reinstated Charles IV
Isabella II	1833–1870	Abdicated in favor of son
Alphonse XII	1875–1885	
Alphonse XIII	1886–1931	Deposed by Franco
Juan Carlos	1976	Restored by Franco

[1]Ferdinand V of Aragon married Isabella I of Castille in 1469, and by that act united all of Christian Spain. Both were fanatical Catholics and together they succeeded in expelling the last of the Moors from the Iberian Peninsula, a feat that they termed a "holy war." Isabella died in 1504 leaving her Castillian domains to her daughter, Juanna (Joanna), who was married to Philip, King of the Netherlands and son of Maximilian I, the Hapsburg Holy Roman Emperor. Juanna and Philip ruled jointly in Castille. He officially became Philip I, but on their way to Granada in 1505 Philip died and Ferdinand mysteriously incarcerated Juanna, claiming her insane. (At the time of Philip's death she was pregnant with their sixth child, a daughter, Catherine). Ferdinand ruled "in her name" until his death in 1516. Her son, Charles V, the Holy Roman Emperor, ruled Spain "in her name" until her death in 1555. In Spain he became Carlos I.

Table 13–6.   Line of the Romanovs of Russia

Michael[1]	1613–1645	
Alexis	1645–1676	
Feodor III	1676–1682	
Ivan V	1682–1689	Ruled jointly with brother, Peter I, until Peter deposed him
Peter I (the Great)	1682–1725	
Catherine I	1725–1727	Servant girl, wife of Peter the Great
Peter II	1727–1730	
Anna	1730–1740	
Ivan VI	1740–1741	Deposed by Elizabeth

[1]Michael Romanov united all the Russias and started "the good times."

Table 13–6. *(Continued)*

Elizabeth	1741–1762	
Peter III	1762	Deposed by his wife, Catherine the Great
Catherine II (the Great)	1762–1796	
Paul I	1796–1801	
Alexander I	1801–1825	
Nicholas I	1825–1855	
Alexander II	1855–1881	
Alexander III	1881–1894	
Nicholas II	1894–1917	Deposed and executed in 1918

Table 13–7. The Dynasties of China

Reischauer, Edwin O. and Fairbank, John K. *East Asia: The Great Tradition* (Boston: Houghton Mifflin Company, 1960).

Hsia[1]	2205 B.C. to 1766 B.C.
Shang (sometimes called Yin)	1766 B.C. to 1122 B.C.
Western Chou	1122 B.C. to 771 B.C.
Eastern Chou	771 B.C. to 256 B.C.
Ch'in	256 B.C. to 206 B.C.
Former Han	206 B.C. to 8 A.D.
Later Han	8 A.D. to 220 A.D.
Wu ⎱ called the	220 A.D. to 280 A.D.
Shu/han ⎰ Three Kingdoms	220 A.D. to 263 A.D.
Wei	220 A.D. to 264 A.D.
Western Chin	280 A.D. to 317 A.D.
Eastern Chin	317 A.D. to 420 A.D.
Northern Wei[2]	386 A.D. to 535 A.D.
Southern Ch'i	479 A.D. to 500 A.D.
Liang	502 A.D. to 557 A.D.
Ch'en	557 A.D. to 589 A.D.
Sui	589 A.D. to 618 A.D.
T'ang	618 A.D. to 907 A.D.

[1]This seems to be a period that was largely mythological, like early Egyptian and biblical times. Documentation starts with the Yin.

[2]After much civil war and the invasion of the northern barbarians, China for a time was divided between two dynasties of equal strength, the Wei controlling the northern half.

Table 13–7. *(Continued)*

Ten Kingdoms[3]	907 A.D. to 979 A.D.
Five Dynasties[3]	907 A.D. to 960 A.D.
Sung	976 A.D. to 1126 A.D.
Southern Sung	1127 A.D. to 1279 A.D.
Yuan	1279 A.D. to 1368 A.D.
Ming	1368 A.D. to 1662 A.D.
Ch-eng	1662 A.D. to 1908
Republic[4]	1908 A.D. to ?
Peoples Republic	1948 A.D. to ?

[3]More civil strife and coexistence of several dynasties at once.
[4]The coexistence of Taiwan and Mainland China, as one can see from this, is not new to the Chinese.

Table 13–8. The Dynasties and Cultures of Japan

Jomon Culture	3000 B.C.–300 B.C.
Yayai Culture	300 B.C.–100 A.D.
Uji Period	100 A.D.–645 A.D.
Taike	645 A.D.–710 A.D.
Nara	710 A.D.–794 A.D.
Heian	794 A.D.–857 A.D.
Fujiware (sometimes called late Heian)	857 A.D.–1160 A.D.
Taira	1160 A.D.–1185 A.D.
Kamakura	1185 A.D.–1333 A.D.
Yoshino	1136 A.D.–1392 A.D.
Ashikaga (sometimes called Muromaghi)	1336 A.D.–1573 A.D.
Nobunaga	1573 A.D.–1582 A.D.
Hideyoshi	1582 A.D.–1598 A.D.
Tokugawa (sometimes called Edo)	1598 A.D.–1867 A.D.
Meiji	1868 A.D.–1912 A.D.
Taisho	1912 A.D.–1926 A.D.
Showa	1926 A.D.– ?

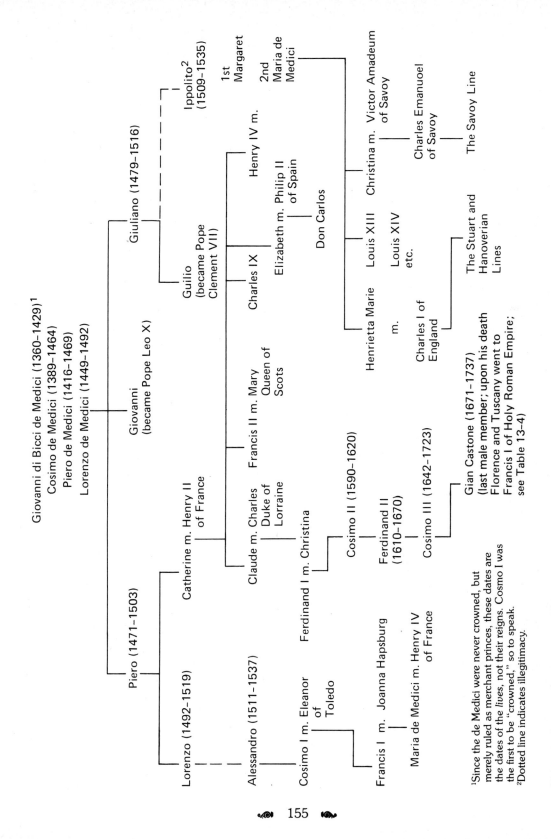

Giovanni di Bicci de Medici (1360–1429)[1]
Cosimo de Medici (1389–1464)
Piero de Medici (1416–1469)
Lorenzo de Medici (1449–1492)

Piero (1471–1503)

Giuliano (1479–1516)

Giovanni (became Pope Leo X)

Lorenzo (1492–1519)

Catherine m. Henry II of France

Guilio (became Pope Clement VII)

Ippolito[2] (1509–1535)

1st Margaret

2nd Maria de Medici

Alessandro (1511–1537)

Claude m. Charles Duke of Lorraine

Francis II m. Mary Queen of Scots

Charles IX

Henry IV m.

Elizabeth m. Philip II of Spain

Don Carlos

Cosimo I m. Eleanor of Toledo

Ferdinand I m. Christina

Cosimo II (1590–1620)

Henrietta Marie m. Charles I of England

Louis XIII

Louis XIV etc.

Christina m. Victor Amadeum of Savoy

Charles Emanuoel of Savoy

The Savoy Line

Francis I m. Joanna Hapsburg

Maria de Medici m. Henry IV of France

Ferdinand II (1610–1670)

Cosimo III (1642–1723)

Gian Castone (1671–1737) (last male member; upon his death Florence and Tuscany went to Francis I of Holy Roman Empire; see Table 13-4)

The Stuart and Hanoverian Lines

[1]Since the de Medici were never crowned, but merely ruled as merchant princes, these dates are the dates of the *lives*, not their reigns. Cosmo I was the first to be "crowned," so to speak.
[2]Dotted line indicates illegitimacy.

Figure 13–1. *The House of Medici*

Family Trees of the War of the Roses

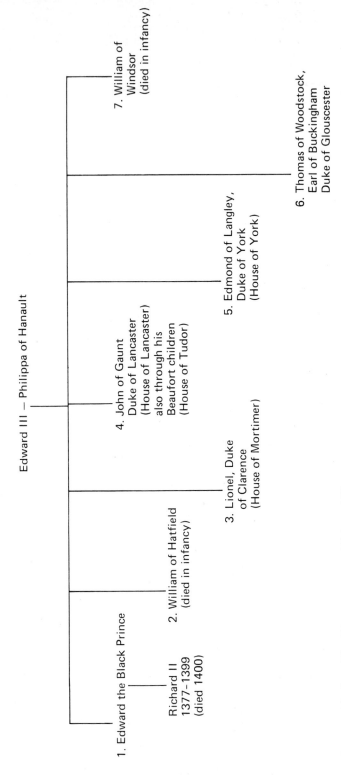

Figure 13–2. *The Plantagenets of Edward III*

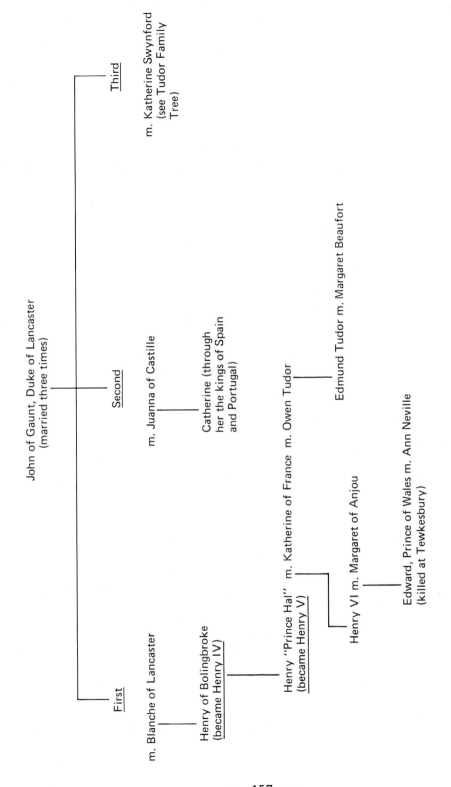

LANCASTER LINE

Figure 13–3. *House of Lancaster* *(Red Rose)*

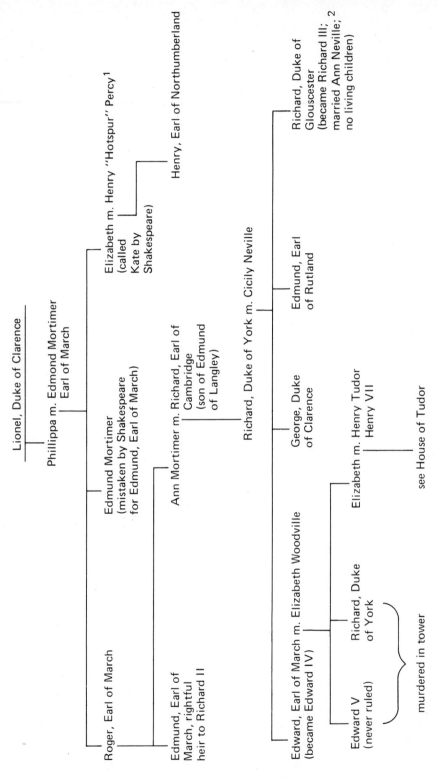

Figure 13–4. *House of York   (White Rose)*

[1]See Percy family tree
[2]See Neville family tree

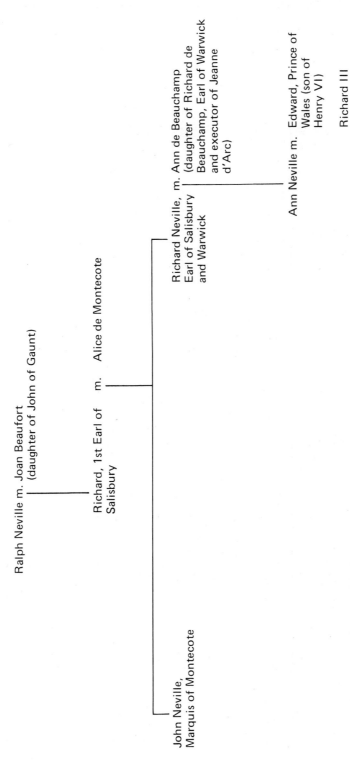

Figure 13–5. *Neville Family Tree*

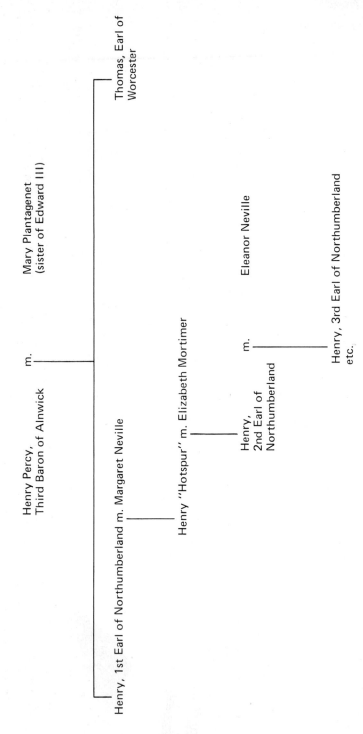

Figure 13–6. *Percy Family Tree*

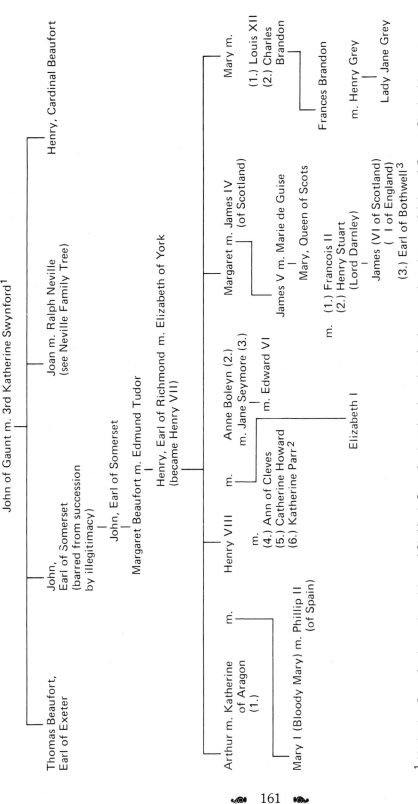

[1] Katherine Swynford was the widow of Sir Hugh Swynford at the time that she became the mistress of John of Gaunt. She had borne two children to Hugh, a daughter named Blanche after Blanche of Lancaster and a son, Thomas. It was this Thomas Swynford who became Richard II's jailer at Pontefact. She had four illegitimate children by John of Gaunt, who gave them the name Beaufort and legitimized them when he finally married their mother. Katherine's sister, Philippa, was married to Geoffrey Chaucer the poet and secretary to John of Gaunt.

[2] An easy way to remember Henry VIII's wives and their fates was told to me by a delightful guide through the Tower of London: K,A,J,A,C,K, – Divorced, Beheaded, Died; Divorced, Beheaded, Survived.

[3] Mary Queen of Scots had twins to Bothwell, but they died in infancy.

Figure 13–7. *House of Tudor*

Table 13–9.   Artists—Period, Nationality, and Style

This has been compiled from *The Tudor History of Painting,* Maillard, Robert (editor), New York: Tudor Publishing Company, 1961.

Period	Artist	Nationality	Style
Gothic	Pietro Cavallini	Italian	Sienese School
Gothic	Cimabue	Italian	Sienese School
Gothic	Duccio	Italian	Sienese School
Gothic	Gentile	Italian	Sienese School
Gothic	Giotto	Italian	Sienese School
Gothic	Ambrogio Lorenzetti	Italian	Sienese School
Gothic	Pietro Lorenzetti	Italian	Sienese School
Gothic	Simone Martini	Italian	Sienese School
Gothic	Pinacoteca	Italian	Sienese School
Gothic	Pisarello	Italian	Sienese School
Gothic	San di Pietro	Italian	Sienese School
Gothic	Sassetta	Italian	Sienese School
Gothic	Guido Da Siena	Italian	Sienese School
High Gothic	Fra Angelico	Italian	Florentine School
High Gothic	Luis Barrassa	Spanish	Iberian School
High Gothic	Hieronymus Bosch	Dutch	Netherlandish School
High Gothic	Dieric Bouts	Dutch	Netherlandish School
High Gothic	Robert Campin	Dutch	Netherlandish School
High Gothic	Enguerrand Charton	French	Avignon School
High Gothic	Petrus Christus	Dutch	Netherlandish School
High Gothic	Gerard David	Flemish	German Classicism
High Gothic	Guileaume Dombet	French	[1]
High Gothic	Giovanni di Fiesole	Italian	Florentine School
High Gothic	Jean Fouquet	French	[1]
High Gothic	Nicolas Fronent	French	Avignon School
High Gothic	Friedrich Herlin	German	Germanic School
High Gothic	Jaume Huguet	Spanish	Iberian School
High Gothic	Geertgen Lat dint Jans	Dutch	Netherlandish School
High Gothic	Stephen Lochner	German	Germanic School
High Gothic	Hans Maler	German	Germanic School

Table 13–9. *(cont.)*

Period	Artist	Nationality	Style
High Gothic	Simon Marmion	Flemish	Franco-Flemish School
High Gothic	Quentin Massys	Flemish	German Classicism
High Gothic	Memlinc	Dutch	Netherlandish School
High Gothic	Michael Packer	German	Germanic School
High Gothic	Martin Schongauer	German	Germanic School
High Gothic	Pol de Timbourg	French	Illustrations for The Duc du Berry's *Book of the Hours*
High Gothic	Nuno Unocalves	Portuguese	Iberian School
High Gothic	Jan Van Eyck	Dutch	Netherlandish School
High Gothic	Hugo Van Der Goes	Dutch	Netherlandish School
High Gothic	Marinus Van Reymaswael	Flemish	Germanic Classicism
High Gothic	Rogier Van Der Weylen	Dutch	Netherlandish School
High Gothic	Conrad Wity	German	Germanic School
Early Renaissance	Paolo Doni	Italian	Florentine School
Early Renaissance	Tomaso Masaccio	Italian	Florentine School
Early Renaissance	Uccella	Italian	Florentine School
Early Renaissance	Domenico Veneziano	Italian	Florentine School
Renaissance	Albrecht Altdorfer	German	German Classicism
Renaissance	Hans Baldung	German	German Classicism
Renaissance	Evaristo Baschenis	Italian	Luminism
Renaissance	Baugin	French	Luminism
Renaissance	Valentin de Baullongne	French	Luminism
Renaissance	Gentile Bellini	Italian	Venetian School
Renaissance	Giovanni Bellini	Italian	Venetian School
Renaissance	Sandro Botticelli	Italian	Florentine School
Renaissance	Brueghel the Elder	Flemish	German Classicism[3]
Renaissance	Caravaggio	Spanish	Luminism
Renaissance	Vittore Carpaccio	Italian	Venetian School
Renaissance	Andrea Del Castagno	Italian	Florentine School
Renaissance	Jean Clouet	French	Clouet School

Table 13–9. (*cont.*)

Period	Artist	Nationality	Style
Renaissance	Piero di Cosimo	Italian	Florentine School
Renaissance	Jean Cousin	French	Mannerism
Renaissance	Lucas Cranoch the Elder	German	German Classicism
Renaissance	Lucas Cranoch the Younger	German	German Classicism
Renaissance	Albrecht Durer	German	German Classicism
Renaissance	Melozzo da Farli	Italian	Umbrian School
Renaissance	Piero Della Francesca	Italian	Umbrian School
Renaissance	Orazio Gentileschi	Italian	Luminism
Renaissance	Ghirlandaio	Italian	Florentine School
Renaissance	Jean Gossaert	Flemish	German Classicism[3]
Renaissance	Benozzo Gozzoli	Italian	Flemish School
Renaissance	El Greco	Spanish (Greek by birth)	[2]
Renaissance	Grien	German	German Classicism
Renaissance	Grunewald	German	German Classicism
Renaissance	Hans Holbein the Younger	German	German Classicism[2]
Renaissance	Filippino Lippi	Italian	Florentine School
Renaissance	Fra Filippo Lippi	Italian	Florentine School
Renaissance	Francois Liesnel	French	Clouet School
Renaissance	Corneille de Lyon	French	Clouet School
Renaissance	Niklaus Manuel	German	German Classicism
Renaissance	Antonio Maro	Spanish	Italian School
Renaissance	Antonello da Messina	Italian	Venetian School
Renaissance	Andrea Montegna	Italian	School of Padua
Renaissance	Luis de Morales	Spanish	Italian School
Renaissance	Pallaiuolo	Italian	Florentine School
Renaissance	Joachino Patenir	Flemish	German Classicism[3]
Renaissance	Ercole de Roberti	Italian	Venetian School
Renaissance	Alonso Sanchez	Spanish	Italian School
Renaissance	Jan Van Scorel	Flemish	Italian School[3]
Renaissance	Luca Signorelli	Italian	Umbrian School
Renaissance	Hendrik Terbugghen	Dutch	[1]
Renaissance	Cosimo Tura	Italian	Venetian School
Renaissance	Martin Van Heemskerch	Flemish	Italian School[3]
Renaissance	Lucas Van Leyden	Flemish	German Classicism[3]

Table 13–9. *(cont.)*

Period	Artist	Nationality	Style
Renaissance	Bernard Van Orley	Flemish	German Classicism[3]
Renaissance	Verrochino	Italian	Florentine School
High Renaissance	Paris Bordone	Italian	Venetian School
High Renaissance	Angelo Bronzino	Italian	Tuscan Mannerism
High Renaissance	Jacapo Carrucci	Italian	Tuscan Mannerism
High Renaissance	Correggio	Italian	Tuscan Mannerism
High Renaissance	Dasso Dassi	Italian	Tuscan Mannerism
High Renaissance	Giorgione	Italian	Venetian School
High Renaissance	Lorenzo Latto	Italian	Venetian School
High Renaissance	Michelangelo	Italian	Florentine School
High Renaissance	Parmigianino	Italian	Tuscan Mannerism
High Renaissance	Penturicchio	Italian	Sienese School
High Renaissance	Perugino	Italian	[1]
High Renaissance	Sebastiano Del Piombo	Italian	Venetian School
High Renaissance	Raphael	Italian	Florentine School
High Renaissance	Andrea Del Sarto	Italian	Florentine School
High Renaissance	Tintoretto	Italian	Venetian School
High Renaissance	Titian	Italian	Venetian School
High Renaissance	Palma Vecchino	Italian	Venetian School
High Renaissance	Veronese	Italian	Venetian School
High Renaissance	Leonardo da Vinci	Italian	Florentine School

Table 13–9. *(cont.)*

Period	Artist	Nationality	Style
Baroque	Gerard Ter Barch	Dutch	Dutch School
Baroque	Adriaen Brouwer	Flemish	Flemish School
Baroque	Charles Le Brun	French	French Classicism
Baroque	Phillippe de Champaigne	French	Italian Classicism
Baroque	Pieter Claesy	Dutch	Dutch School
Baroque	William Claesy	Dutch	Dutch School
Baroque	Verard Dau	Dutch	Dutch School
Baroque	Carel Frabritws	Dutch	Dutch School
Baroque	Claude Gellee	French	Italian Classicism
Baroque	Frans Hals	Dutch	Rustic School
Baroque	Pieter de Hooch	Dutch	Dutch School
Baroque	Jacob Isaacksz	Dutch	Dutch School
Baroque	Pieter Jansy	Dutch	Dutch School
Baroque	Jacob Jordaens	Flemish	Flemish School
Baroque	Claude Lorrain	French	Italian Classicism
Baroque	Pierre Megnard	French	French Classicism
Baroque	Murillo	Spanish	Luminism
Baroque	Antoine Le Nain	French	Miniaturist
Baroque	Louis Le Nain	French	Rustic School
Baroque	Mathieu Le Nain	French	Court Portraitist
Baroque	Nicolas Poussin	French	French Classicism
Baroque	Rembrandt	Dutch	Luminism
Baroque	Jose de Ribera	Spanish	Luminism
Baroque	Hyacinthe Rigaud	French	French Classicism
Baroque	Peter Paul Rubens	Flemish	Flemish School
Baroque	Solomon Van Ruisdael	Dutch	Dutch School
Baroque	Frans Snyders	Flemish	Flemish School
Baroque	Jan Steen	Dutch	Dutch School
Baroque	Justus Suttermane	Flemish	Flemish School
Baroque	Nicolas de Targilliere	French	French Classicism
Baroque	David Teniers	Flemish	Flemish School
Baroque	Georges de la Tour	French	Luminism
Baroque	Anthony Van Dyck	Flemish	Flemish School
Baroque	Jan Van Goyen	Dutch	Dutch School
Baroque	Adriaen Van Ostado	Dutch	Dutch School

Table 13–9. (*cont.*)

Period	Artist	Nationality	Style
Baroque	William Van de Velde	Dutch	Dutch School
Baroque	Cornelius de Vas	Flemish	Flemish School
Baroque	Velasquez	Spanish	Realism
Baroque	Jan Vermeer	Dutch	Dutch School
Baroque	Joseph Vivien	French	French Classicism
Baroque	Emanuel de Witte	Dutch	Dutch School
Baroque	Zurbaran	Spanish	Luminism
Rococo	Louis Leopold Boilly	French	French Romanticism
Rococo	Francois Boucher	French	French Romanticism
Rococo	Giovanni Canale	Italian	Venetian Romanticism
Rococo	Jean Baptiste Chardin	French	Rustic School
Rococo	John Singleton Copley	American	Classicism, Italian School
Rococo	Ralph Earl	American	Classicism
Rococo	Jean Honore Fragonard	French	French Romanticism
Rococo	Hans Heinrich Fussle	German	German Romanticism
Rococo	Thomas Gainsborough	English	English Classicism
Rococo	Jean Baptiste Greuye	French	French Romanticism
Rococo	Francisco Guardi	Italian	Venetian Romanticism
Rococo	William Hogarth	English	Rustic School
Rococo	Nicolas Lancert	French	French Romanticism
Rococo	Pietro Longhi	Italian	Venetian Romanticism
Rococo	Jean-Marc Nattier	French	French Romanticism
Rococo	Maurice Quentin	French	French Romanticism
Rococo	Henry Raeburn	English	English Classicism
Rococo	Joshua Reynolds	English	English Classicism
Rococo	Hubert Robert	French	French Romanticism
Rococo	George Romney	English	English Classicism
Rococo	Edward Savage	American	Classicism
Rococo	Gilbert Stuart	American	Classicism
Rococo	George Stubbs	English	English Classicism
Rococo	Giambattista Tiepolo	Italian	Venetian Romanticism
Rococo	Giandomenico Tiepolo	Italian	Venetian Romanticism
Rococo	John Trumbull	American	Classicism
Rococo	Joseph Vernet	French	French Romanticism

Table 13–9. *(cont.)*

Period	Artist	Nationality	Style
Rococo	Antoine Watteau	French	French Romanticism
Rococo	Richard Wilson	English	German Romanticism
Rococo Empire	William Blake	English	German Romanticism
Rococo Empire	John Constable	English	English Classicism
Rococo Empire	John Crome	English	English Classicism
Rococo Empire	Francisco Goya	Spanish	[1]
Rococo Empire	Thomas Sully	American	Classicism
Rococo Empire	Tischluein	German	German Romanticism
Empire	Marie-Guehelmine Benoist	French	Neo-Classicism
Empire	Jacques Louis David	French	Neo-Classicism
Empire	Arthur W. Devis	English	English Classicism
Empire	Francois-Pascal Gerard	French	Neo-Classicism
Empire	Theodore Gericault	French	[1]
Empire	Jean-Antoine Gros	French	Neo-Classicism
Empire	Ann-Louis Guodet-Trisson	French	Neo-Classicism
Empire	Richard Parker	English	English Classicism
Empire	Pierre Paul Prod'hon	French	Neo-Classicism
Empire	Jean-Baptiste Regnault	French	Neo-Classicism
Empire	Elizabeth Virgee-Lebrun	French	Neo-Classicism
Empire Victorian	Caspar Friedrich	German	German Romanticism
Empire Victorian	J. A. Dominique Ingres	French	Academician
Empire Victorian	Edward Hicks	American	Primitive
Victorian	John James Audubon	American	Realism
Victorian	Frederic Bazille	French	Impressionism
Victorian	George Caleb Bingham	American	Rustic School
Victorian	Rosa de Bonhuere	French	Ecole Barbizon
Victorian	Eugene Boudin	French	Impressionism
Victorian	Ford Madox Brown	English	Pre-Raphaelite
Victorian	Edward Burne-Jones	English	English Classicism
Victorian	Mary Cassatt	American	Impressionism
Victorian	Paul Cezanne	French	Impressionism
Victorian	Theodore Chasseriau	French	Academician
Victorian	Puvis de Chavannes	French	Symbolism
Victorian	Jean Baptiste Corot	French	Ecole Barbizon
Victorian	Erich Correns	German	Academician

Table 13–9. (*cont.*)

Period	Artist	Nationality	Style
Victorian	Gustave Courbet	French	Ecole Barbizon
Victorian	Jaspar E. Crosbey	American	Romanticism
Victorian	Honore Daumier	French	[1]
Victorian	Edgar Degas	French	Impressionism
Victorian	Eugene Delacroix	French	[1]
Victorian	Henry-Edmond Delacroix	French	Pointilism
Victorian	Maurice Denis	French	Symbolism
Victorian	Asher Durand	American	Romanticism
Victorian	Paul Gaugin	French	Primitivism
Victorian	Victor De Grailly	American (born in France)	Romanticism
Victorian	Edward Lamson Henry	American	Realism
Victorian	Winslow Homer	American	[1]
Victorian	William Hornett	American	Realism
Victorian	Thomas Eakins	American	English Classicism
Victorian	George Inness	American	English Classicism
Victorian	Jongkind	Dutch	Impressionism
Victorian	Henri Fantin Latour	French	Symbolism
Victorian	Edouard Manet	French	Impressionism
Victorian	John Everett Millais	English	Pre-Raphaelite
Victorian	Jean-Francais Millet	French	Romanticism Rustic School
Victorian	Claude Monet	French	Impressionism
Victorian	Gustave Moreau	French	Symbolism
Victorian	Berthe Morisot	French	Impressionism
Victorian	William S. Mount	American	Rustic School
Victorian	Samuel Palmer	English	German Romanticism
Victorian	Camille Pissarro	French	Impressionism
Victorian	Odilon Redon	French	Symbolism
Victorian	Pierre Auguste Renoir	French	Impressionism
Victorian	Gustav Richter	German	Academician
Victorian	Dante Gabriel Rossetti	English	Pre-Raphaelites, English Romanticism
Victorian	Charles Russell	American	Realism
Victorian	Albert P. Ryder	American	Romanticism
Victorian	Georges Seurat	French	Pointilism

Table 13–9. *(cont.)*

Period	Artist	Nationality	Style
Victorian	Paul Signac	French	Pointilism
Victorian	Alfred Sisley	French	Impressionism
Victorian	Henri de Toulouse-Lautrec	French	Neo-Impressionism
Victorian	William Turner	English	[1]
Victorian	Vincent van Gogh	Dutch	Neo-Impressionism[3]
Victorian	Edouard Vuillard	French	Symbolism, Neo-Impressionism
Victorian	James McNeill Whistler	American	Symbolism[3]
Victorian	Hugo Winterhalter	French (German by birth)	Academician[1]
Victorian 20th Century	George Bellows	American	Impressionism
Victorian 20th Century	James Cnsor	Belgian	Expressionism
Victorian 20th Century	William Glackens	American	Surrealism
Victorian 20th Century	Carl Larson	Swedish	Rustic
Victorian 20th Century	Modigliani	Italian	Expressionism
Victorian 20th Century	Eduard Munch	Norwegian	Expressionism
Victorian 20th Century	Geroge Ravalts	French	Expressionism
Edwardien	Aubrey Beardsley	English	Art Nouveau
Edwardien	Mucha	French	Art Nouveau
20th Century	Hans Arp	German	Dadaism
20th Century	Giacomo Balka	Italian	Futurism
20th Century	Andre Bauchant	French	Modern Primitive, Naive School
20th Century	Thomas Hart Benton	American	Naive School
20th Century	Streeter Blair	American	Primitive
20th Century	Umberto Boccinoni	Italian	Futurism
20th Century	Camille Bombois	French	Modern Primitive, Naive School
20th Century	Pierre Bonnard	French	Neo-Impressionism[3]

Table 13–9. *(cont.)*

Period	Artist	Nationality	Style
20th Century	Marc Chagall	French	Modern Primitive, Naive School
20th Century	Giorgio de Chirico	Italian	Metaphysicalism
20th Century	Salvador Dali	Spanish	Surrealism
20th Century	Robert Delauncey	French	Cubism
20th Century	Andre Derain	French	Expressionism
20th Century	Marcel Duchamp	French	Dadaism
20th Century	Raoul Dufy	French	Expressionism
20th Century	Max Ernst	German	Surrealism
20th Century	Roger de la Fresnoye	French	Cubism
20th Century	Albert Gleizes	French	Cubism
20th Century	Juan Gris	Spanish	Cubism
20th Century	Hans Hoffmann	American	Abstract
20th Century	Edward Hopper	American	Realism
20th Century	Alexei Jawlensky	Russian	Expressionism and Abstract
20th Century	Wassily Kandinsky	Russian	Expressionism and Abstract
20th Century	Rockwell Kent	American	Romanticism
20th Century	Ernst Ludwig Kirchner	German	German Expressionism
20th Century	Paul Klee	German	Expressionism and Abstract
20th Century	Oskar Kokoshka	Austrian	German Expressionism
20th Century	Grank Kupka	Czechoslovakian	Abstract
20th Century	Joseph Kutter	Flemish	Expressionism
20th Century	Jack Levine	American	Expressionism
20th Century	Franz Marc	German	Expressionism and Abstract
20th Century	Albert Marquet	French	Expressionism
20th Century	Louis Marcoussis	Spanish	Cubism
20th Century	Rene Magritte	Belgian	Surrealism
20th Century	Casimir Malevitch	Russian	Abstract
20th Century	Henri Matisse	French	Expressionism
20th Century	Jean Metzinger	French	Cubism
20th Century	Joan Miro	Spanish	Surrealism
20th Century	Giorgio Mordnhi	Italian	Metaphysicalism

Table 13–9.   *(cont.)*

Period	Artist	Nationality	Style
20th Century	Piet Mondrian	Dutch	Abstract
20th Century	Grandma Moses	American	Modern Primitive, Naive School
20th Century	Paul Nash	English	Surrealist
20th Century	Jackson Pollack	American	Abstract
20th Century	Constant Permeke	Flemish	Expressionism
20th Century	Francis Picabia	French	Dadaism
20th Century	Pablo Picasso	Spanish	Multi-phased
20th Century	Robert Rauschenberg	American	Surrealism
20th Century	Frederic Remington	American	Realism
20th Century	Henri Rousseau	French	Modern Primitive, Naive School
20th Century	Chaim Sautine	French	Expressionism
20th Century	Karl Schmidt-Rottluf	Norwegian	German Expressionism
20th Century	Gino Severini	Italian	Futurism
20th Century	Yves Tanguy	French	Surrealism
20th Century	Fernand Leger	French	Cubism
20th Century	Lyonel Treininger	American	Cubism and Surrealism
20th Century	Andre Thoti	French	Cubism
20th Century	Maurice Utrillo	French	Impressionism
20th Century	Kees Van Dongen	Dutch	Expressionism, Cubism
20th Century	Jacques Villon	French	Cubism
20th Century	Louis Viven	French	Modern Primitive, Naive School
20th Century	Maurice de Vlaminck	Flemish	Expressionism
20th Century	Grant Wood	American	Modern Primitive, Naive School
20th Century	Andrew Wyeth	American	Realism

[1]Not all artists are classifiable as to style. Some are far ahead of their time, some return to a previous influence, and some stand alone. This last reason seems to be the case with El Greco and Goya in particular.

[2]Hans Holbein the younger, although born and schooled a German, spent the majority of his life painting the English Court of Henry VII and VIII.

El Greco was the name the Spaniards gave to Comenidos Theotokopoulos because of his place of birth, but he lived and painted in Spain. Wherever this occurs I have tried to point it out. James McNeill Whistler was American-born, but never fully adopted either England or France as his home, although he spent the majority of his life abroad.

[3]Vincent Van Gogh is one of those that stands alone, but several painters come so close to impressionism that sometimes they are classified with it. I have named them neo-impressionists for my own classification.

Table 13–10. Musicians—Period, Nationality, and Main Contribution

This listing has been compiled from Grout, Donald Jay, *A History of Western Music,* Revised Edition, (New York: W. W. Norton & Company, 1973).

Period	Musician	Nationality	Main Contributions
Gothic	Jacob Albrecht	Dutch	Masses, motets, secular songs
Gothic	Guillaume Dufay	Burgundian	Masses, Magnificat and secular songs
Gothic	Costanzo Festa	Italian	Madrigals
Gothic	Alan de la Hale	French	Robin and Marian[1]
Gothic	Jacob of Liege	French	Secular motets
Gothic	Guillaume de Machaut	French	sacred masses for Notre Dame
Gothic	Jean du Muris	French	Secular motets
Gothic	Marchetto de Padua	Italian	Secular motets
Gothic	Jacques des Pres	Hainult (Belgian)	Masses and motets
Gothic	Phillip Verdelas	Italian	Madrigals
Gothic	Philippe de Vitry	French	Roman di Fauvel
Renaissance	Jacob Arcadelt	Dutch	Madrigals
Renaissance	William Byrd	English	Dance compositions
Renaissance	Franchino Gafori	Italian	Secular songs—a transition from Middle Ages to Renaissance
Renaissance	Claude Gaudimel	French	Psalms
Renaissance	Orlando Gibbons	English	Dance compositions
Renaissance	Jacob Handl	Czech	Italian School
Renaissance	Hans Leo Hassler	German	Italian School
Renaissance	Martin Luther	German	Chorals
Renaissance	Phillippe de Monte	French	Madrigals
Renaissance	Claude Monteverdi	Italian	Madrigals
Renaissance	Giovanni Palestrina	Italian	Masses
Renaissance	Hieronymus Praetorius	German	Italian School
Renaissance	Cipriano de Rore	Italian	Madrigals
Renaissance	Heinrich Schutz	German	Italian School
Renaissance	Johann Walter	German	Chorales
Renaissance	Adrian Willaert	Venetian	Madrigals
Renaissance-Baroque	Giulio Caccine	Italian	Opera (*Euridice*)
Renaissance-Baroque	Emilio de Cavalieri	Italian	Oratorio

Table 13–10. *(cont.)*

Period	Musician	Nationality	Main Contributions
Renaissance-Baroque	Andrea Giovanni Gabrielli	Venetian	All forms except opera
Renaissance-Baroque	Thomas Morley	English	Dance music
Renaissance-Baroque	Jacapo Peri	Italian	Early dance music
Renaissance-Baroque	Samuel Scheidt	German	Instrumental[2]
Baroque	Heinrich Albert	German	Solo arias and dance music
Baroque	Johann Sebastian Bach	German	Everything but opera
Baroque	Giovanni Battista Bassani	Italian	Chamber music
Baroque	Franz Biber	German	Violin music
Baroque	John Blow	English	Opera and sacred music
Baroque	George Bohm	German	Keyboard music
Baroque	Dietrich Buxtehude	German	Sacred music
Baroque	Juan Baptista Jose Cabanilles	Spanish	Keyboard music
Baroque	Giacomo Carissimi	Italian	Secular cantatas and oratorio
Baroque	Marc-Antonio Cesti	Italian	Secular cantatas
Baroque	Corelli	Italian	Chamber music
Baroque	Francois Couperin	French	Keyboard music
Baroque	William Craft	English	Sacred music
Baroque	Froberger	German	Keyboard music
Baroque	Francesco Geminiani	English	Violin music
Baroque	George Frederick Handel	German	Everything including opera
Baroque	Reinhard Keiser	German	Opera, tragic and comic
Baroque	Nicolas Lanier	French	Solo arias and dance music
Baroque	Henry Lawes	English	Solo arias and dance music
Baroque	Jean Baptiste Lully	French	Originator of French opera and ballet

Table 13–10. *(cont.)*

Period	Musician	Nationality	Main Contributions
Baroque	Virgilio Marco Mazzocchi	Italian	First comic opera (*Chi Soffre Speri*)
Baroque	Theophil Muffet	German	Keyboard music
Baroque	Erdman Neumeister	German	Sacred cantatas—a forerunner of the style Bach employed in *St. Matthew Passion*
Baroque	Pachelbel	German	Keyboard music
Baroque	Henry Purcell	English	Opera and sacred music
Baroque	Esajas Reusner	German	Lute music
Baroque	Luigi Rossi	Italian	Secular cantatas
Baroque	J. H. Schein	German	Compositions and oratorios
Baroque	Georg Kasper Schurmann	German	Opera, tragic
Baroque	Heinrich Schutz	German	Compositions and oratorios
Baroque	Pietro Tocatelli	Italian	Violin music
Baroque	Francesco Maria Veracini	Italian	Violin music
Baroque	Johann Jakob Walther	German	Violin music
Baroque	Silvius Leopold Weiss	German	Lute music
Baroque	John Wilson	English	Solo arias and dance music
Late Baroque Rococo	Jean-Marie Leclair	Italian	Violin music
Late Baroque Rococo	Jean-Philippe Rameau	French	All forms
Late Baroque Rococo	Guiseppi Torelli	Italian	Concerti
Late Baroque Rococo	Antonio Vivaldi	Italian	All forms
Rococo	Thomas Augustine Arne	English	Italian School of opera
Rococo	C.P.E. Bach	German	Symphony-keyboard
Rococo	Johann Christian Bach	German by birth, Italian by influence	Operas and symphonies
Rococo	Giovanni Bononcini	Italian	Italian School of opera
Rococo	William Boyce	English	Symphonies

Table 13–10.   *(cont.)*

Period	Musician	Nationality	Main Contributions
Rococo	Rinaldo di Capua	Italian	Symphony, opera
Rococo	Christian Cannabich	?	Founder of Mannheim school
Rococo	Carl Ditters von Dittersdorf	German	Singspiel, opera[3]
Rococo	Giovanni Gambini	Italian by birth, French school	Symphonies
Rococo	Francois Joseph Gasser	Belgian by birth, French school	Symphonies and comic operas
Rococo	Baldassau Goluppi	Italian	Italian comic opera
Rococo	Christoph Willebald Gluck	Bohemian	Italian school of opera
Rococo	Karl Heinrich Graen	German	Italian school of opera
Rococo	Franz Joseph Haydn	Austrian	All forms
Rococo	Michael Haydn	Viennese	Symphonies
Rococo	Johann Adolph Hasee	German	Italian school of opera
Rococo	Nicola Logroscino	Italian	Italian comic opera
Rococo	George Matthais Mann	Austrian, Viennese school	Symphonies
Rococo	Andre Ernest Modeste	Belgian	French opera comique
Rococo	Pierre Alexander Monsigny	French	French opera comique
Rococo	Wolfgang Amadeus Mozart	Austrian	All forms
Rococo	Pieccini Giovanni Paisiello	Italian	Italian comic opera
Rococo	G. B. Pergolesi	Italian	Chamber music
Rococo	F. A. Danican-Philidier	French	French opera comique[4]
Rococo	G. B. Sammartini	Italian	First to write symphonies
Rococo	Domenico Scarlatti	Italian	Keyboard music
Rococo	Giuseppi Tartini	Italian	Chamber music
Empire	Ludwig von Beethoven	German (influenced by Vienna)	All forms
Empire	Gasparo Spontini	Italian (influenced by France)	United lesser character of Gluck with German "rescue" into grand opera
Romantique[5]	Frederic Chopin	Polish	Keyboard music
Romantique	Muzio Clementi	Italian	Keyboard music

Table 13–10.　*(cont.)*

Period	Musician	Nationality	Main Contributions
Romantique	Johann Hummel	Austrian	Keyboard music
Romantique	Franz Peter Schubert	Viennese	All forms
Victorian	Francois Auber	French	Grand opera and grand bouffe[6]
Victorian	Vincenzo Bellini	Italian	Grand opera
Victorian	Hector Berlioz	French	All forms
Victorian	Georges Bizet	French	Opera, symphony
Victorian	Alexander Borodin	Russian	All forms
Victorian	Johannes Brahms	German	All forms
Victorian	Anton Bruckner	German	Everything but opera
Victorian	Luigi Cherubini	Italian	Opera, sacred music
Victorian	Gaetano Donizetti	Italian	Grand opera
Victorian	Anton Dvorak	Czech	All forms
Victorian	Stephen Foster	American	Made use of nationalistic melodies
Victorian	Cesar Franck	French	Symphony, chamber music
Victorian	Gilbert & Sullivan	English	Opera bouffe
Victorian	Edvard Grieg	Norwegian	All forms
Victorian	Charles Gounod	French	Opera, sacred music
Victorian	Jacques Halavey	French	Grand opera
Victorian	Engelbert Humperdinck[7]	German	Opera
Victorian	Franz Liszt	Hungarian	All forms
Victorian	Felix Mendelssohn	German	All forms
Victorian	Giacomo Meyerbeer	French	Grand opera
Victorian	Modest Mussorgsky	Russian	Symphonies
Victorian	Jacques Offenbach	French	Opera bouffe
Victorian	Nicolas Rimsky-Korsakov	Russian	Symphonies, ballets
Victorian	Gioacchino Rossini	Italian	Opera, sacred music
Victorian	Anton Rubinstein	Russian	Keyboard music
Victorian	Robert Schumann	German	Lieder and keyboard
Victorian	Bedrich Smetana	Czech	Opera
Victorian	Johann Strauss, younger	Austrian	Opera bouffe, waltzes
Victorian	Peter Ilich Tchaikovsky	Russian	Opera, ballet, symphony

Table 13–10.   *(cont.)*

Period	Musician	Nationality	Main Contributions
Victorian	Giuseppe Verdi	Italian	Opera, sacred music
Victorian	Richard Wagner	German	Grand opera
Late Victorian	Claude Debussy[8]	French	All forms
Late Victorian	Gabriel Faure[8]	French	All forms
Late Victorian	Hugo Von Hofmannsthal	German	Opera
Late Victorian	Charles Ives	American	Instrumental pieces
Late Victorian	Edward MacDowell	American	Keyboard
Late Victorian	Gustav Mahler	Austrian	Symphonies
Late Victorian	Jules Massenet	French	Opera
Late Victorian	Maurice Ravel	French	Symphonies, ballet
Late Victorian	Camille Saint-Saens[8]	French	Symphonies[9]
Late Victorian	Erik Satie	French	Keyboard and piano[9]
Late Victorian	Jean Sibelius	Finnish	Symphonies
Late Victorian	Richard Strauss	German	Symphonies
20th century	Alder & Ross	American	Musicals
20th century	Harold Arlen	American	Broadway and movie musicals
20th century	Bela Bartok	Hungarian	Influence of folk idiom in symphonic work
20th century	Irving Berlin	American	Musicals
20th century	Elmer Bernstein	American	Hollywood sound-track, symphonies
20th century	Leonard Bernstein	American	Musicals, sacred music, opera
20th century	Benjamin Britten	English	Sacred music and opera
20th century	Carlos Chauvey	Mexican	Keyboard music
20th century	George M. Cohan	American	Ragtime, musicals
20th century	Aaron Copland	American	Symphonies, ballet
20th century	De Silva, Brown, and Henderson	American	College musicals
20th century	Vernon Duke[10]	Russian born, worked in America	Musicals, but under his real name, ballet and symphonies
20th century	Rudolph Frimmel	American	Operettas

Table 13–10.   *(cont.)*

Period	Musician	Nationality	Main Contributions
20th century	Victor Herbert	Ireland born, worked in America	Operettas
20th century	Alberto Genastera	Argentina	Opera
20th century	George Gershwin	American	Musicals, symphonies
20th century	Paul Hindemith	German	Symphonies
20th century	Arthur Honegger	French	Oratorio, symphony, sacred music
20th century	Zoltan Kodaly	Hungarian	Adaptation and collection of folk music
20th century	Jerome Kern	American	Musicals
20th century	Burton Lane	American	Broadway and movie musicals
20th century	Lerner and Loewe	American	Musicals
20th century	Frank Loesser	American	Musicals
20th century	Heitor Villa Lobos	Brazil	Use of Latin rhythms and themes in his instrumental compositions
20th century	Darius Milhaud	French	All forms
20th century	Carl Orff	German	Choral music, opera, creator of children's musical instruments
20th century	Cole Porter	American	Musicals
20th century	Francis Poulenc	French	Opera, sacred music
20th century	Sergei Prokofiev	Russian	Opera, ballet, symphonies
20th century	Rodgers & Hammerstein	American	Musicals
20th century	Rodgers and Hart	American	Musicals
20th century	Sigmund Romberg	Born Austria, worked in America	Operettas
20th century	Mikles Rosjos	(?)	Hollywood soundtrack, symphonies
20th century	Arnold Schoenberg	German	Symphonies
20th century	Schwartz & Dietz	American	Broadway and movie musicals
20th century	John Phillip Sousa	American	Band music

Table 13–10. *(cont.)*

Period	Musician	Nationality	Main Contributions
20th century	Max Steiner	American	Hollywood sound-track, symphonies
20th century	Dimitri Shostakovich	Russian	Keyboard music, symphony
20th century	Igor Stravinsky	Russian	Opera, ballet, symphony
20th century	Jule Styne	American	Musicals
20th century	Virgil Thompson	American	Opera, sacred music
20th century	Kurt Weill	German born, but influenced by and worked in America	Musicals, opera
20th century	Meredith Wilson	American	Musicals
20th century	Vaughn Williams	English	Symphony, sacred music
20th century	Vincent Youmans	American	Musicals

[1]This was an epic poem put to music and then acted as a sort of play. In a sense this could qualify as the first opera or musical.

[2]In music history the Baroque period is considered 1600 to 1750, but in this list, which goes only to 1720, composers are placed according to their productive periods, not year of birth.

[3]Singspiel opera was based on the English form of ballad opera. *The Beggars Opera* is the best example of this. Native popular songs were incorporated into a plot and often the plot was both funny and heroic. Sometimes these were called "rescue" operas and gave rise to the old-fashioned melodrama.

[4]French opera comique simply meant that the recitative was spoken as dialogue rather than sung. It had nothing to do with plot. *Carmen* was written for the opera comique.

[5]The Romantic period in music somewhat corresponds to the 1820–1840 time period. It is characterized by a flowing melodic line and a rise in nationalistic themes.

[6]After the various nationalistic treatments of opera, Spontini melted them together and came up with an alloy called "grand opera" by the French. It came to mean massiveness and sung recitative. Francois Auber almost immediately developed a new style called opera bouffe (not to be confused with the old Italian comic opera style called "opera buffa"). This would be what we in America call operettas.

[7]Humperdinck wrote opera in the style of the folk opera, and often for children's tales.

[8]Saint-Saens, Faure, and Debussy epitomized the "impressionist" movement in music.

[9]Erik Satie started an anti-impressionist movement which corresponds well to "primitivism" in the art world.

[10]Vernon Duke's real name, under which he wrote classical pieces, was Vladimir Dukelsky.

Table 13–11. Illustrators, Costume Designers, Fashion Designers

I have compiled this table partly from research done for Part II and partly from a vast supply of theater programs too numerous to list. I would also like to thank Robert Jones of Butler, Pennsylvania for his donation of a complete set of *Theater Arts*, a magazine that unfortunately is no longer in print.

Period	Name	Nationality	For What They Are Known
Renaissance	Leonardo da Vinci	Italian	Designed theatrical scenery and costumes, as well as weapons
Baroque	Inigo Jones	English	Architect, designed sets and costumes for Court of James I and Charles I
Rococo	Rose Bertin	French	Dressmaker to Marie Antoinette
Rococo	Léonard	French	Hair stylist to Marie Antoinette
Empire Regency	George Bryan Brummel	English	Male style setter; invented long trousers
Empire	Jean Baptiste Isabey	French	Designed all gowns for the coronation of Napoleon I
Empire	Leroy	French	Dressmaker and designer to the Empress Josephine
Empire	Madame Recamier	French	Leading beauty of her day, who set makeup and hair styles; also invented a reclining couch named for her
Victorian	Amelia Bloomer	American	Advocate of women's rights to freedom of movement; designed pants outfits for sportswear, which became standard undergarments; named for her.
Victorian	Prof. Dr. Gustave Jaeger	German	Designer of elaborate ladies' underwear in England
Victorian	Worth	French	He was born in England, but became the chief designer for the Empress Eugenie in Paris and continued designing until 1900.

Table 13–11. *(cont.)*

Period	Name	Nationality	For What They Are Known
Late Victorian	Drecole	French	Fashion designer
Late Victorian	Paquin	French	Fashion designer
Late Victorian	Redfern	English	Fashion designer of tailored suits for women
Late Victorian	Rouff	French	Fashion designer
Victorian to World War I	Fabergé	Russian	Designer of jewelry and objects d'art
Art Nouveau	Léon Baskt	Russian	Costume and set designer for the Russian Ballet
Art Nouveau	Aubrey Beardsley	English	Black and white sketches, illustrator for the *Yellow Book Magazine* and editions of *The Rape of the Lock* and *Mort d'Arthur*
Art Nouveau	Benois	Russian	Set designer for Russian Ballet
Art Nouveau	Joseph Mierhoffer	Czech	Stained glass windows, including the large cathederal in Friberg, Switzerland
Art Nouveau	Mucha	French	Illustrator and artist; did theatrical posters for Sarah Bernhardt
Edwardian	Arthur Lasenby Liberty	English	Fashion designer who first designed oriental flowing garments for every day wear
Edwardian	Lavin	French	Fashion designer
Edwardian	Maxfield Parrish	American	Book illustrator and artist of a luminous romanticism
Edwardian	Paul Poiret	French	Fashion designer
Early 20th century (Edwardian to 1920's)	N. C. Wyeth	American	Book illustrator and artist, including editions of *Robinson Crusoe* and *The Knights of King Arthur*; very romantic

Table 13–11. *(cont.)*

Period	Name	Nationality	For What They Are Known
World War I	Doeuillet	French	Fashion designer
World War I until present time	Erté	French	Artist, fashion designer and theatrical designer, famous for extravanganzas like the Follies Bergere
World War I	Callot Soeurs	French	Fashion designer
20th century '30s–'50s	Adrian	American	Hollywood designer; did *Camille* for Garbo
20th century '60s on	Theoni Aldridge	American	Theatrical costume designer, including *Annie*
20th century '50s–'70s	Alexander of Paris	French	Known for his elegant and elaborate hair styles, particularly his intricate curl cluster and braids; almost the exact opposite of Vidal Sassoon
20th century '20s –on	Elizabeth Arden	American	Started in the cosmetic business in late teens; emphasized the pink and white feminine look; never extreme
20th century '30s–'50s	Travis Banton	American	Hollywood designer
20th century '30s (?) on	Cecil Beaton	English	Designed both scenery and costumes for everything from opera, to theater, to films; best known for his costumes for the movie and both stage versions of *My Fair Lady* and also the movie *Gigi*
20th century '30s and '40s	Norman Bel Geddes	American	Theatrical scenic designer
20th century '40s on	Oleg Cassini	American	Hollywood designer, who switched successfully to high fashion; also designs fabrics

Table 13–11.   *(cont.)*

Period	Name	Nationality	For What They Are Known
20th century 1920–1970s	Coco Chanel	French	Fashion designer
20th century	Chandler Christy	American	Illustrator and artist of realistic landscapes and people, but of the antebellum South, particularly illustrations on the life of Stephen Foster
20th century '50s on	Sybil Connelby	Irish	Dublin designer who designs beautifully tailored ensembles and makes excellent use of Irish fabrics, tweeds, linen, and woolen goods
20th century Edwardian thru '30s	Gordon Craig	English	Designer of scenery, whose theories revolutionized the theatrical world, but he actually built very little
20th century '30s–60s	Lille Dacheé	American	Fashion designer known primarily for her hats
20th century '40s–'60s	Dior	French	Fashion designer
20th century	Walt Disney	American	Cartoonist and film maker; his films use many artists, but they come up with a unified style that has left an indelible imprint on all of us born after 1936.
20th century '30s on	Frazetti	American	Creator of Buck Rogers comic strip and artist and illustrator, primarily of barbarian and futuristic times, also illustrated Tarzan; known for voluptuous women

Table 13–11. *(cont.)*

Period	Name	Nationality	For What They Are Known
20th century '60s on	Margaret Furse	English	Primarily British films and B.B.C. television
20th century '50s on	Givenchy	French	Fashion designer
20th century	Cecil Golding	American	Illustrator and artist known for his ballet figures and his paintings of birds
20th century '50s on	Gucci	Italian	Fashion designer known primarily for leather goods
20th century '40s on	Morey Hamburger	American	Designer of exclusive and sumptuous wedding gowns
20th century '20s on	Edith Head	American	Hollywood designer, primarily for Paramount Studios, including Cecil B. DeMille's *Sampson and Delila* and *The Sting*
20th century	Alejander Rangel Hidalgo	Mexican	Illustrator known for his little doll-like figures and pure palette.
20th century	Huldah	?	Illustrator and artist known for his impressionistic techniques used to paint ballerinas or young girls dressed in the styles of the 1880s
20th century '50s and '60s	Mr. John	American	Designer of hats
20th century '20s–'40s	Robert Edmond Jones	American	Primarily a scenic designer, who believed in "less is more"
20th century	Keanne	American	This is one name, shared by a husband and wife, who draw in a very similar manner. They are noted for their large-eyed children.

Table 13–11. *(cont.)*

Period	Name	Nationality	For What They Are Known
20th century '40s(?)–'60s	Orry Kelly	American	Hollywood designer
20th century '50s on	Sean Kenny	English	Set designer, who does most of Anthony Newley's shows such as *Stop the World*
20th century '20s on	Rockwell Kent	American	Artist and book illustrator whose edition of *The Complete Works of Shakespeare* is typical of Art Deco
20th century '40s	Charles de Lamaire	American	Hollywood designer
20th century '60s on	Ming Chou Lee	American	Theatrical set designer
20th century '50s and '60s	Jean Louis	American	Hollywood designer; famous for his evening gowns worn by Doris Day, among others
20th century '60s on	Bob Mackey	American	Films and TV work, as well as high fashion; designs a great deal for Cher and Carol Burnett; known for his beaded dresses
20th century	Mainbocher	American	Fashion designer, who also designed for the theater, including wedding dress for Mary Martin in *Sound of Music*
20th century '20s–'30s	Marcel	French	Fashion designer and hair stylist, who invented the permanent wave
20th century '30s–'70s	Jo Melziner	American	Theatrical scenic designer of the R. E. Jones tradition; designs include *South Pacific, Death of a Salesman,* and *Street Scene*
20th century '20s–'50s	Molyneux	American	Fashion designer

Table 13–11.   *(cont.)*

Period	Name	Nationality	For What They Are Known
20th century '50s on	Motley	English	This is a name for several designers, who work together designing scenery, props, and costumes for all types of theatrical and cinematic productions
20th century 1920–1940	Patou	French	Fashion designer
20th century '30s on	Walter Plunkett	American	Hollywood designer famous for his knowledge of the 19th century fashions; designed *Gone With the Wind, Raintree County,* and the technicolor version of *Show Boat,* to name a few
20th century '50s on	Pucci	Italian	Fashion designer, who also designs fabrics
20th century '60s on	Lillie Pulitzer	American	Designer of silk screened dresses
20th century '60s	Mary Quant	English	Fashion designer, who invented the mini skirt
20th century '60s on	Oscar de la Renta	Italian	Fashion designer noted for his intricately draped creations
20th century '30s on	Charles Revson (Revlon)	American	Cosmetic business; first perpetrator of nail polish for hands and feet
20th century '20s–'40s	Rochas	French	Fashion designer
20th century	Norman Rockwell	American	Artist and illustrator who best captures everyday American life. His mural of the peoples of the world is in the U.N. Building. He did countless covers for *The Saturday Evening Post* magazine.

Table 13–11.   *(cont.)*

Period	Name	Nationality	For What They Are Known
20th century '40s on	Helen Rose	American	Hollywood designer at M.G.M. Her musicals are delightful as are her many costumes for ice shows and circuses.
20th century '60s on	Ann Roth	American	Theatrical costume designer, including *Purlie Victorious*
20th century '20s on	Helena Rubenstein	Polish, but went first to Paris, then to U.S.A.	Started in cosmetic business at the same time as Arden; was Arden's chief competitor; emphasized a more dramatic look to makeup.
20th century '50s on	Yves St. Laurent	French	Fashion designer
20th century '60s and '70s	Vidal Sassoon	English American	Hair stylist, who cut women's hair exactly like a man's, a la Mia Farrow
20th century '30s–'50s	Elsa Schiaparelli	French	Fashion designer
20th century '60s on	Peter Seddon	English	Primarily films and B.B.C. television work; did both sets and costumes for *The Six Wives of Henry VIII*
20th century '40s on	Oliver Smith	American	Theatrical scenic designer best known for his sets for *My Fair Lady* and *Camelot*

Table 13–11.   *(cont.)*

Period	Name	Nationality	For What They Are Known
20th century '50s on	Bill Thomas	American	Hollywood costume designer
20th century '70s	Toyobo	Japanese	Fabric designer
20th century '60s on	Gloria Vanderbilt	American	Fabric designer (also jeans)
'50s on	Vera	American	Fabric designer
20th century '70s	Diane Von Furstenberg	American	Designs both fashions and fabric.
20th cent.	August Von Munchhausen	(?)	Illustrator and artist known for his charcoal and pastel ballet figures
20th century '60s on	Tony Walton	English	Designs scenery and costumes for theater and films; his films include *Mary Poppins, The Boyfriend, The Wiz,* and *All That Jazz.*
20th century '50s on	Franco Zeffirelli	Italian	Designs both scenery and costumes as well as directs everything, including opera, ballet, plays, and films; designed and directed the '60s Shakespearean movies of *Romeo and Juliet* and *Taming of the Shrew*
20th century '70s	Patricia Zipprott	American	Theatrical costume designer

Well-known Egyptian Gods and Goddesses

Hathar	Tall horned cow (sometimes holds a round dish between horns); originally goddess creator of the world and symbol of the living; became goddess of the dead
Bast	Cat goddess of pleasure
Ra	Falcon-headed god of the sun
Khepri	Scarab (beetle) god, mover of the sun, symbol of eternal life
Mertseger	Snake goddess
Sebek	Crocodile god of the Nile and of the dead on their journey to the underworld
Sekhmet	Lioness-headed goddess of war
Anubis	Jackal god, guardian of the dead
Thoth	Baboon god (sometimes represented by the head of an ibis), god of learning

The "Holy Three"

Horus, Osiris, and Isis were the most revered of all Egyptian deities; they were not necessarily represented by animals, although Horus is sometimes shown as the hawk, similar to Ra, because he, too, represented the sun. Figure 13–8 shows the mythical family tree.

Keb and Nut had three children, Set, Osiris, and Isis. Set murdered Osiris, the original sun god, and cut him into one thousand pieces and scattered him to the four winds. Isis gathered all the pieces and put Osiris together again, married him, and gave birth to Horus, the new sun god, representing the triumph of day over night and the eternal cycle of everlasting life. Osiris then became god of the underworld.

These "Holy Three" gods were adapted into both the Greek and Roman religions. Isis became associated with all magic and was worshipped well into the five hundreds A.D.

Note: This has been compiled from Aldington, Richard and Ames, Delano (translators), *New Larousse Encyclopedia of Mythology* (London: The Hamlyn Publishing Group Ltd., 1968), ninth printing, 1974.

The Roman and Greek Gods and Goddesses

Space does not permit inclusions of all the gods and goddesses of ancient Greece and Rome. The following list shows the correlation between the two religions. As with almost everything else (style of dress, architecture, etc.) the Greeks originated, the Romans copied, adapted and embellished.

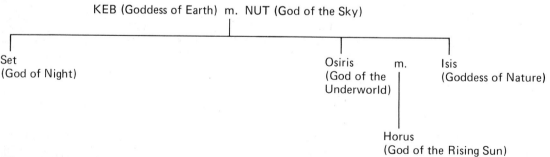

Figure 13–8. *Mythical Family Tree*

Greek Name	Roman Name	Purpose
Uranus	?[1]	Old god of the sky,[2] originally all-powerful god, married to Gaea
Gaea	?[1]	Old goddess of the earth, original goddess of fertility
Cronus	Saturn ⎫ married	God of the harvest
Rhea	Ops ⎭	Goddess of fertility, wife of Cronus, mother of Zeus
Zeus	Jupiter (or Jove)	All-powerful God of Gods
Hera	Juno	Sister and wife of Zeus
Poseidon	Neptune	God of the sea
Hades	Pluto	God of the underworld
Aphrodite	Venus	Goddess of beauty
Artemis	Diana	Goddess of night and the hunt
Hestia	Vesta	Goddess of hearth and home
Hermes	Mercury	Messenger of the gods
Apollo	Helios	God of music and the sun
Athena	Minerva	Goddess of wisdom
Iris	?[1]	Goddess of the rainbow

Greek Name	Roman Name	Purpose
Ares	Mars	God of war
Demeter	Ceres	Goddess of the bountiful harvest
Cupid	Eros	God of love
Dionysus	Bacchus	God of revelry and wine
Pan	Faunnus	God of mischief[3]

Mythological Creatures

The satyr: Half man, half goat
The minotaur: Half man, half bull
The centaur: Half man, half horse

[1]There do not seem to be accurate correlations of Roman deities for these three. The Romans seem to confuse Gaea and Rhea, as they do Uranus and Cronus, as if ignoring one whole generation. As for Iris, some believe that the Romans substituted the Egyptian goddess Isis for her; however, the Romans had Aurora, who was the goddess of the dawn, and there does not seem to be any Greek correlation. Perhaps one was substituted for the other.

[2]Uranus and Gaea were the original gods. They were married and gave birth to Cronus and Rhea, who married each other and disposed of their parents. They in turn had children, including Zeus and Hera, who married and took over. Zeus divided the universe among his brothers, sisters, and children.

[3]Pan and Dionysus were part of the same cult. Dionysus was also considered by some to rule fertility, as was Aphrodite. Pan was associated with music because he plays a set of reed pipes. He once fell in love with the nymph Syrinx, who turned herself into a reed. Pan plays his reed pipes in memory of her. Pan is also portrayed as the first satyr, but he is more accurately half god-man, half deer.

The Best Known of the Norse Gods and Goddesses

Odin	God creator of all (Sometimes Wodin)
Frigg	Odin's wife
Thor	God of war and thunder
Freyja	Goddess of fertility
Loki	God of mischief
Balder	God of light and lightning

14

A Knowledge of Fabrics

The only way to know exactly what a fabric will and will not do is to buy one-quarter of a yard and play with it until you discover for yourself if you can (1) distress it by wrinkling, burning, overdying, fraying, etc., (2) make it float, or (3) hold a particular shape. Whatever you want it to do, there are certain rules of thumb, however.

1. Loosely woven fabrics fray more easily than tightly woven fabric, particularly if they are of a square weave. Therefore, if you want to fringe something, pick a loosely woven fabric.
2. Pure fibers are porous. Air moves freely through them, as do dye and bleach.
3. Generally, the finer the thread, the lighter the weight, and the more inherent the drapability, excluding starches and finishes. Also, the number of threads per square inch can account for weight. The fewer the threads used, the lighter the weight. This is particularly true of certain muslins and gauzes.

4. Napped fabrics show wrinkles and "sit" a shiny seat.
5. Water spots and rings silk.
6. Never totally trust navy, red, or black not to run when washed. Expect Oriental fabrics to run. They are often dyed with vegetable dyes.
7. Never wash felt. It is not a woven fabric.

The following is a table of fabrics by common name and classified by basic fiber, weave, weight, and description or illustratation (see Table 14–1). This name may be for the pattern (polka-dot), the weave (twill), the fiber (mohair), or a combination (calico). The table contains only fabrics that will be found today.

A word to the wise: when you take your samples home to play, be sure you do so under the proper light. What works under bastard amber may look very different under surprise pink or natural sunlight. Fluorescent work lights tend to accent blue tones, certainly the cooler tones. Candescent light accentuates the warm tones.

Table 14–1.   Fabrics by Common Name

Fabric	Fiber	Weave	Weight	Description or Illustration
acrylic—synthetic from oil	bulky fiber used as a wool substitute	knits mostly	light to heavy	does not breathe or dye; good for fake furs.
antique velvet	silk, often with a cotton "backing" in which warp threads are cotton	square and single looped	heavy	only every other woof thread is woven with a loop and therefore when cut, it leaves tiny ridges not big enough to be called wales
bombazine	a combination of wool and cotton	square	heavy	Although this is a heavy and warm fabric, it is not stiff and has a soft look to it. It is, however, very difficult to find today. A brushed denim used brushed side out makes a good substitute.
broadcloth	cotton or wool	square	medium to heavy	square weave of a heavy thread as compared to denim, which has a double thread
brocade (self brocade)	silk	square with a twilled over-weave forming a design	light to heavy	"Self brocade" means threads all of a color; brocade can have a design overwoven in other colors.
burlap	hemp	square	medium to heavy	Moisture tends to destroy this very rough fabric. It is exceedingly stiff and can sometimes be substituted for horsehair as a stiffening. Many people are allergic to it, however, and it should be used with caution for costume purposes.

Table 14—1.   *(cont.)*

Fabric	Fiber	Weave	Weight	Description or Illustration
calico	cotton	square	medium	
canvas	cotton	square	extra heavy	the heaviest grade of a muslin-like fabric
carved velvet (sometimes called velvet brocade)	silk	square and single looped	light to medium	By cutting some of the pile shorter than the other, a design can be achieved merely from the difference in reflected light cast off by the depth of the pile.
cashmere	wool of Indian goat hair	can be any weave or knit, but is usually twilled	fine	luxuriously soft wool and although light in weight, is quite warm and pliable, but expensive
challis	wool	square	very fine	This is woven of very fine thread and is soft and very movable.
chamois	hide of a doe	not woven	light	very fine and pliable leather
chiffon	silk	square	sheer	completely unstiffened
chintz	cotton	square	medium	glazed and usually printed in a floral pattern

Table 14–1.   *(cont.)*

Fabric	Fiber	Weave	Weight	Description or Illustration
corduroy	cotton	square and single looped	medium to heavy	The woof thread is looped across only so many of the warp threads in an even spacing; therefore, when cut, it leaves a piled ridge called a wale. Corduroy is a good substitute for velvet.
corduroy— uncut	cotton	square and single looped	medium to heavy	This is a misnomer, as it is indeed cut but not ridged, and the pile is considerably shorter than velveteen. It makes a good substitute for suede.
corduroy—wide wale	cotton	square and single looped	medium to heavy	The plush or piled area is wider.
crepe	wool or silk	woven in a step pattern	light	This has usually been crinkled, or at least given that effect.
crepe—satin backed	silk	double weave of step pattern	light	This shows all charac-teristics of regular crepe, but it has a shiny side and dull side.
crushed velvet	silk	square and single looped	medium	Because velvet marks so readily from normal use, someone got the bright idea to do it pur-posely by steaming in wrinkles so that new ones would not show.
denim	cotton	double thread square	heavy	heavy cotton, usually blue
dotted swiss	cotton	square	fine	Real dotted swiss has looped threads woven at regular intervals in a very tiny, almost polka-dot pattern. These threads are then cut.

Table 14—1.   *(cont.)*

Fabric	Fiber	Weave	Weight	Description or Illustration
				They leave a little velvety bump. Too often on today's market the bump is merely flocked on.
duck	cotton	square	heavy	between muslin and canvas weight
eyelet (This is cutout work and each cutout has been surrounded by a buttonhole stitch. This also refers to a type of trim done the same way and through which ribbon may be threaded.)	cotton	square	medium	
flannel	wool	square	medium to heavy	basic woven wool
felt	wool	not woven, but pressed	varying thickness, from thin to thick carpet padding	The quality of felt depends upon the fibers used. Certain hatweight felts have a shine and others a velvety look. Has many universal uses, but it *must* be dry-cleaned as moisture destroys it.
flocked fabric	usually cotton	can be any weave	medium	This is a process of fabric design in which a pattern is put on in glue and loose fibers dusted on top. When the glue dries the excess loose fibers are dusted off and those that made contact with the glue design leave a raised pattern on the fabric.

Table 14—1.   *(cont.)*

Fabric	Fiber	Weave	Weight	Description or Illustration
gabardine	cotton or wool	twilled diagonal	light to medium	very like twill, but much lighter in weight
gingham	cotton	square	medium	
herringbone	wool	type of tweed, woven of at least two colors or tones in an alternating zigzag pattern	medium to heavy	
horsehair	hair from mane and tail of horse	can be square woven or plaited	heavy, but pliable	used as stiffening or stuffing
jersey	can be any fiber	not woven but knitted with a fine stockinette stitch	sheer to heavy	used for everything from nylon stockings to wool suits
kettlecloth	cotton (often combined with polyester)	square	medium	a very durable fabric which holds a good shape and is used for sportswear and tailored summer apparel

Table 14—1. *(cont.)*

Fabric	Fiber	Weave	Weight	Description or Illustration
khaki (technically a dull yellow color; now seems to also represent a specific dull tan cloth)	cotton	twill	medium to heavy	extremely serviceable; used for safari clothes and by the military for hot climates
lawn	linen or cotton	square	sheer to light	like organdy, but without stiffness
madras	cotton from India and dyed with vegetable dyes (runs)	type of plaid, usually with large blocks of color	medium	
metallic brocade	silk	square with a twilled overweave forming a design	sheer to heavy	The overwoven design is worked in metallic thread, generally gold or silver. In India they use real silver, but it tarnishes.
mohair	the "wool" of an angora goat	can be any weave	can be any weight	very warm, but sometimes is scratchy; used often in combination with other wools
moiré (sometimes called watered silk)	silk	square	light to medium	silk, particularly peau de soie; water spots, so someone decided to do it purposely so that other spots would not show
monks cloth	cotton	square	heavy	This is woven just like osnaberg, but is less scratchy and is readily dyable.

Table 14–1.   *(cont.)*

Fabric	Fiber	Weave	Weight	Description or Illustration
moqueshel	linen	square	light to medium	linen from Ireland; excellent quality
muslin	cotton	square	fine to medium heavy	Muslin is either bleached or unbleached, combed cotton. It is bought by weight: 80–80 means eighty warp threads to eighty woof threads per square inch.
nylon	fiber made from oil as a silk substitute	any weave or knit	sheer to heavy	the best of the synthetics
organdy	cotton	square	sheer	can be seen through, but heavily starched
organza	silk	square	sheer	same as organdy, only silk and therefore finer in quality
osnaberg	several fibers, including linen, cotton, and hemp	square	heavy	This is a rough fabric made of uncombed threads and although each individual thread is somewhat thick and uneven, it is loosely woven.
paisley	can be any fabric (this is a particular design that resembles a paramecium)	can be any weave	can be any weight	

Table 14—1.   *(cont.)*

Fabric	Fiber	Weave	Weight	Description or Illustration
panne velvet	silk	square and single looped	light	This is a flattened pile done by heat and steam, which gives the velvet an extra shine.
peau de soie	silk	square	medium to heavy	a rich dull lustre to one side of fabric
percale	cotton	square	medium	lightly starched sheeting fabric
pique	cotton	square	heavy	heavy cotton with corded wales
even plaid	can be any fabric	must be a square weave and colored threads in exact proportion warp to woof	can be any weight	
uneven plaid	can be any fabric	must be a square weave and colored threads *not* in even proportion, warp to woof	can be any weight	
plush	silk or cotton	square and single looped	heavy	extra thick pile

Table 14–1. *(cont.)*

Fabric	Fiber	Weave	Weight	Description or Illustration
polka-dot (this is a type of print) dots are usually of uniform size but not necessarily; and usually evenly spaced but not always.	can be any fiber	can be any weave	can be any weight	
polyester	fiber made from oil; a wool and cotton substitute	any weave or knit	sheer to heavy	cannot be home dyed easily as rayon cannot; it is constantly being improved
raw silk	silk	square	medium	shantung-like, only unbleached and undyed
rayon (called "artificial silk") from its conception in 1884 until the 1920s when Dupont coined the term "Ray" meaning shiny and "on," the last sound in the word cotton.	"synthetic" silk; composed of cellulose fibers derived from milk, wood, seaweed, etc.	any weave	any weight that silk can be	Generally dry clean only. Rayon does not like heat and it does wrinkle; best used with a natural fiber.
sateen (sometimes called polished cotton)	cotton	square	light	glazed to look like satin; actually more of an unprinted chintz
satin	silk	square	fine to light	highly shiny surface on one side
seersucker	cotton and linen	square, some warp threads are strung tighter than others	medium	This is often done in stripes, but where the warp thread is tight the stripe is flat, where loose it allows for a crinkly look

Table 14—1. *(cont.)*

Fabric	Fiber	Weave	Weight	Description or Illustration
serge	wool	diagonal	medium to heavy	This is a wool twill and has a hard look to it. It sits a shine quickly
shantung	silk or linen	square	medium	Woven of uncombed threads and therefore somewhat uneven and with occasional bumps
sharkskin	rayon coated with chemicals to make it durable, very popular in the '30s	square	medium, but hard	Due to rayon (or like synthetics) this has a shine to it. Very durable and somewhat water resistant, therefore often used for seafaring and sportclothes
suede	hide of cattle	not woven	heavy	Using the dull side of leather, the side that looks somehow matted
taffeta	silk	square	light to medium	shiny to both sides and glazed to give a certain hardness; makes a distinct noise in motion
terry cloth	cotton	square and double looped	medium to heavy	The woof threads are looped and the loops are left uncut; used for toweling
ticking	cotton	square with a diagonal overweave similar to twill	heavy	
toile	linen	square	fine	handkerchief quality

Table 14–1. *(cont.)*

Fabric	Fiber	Weave	Weight	Description or Illustration
tissue velvet	silk	square and single looped	fine to light	This is a chiffon on which certain areas of woof thread are looped and then cut to form a design. Sometimes colored threads are over-woven and looped and then cut; very expensive.
tweed	wool	square with a diagonal over-thread	medium to heavy	
twill (there is a twill weaving process. The above is strictly a fabric name)	cotton	diagonal	heavy	woven with a diagonal twisted thread. When of a light khaki color, it is called "chino."
velour	can be any fiber, except wool or hemp	square and single looped	heavy	Originally this was an extra sturdy velvet made by having cotton warp threads and silk woof ones; now it refers to synthetic velvet.
velvet	silk	square and single looped	medium to heavy	woven exactly like terry cloth, but the loops are on one side of the fabric only, and then they are cut to give a pile. Silk crushes easily, is readily waterspotted, and sits a shiny seat.
velveteen	cotton	square and single looped	medium to heavy	woven exactly like velvet but of cotton fibers and therefore much more durable

15

The Sketch:
What it Should Convey

Nowhere in this book are attempts made to tell you how to actually draw or paint your sketches. This is one area of trial and error and "every man for himself," but it is necessary to talk briefly and in general terms about what the sketches should convey.

First of all you have to decide your exact purpose. Is this just a pretty little picture or is this a working drawing? There may be times when it is one or the other, but generally it is both.

Faces

We all agree that the sketch should convey all the visual elements of the character—social position, age, physical characteristics, relationship with other characters. Should you include faces? How well do you draw faces? Hair styles and facial hair on men are important period details. Sometimes faces detract from what you are trying to sell, which is the costume. Many designers just indicate where the center of the face should be. Some just do noses.

My own personal belief is to go with the situation. There are many times when a show is designed long before it has been cast and then it is cast to type, so there would be little point in faces, as witness the sketches for *Tartuffe* in the insert. On the other hand, when the cast is known beforehand, exact sketches give the director a more accurate picture of exactly how that particular person will really look. Also, when you have specific bodies it is always easier to do a specific design.

It may not be your choice. Several directors request blank faces, because they find illustrated faces distracting, particularly an influence in casting, and do not wish that. Other directors like them for the same reason. They want that visual influence.

Every Button and Bow?

You have all probably seen the kind of sketch that has a line here and a squiggle there and it's great fun in an abstract sort of way, even vaguely period, but how on earth would you build it? Should you draw in every button and bow, or not? If this is the kind of sketch you do, you must either draw a lot of details on the side, write copious notes, or build it yourself. If you are fussy about having the finished costume look like your sketch, you had better count the buttons and bows. Often with commercial houses, what you see is what you get. Always add your samples, so that the right fabric goes the right place.

It is also a good idea to write important notes, draw a back view, and give any cutting suggestions you may have. This will help you achieve what you want, as well as save the commercial construction house time and everybody money. The sketches for *Albert Herring,* an opera by Benjamin Britten, are an example of this.

Backgrounds

Should you put in backgrounds? Again, that's a matter of choice. It takes time to do much detail. Some like a light wash, particularly when using all white paper. A ground line stops the sketch from floating in white space. Try colored paper. Have you tried painting on mat board? It comes in silk and nubby linen, as well as all those colors. (I've had great luck with it and maybe you will too.)

Sometimes a little background gives an idea of scene, which helps, particularly in big musicals or operas. See, for example, the *Mikado* sketches. That particular production was done in front of paper screens painted in black on white. It helped to give a more accurate flavor to the sketch.

More Than One Figure per Plate

Should you put more than one figure per plate? Again, that depends on the show and what you want to do to it. As you will see in the color plates, the *Amelia Goes To The Ball* sketches have three and four figures per plate. For large

shows this is a necessity, just to save on paper. But they should be arranged with a semblance of continuity—either by pairs of lovers, as some shows so conveniently arrange themselves, or by scenes or acts. These, then, become costume plates and should be labeled and numbered in a chronological order. (Each individual costume should also be labeled.)

Medium

What medium should you use? Any one at all, or several, in combination. Watercolor and acrylic go very well together. A quick way to do skin tone is by pastel pencil. Wax crayon over watercolor on a bumpy surface gives the greatest wool effect you ever saw. White pastel pencil over a dark water color or acrylic gives a marvelous velvet look. Tiny cotton lace glued down and painted over produces a fascinating effect, as do glued on glitter dust, rhinestones, and seed pearls. Try doing a sketch in bas relief coulage. Some shows cry for a pen and ink cartoon effect.

Style

What style of presentation should you choose? If you can afford it, matting always gives a polished look to a sketch, but this can be saved for the future, when you add these to your portfolio (See Chapter 19.)

Matting certainly is not a necessity, however. Some directors like an "unfinished" look. Recently, there seems to be a movement away from the formality of a matted sketch. You do need to sell your ideas when you show these to the director. Be sure to have your "spiel" ready to go along with your visual effects.

This brings to mind the one great disadvantage of doing more than one figure to a plate. If one costume is rejected, the whole plate must be done over, whereas with the single figure sketch, you merely tear that up and do one more.

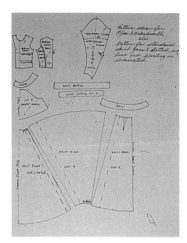

Two sketches plus pattern notations for the opera *Albert Herring* by Benjamin Britten.

Koko and Katisha of *The Mikado* as done for the Butler Musical Theatre, Butler, Pennsylvania.

Four plates for *Amelia Goes to the Ball* by Gian-Carlo Menotti, designed for the Palm Beach Opera.

Three sketches, Caliban, Stephano, and Trinculo, and a production slide of *The Tempest* by William Shakespeare as done by Florida Atlantic University.

Three sketches, Elmire, Madame Paenelle, and Orgon, and a production slide from *Tartuffe* by Molière as produced by the University of Montana.

Finally, the proof of the pudding is in the tasting. The proof of the sketch is in the finished costume. You have an obligation to have the final result look like the approved sketch. See production photos for *Tartuffe* (University of Montana, Department of Theater, 1967) and sketches and photos of *The Tempest* (Florida Atlantic University, Department of Theater, 1972) at the end of this chapter as an illustration of this point. A helpful hint is to gather your fabric samples before you paint your final sketches. This saves a lot of grief and you and the director together may share the praise or the blame for the design concept.

With your sketches approved, you can now go on to what often seems to be the nemesis of great and glorious ideas—the budgeting and buying for the production.

16

Budgeting

"T.T.D." List

Before your next conference with the producer, you will want to have a fairly accurate *estimated* budget. The next step is to make out a complete "Things To Do" list, here shortened to "T.T.D. List." You make this with the aid of your finished sketches. For a hypothetical example we shall use *Amelia Goes to the Ball* by Gian-Carlo Men-

otti, a one-act opera set in the early 1900s. The design concept was to set it in the 1860s so the costumes could be reused in *La Traviata*, which was scheduled for a future season.

Please compare the T.T.D. List to the sketches.

Table 16–1. T.T.D. List for *Amelia Goes to the Ball*

(undergarments—female)

 1. 4 pr. women's white tights
 2. 2 pr. women's black tights
 3. 5 "merry widow" corsets
 4. 5 hoop skirt petticoats
 5. 1 double petticoat—Amelia
 6. 2 black petticoats—Maids
 7. 2 white petticoats—Friend and Passerby Lady
 8. 1 white nightgown
 9. 1 fancy wrapper
10. 1 plaid wrapper
11. 1 fancy camisole—Amelia

(undergarments—male)

12. 5 pr. black socks[1]
13. 1 white nightshirt

(men's attire)

14. 1 white ruffled front shirt (collarless)
15. 1 white tucked front shirt (collarless)
16. 2 regular front white shirts (collarless)
17. 1 doz. linenex collars—gladstone type
18. 1 pr. cabineri uniform pants
19. 1 cabineri uniform jacket
20. 1 caped frock coat—Chief of Police
21. 1 pr. pants—Chief of Police
22. 4 stocks of various colors
23. 3 vests of various fabrics
24. 1 robe—woolen
25. 1 frogged lounge coat
26. 1 pr. plaid pants
27. 1 black evening tails—coat and pants
28. 1 frock coat—Passerby
29. 1 pr. pants—Passerby

(hats and headdresses)

30. turkish toque
31. high silk hat
32. high bell topper hat
33. stocking cap
34. cabineri tricorn hat

Table 16–1. *(cont.)*

35. black corded snood and flower bunches—Amelia
36. corded hair piece and flower bunches—Friend
37. victorian bonnet
38. lace boudoir cap
39. 2 maids caps
40. bowler derby

(shoes)

41. 5 pr. of black shoes[1]
42. 1 pr. embroidered slippers
43. 1 pr. spats
44. 5 pr. black character shoes or equivalent[1]
45. 1 pr. ladies slippers

(women's attire)

46. 2 maids aprons
47. 2 maids black bodices

48. 2 maids black skirts
49. 1 skirt with biased striped front
50. 1 bodice with biased striped front
51. 1 scarf paneled skirt
52. 1 fake bolero-bodice top
53. 1 velvet and lace bodice—Amelia
54. 1 velvet, lace and flowered skirt—Amelia

(miscellaneous)

55. 1 reticule
56. 4 pr. men's gloves
57. 3 pr. ladies gloves
58. jewelry (cameo, 3 pr. earrings)
59. 1 feather fan
60. 1 silk fan

A total of 105 separate items.

[1]Items the actors can supply themselves.

The T.T.D. list now allows you to sit down and make a yardage and fabric cost estimate. To this you add labor costs. Labor costs can be figured as follows: It takes an experienced seamstress eight yours to cut and sew one untrimmed dress. (By trim I mean added decoration.) Collars, zippers, buttons, etc. are figured into the eight hours. It takes eight hours to draft and cut four dresses or two men's 3-piece suits, sixteen hours to properly construct a man's three-piece suit; four to eight hours to construct a hat. (It also partially depends on the garment, but this is a general rule of thumb.) It takes at least four hours to trim a dress. Labor gets $4.00 per hour and up for skilled work. Pattern drafters and cutters get at least $5.00 per hour. As you can see, time is also money.

Table 16–2. Yardage and Fabric Cost Sheet for *Amelia Goes to the Ball*

(Lady in nightgown)

2 yds. plaid wool	@ 6.49 =	12.98
5 yds. white cotton	@ 1.98 =	9.90
1 yd. white lace	@ 4.50 =	4.50
½ yd. white organdy	@ 2.29 =	1.15
1 pr. white tights	@ 4.50 =	4.50
1 pr. slippers	@ 5.00 =	5.00
Sub-total:		38.03
Labor:		32.00
Total:		70.03

Table 16–2. *(cont.)*

(Man in night clothes)

1 pr. slippers	@ 10.00 =	10.00
4 yds. white cotton	@ 1.98 =	7.92
1 yd. white cotton knit	@ 2.50 =	2.50
5 yds. wool	@ 6.49 =	32.45
10 yds. cording	@ .79 =	7.90
Sub-total:		60.27
Labor:		32.00
Total:		92.27

(Lady passerby)

6 panels of wool challis	@ 6.49 =	38.94
3 yds. pink panne velvet	@ 11.00 =	33.00
2½ yds. lavender silk	@ 3.95 =	15.80
1½ yds. green silk	@ 3.95 =	
2½ yds. muslin	@ 1.25 =	3.13
hat frame	@ 4.00 =	4.00
8 buttons	@ 2.00 =	2.00
Sub-total:		96.87
Labor:		64.00
Total:		159.87

(Gentleman passerby)

1 yd. brocade	@ 18.00 =	18.00
3 yds. white cotton	@ 2.49 =	7.47
3 yds. linen-like fabric	@ 3.95 =	11.85
4½ yds. broadcloth	@ 4.49 =	19.16
10 yds. bias tape	@ 1.25 (for 3 yd.) =	5.00
½ yd. felt	@ 4.50 =	2.25
1 doz. gladstone collars	@ 7.80 (per doz.) =	7.80
1 bell topper	@ 27.80 =	27.80
8 pearl buttons	@ 1.00 (for 4) =	2.00
2 coat buttons	@ 1.00 (for 2) =	1.00
4 sleeve buttons	@ 1.00 (for 2) =	2.00
6 vest buttons	@ 1.00 (for 3) =	2.00
Sub-total:		106.33
Labor:		64.00
Total:		170.33

(Officer of the cabinerie)

tricorn hat	@ 7.50 =	7.50
6 yds. black wool	@ 6.49 =	38.94
1 yd. white felt	@ 4.50 =	4.50
2 yds. red broadcloth	@ 4.49 =	8.98

Table 16–2.   *(cont.)*

enormous buckle	@ 4.00 =	4.00
12 silver buttons	@ 1.00 (for 3) =	4.00
2 silver stars	@ 1.00 (for 2) =	1.00
1 pr. white gloves	@ 3.00 =	3.00
4 12″ ostrich feathers	@ 1.50 =	6.00
2 yds. interfacing	@ 1.49 =	2.98
3 yds. muslin	@ 1.25 =	3.75
Sub-total:		84.65
Labor:		64.00
Total:		148.65

(Amelia—both outfits)

snood (6.00 worth of silk cord) =		6.00
hoop skirt	@ 21.95 =	21.95
merry widow	@ 12.50 =	12.50
5 yds. black moire silk	@ 2.95 =	14.85
5 yds. black lace	@ 4.49 =	22.45
3 yds. panne velvet	@ 11.00 =	33.00
flowers		60.00
gloves or mitts	@ 5.00 =	5.00
5 yds. white cotton	@ 1.98 =	9.90
3½ yds. 45 ″ wide eyelet	@ 6.75 =	23.63
6 yds. 24″ wide eyelet	@ 3.49 =	20.94
eyelet rushing 3 yds.	@ 1.79 =	5.37
10 yds. ¼″ wide ribbon	@ .89 =	8.90
3 yds. cotton lawn	@ 2.49 =	7.47
1 pr. tights	@ 4.50 =	4.50
Sub-total:		256.46
Labor:		99.00
Total:		355.46

(Chief of Police)

Derby	@ 12.85 =	12.85
3 yds. broadcloth (pants)	@ 4.49 =	13.47
5½ yds. broadcloth (coat lining)	@ 4.49 =	24.70
5½ yds. plaid	@ 5.00 =	27.50
1 pr. gloves	@ 3.00 =	3.00
3 yds. white cotton	@ 2.49 =	7.47
½ yd. felt	@ 4.50 =	2.25
10 shirt buttons	@ 1.00 (for 6) =	2.00
8 coat buttons	@ 1.00 (for 2) =	4.00
4 sleeve buttons	@ 1.00 (for 3) =	2.00
Sub-total:		99.24
Labor:		64.00
Total:		163.24

Table 16–2. *(cont.)*

(The husband)

3½ yds. white cotton	@ 2.49 =	8.72
10 pearl buttons	@ 1.00 (for 4) =	3.00
3 yds. white moire silk	@ 2.95 =	8.85
5 yds. satin coat lining	@ 2.25 =	11.25
7 yds. black wool	@ 6.49 =	45.43
black top hat	@ 27.50 =	27.50
5 vest buttons	@ 1.25 (for 2) =	3.75
6 coat buttons	@ 1.00 (for 2) =	3.00
6 sleeve buttons	@ 1.00 (for 3) =	2.00
Sub-total:		113.50
Labor:		64.00
Total:		117.50

(The lover)

5½ yds. 54″ velvet	@ 10.00 =	55.00
2 frogs	@ 3.00 =	6.00
3 yds. satin	@ 2.25 =	6.75
8 yds. rayon bias tape	@ 1.25 (for 3 yd.) =	3.75
3 yds. plaid linen or broadcloth	@ 4.49 =	13.47
3 yds. moire silk	@ 2.95 =	8.85
3 yds. cotton (white)	@ 2.49 =	7.47
tassel	@ 1.98 =	1.98
gold cord trim	@ 3.00 =	3.00
Sub-total:		106.27
Labor:		64.00
Total:		170.27

(2 maids)

14 yds. black cotton	@ 2.49 =	34.86
6 yds. white cotton	@ 2.49 =	14.94
3 yds. white organdy	@ 2.98 =	8.94
28 pearl buttons	@ 1.00 (for 4) =	7.00
2 cameos	@ 5.00 =	10.00
2 hoop skirts	@ 21.95 =	43.90
6 yds. black cotton petticoats	@ 1.98 =	11.88
2 pr. tights	@ 4.50 =	9.00
2 merry widows	@ 12.50 =	25.00
Sub-total:		165.52
Labor:		96.00
Total:		261.52

Table 16–2. *(cont.)*

(Friend)

4 yds. muslin	@ 1.25 =	5.00
2½ deep orange mussiline	@ 5.50 =	12.25
4 yds. organza	@ 2.50 =	10.00
2½ yds. striped brocade	@ 18.00 =	45.00
6 yds. antique satin	@ 2.50 =	15.00
flowers		10.00
1 yd. buckram	@ 4.50 =	4.50
1 hoop		21.50
3 yds. white cotton	@ 1.98 =	5.94
1 pr. tights	@ 4.50 =	4.50
1 merry widow	@ 12.50 =	12.50
Sub-total:		146.19
Labor:		64.00
Total:		210.19

Design, Fee, Continuing Expenses, and Profit Margin

Then comes the design fee. If you belong to the United Scenic Artists Union there is a proscribed pay scale. The preceding figures refer to what I usually charge for a one-act play, provided I am also paid to draft and cut. (As previously stated, this may not be possible in union situations.)

One must also charge an overhead margin for continuing expenses, such as heat and/or air conditioning, power, water, rent, adequate storage, if necessary, and dry cleaning and laundry costs. If you do not maintain your own shop, you may not have this worry. If you do, at least a 15 percent margin must be added to each production you do.

A word to the wise: Costumes must be kept at a temperate temperature, between 50 and 80 degrees, and humidity-free. Too cold and they dry rot; too hot and they steam apart; too dirty and the bugs eat them, so they must be stored clean. Lastly, you may want to add a profit margin if you run your own shop. On the budgetary totals that follow, this last is not included.

Total yard goods = 231 yards

Total cost of fabric, including hats, trim, hand props:	$1267.81
Total labor costs—based on $4.00 per hour:	704.00
Design fee:	250.00
Overhead margin:	250.00
Drafting and cutting time @ 5.00—70 hrs:	350.00
Total:	$2821.81

Rental vs. Construction Costs

Several points should be discussed when you compare rental prices to construction costs. This particular opera was designed for a children's opera tour to go around to schools for six months.

Recent New York estimates range around $35.00 per week for each costume. There are fourteen costumes here, out for 24 weeks, which comes to $11,760.00. Every month replacement and cleaning costs added to basic outlay make construction worthwhile. Let's hypothetically say they were only touring for six weeks. It would then cost $2,940.00—still better to construct. What if they only toured for three weeks? It would cost $1470.00 to rent, but that is money totally gone; whereas, they will be saving $2800.00 on the total cost of *Traviata* in the future. If you are doing a musical for only three nights, unless you can get free labor, as in civic groups or university situations, you are better off renting. Oftentimes getting the producer over a penny-wise, pound-foolish outlook becomes the job of the costume designer, as well.

These costs were done in the summer of 1978. One year later labor cost had gone to $4.75 an hour for seamstresses and $6.50 to $7.00 for drafter-cutters. There was also a 20 percent increase in the cost of fabrics. Costs also differ by area; New York prices are much higher than those in Florida, for example.

It is also wise to estimate on the *retail* price of fabric in case you have to buy it retail, but your cost goes down (and profit up) if you can buy wholesale. To buy wholesale, however, you must usually buy in ten-yard (and up) bolts. You may not want that much fabric. That may be a penny-wise, pound-foolish pitfall for you.

17

Scheduling an Individual Production

Working Backwards from Opening Night

No matter what the circumstances, the costumes have to be ready for opening night. You work backward from that date, to allow proper construction time, and forward from that date for running time. Technically speaking, running time comes under the prerogative of the wardrobe crew, but the designer should be aware of it, because it may require double sets of some items.

Construction Time

Construction time varies, depending on situations. Repertory theaters generally have full-time shop people who can put in steady, eight-hour days. In the university situation construction time must be juggled around class schedules for the professor and students alike. In the commercial theater the designs are turned over to a professional house and the designer does not have to worry about it. He or she may have two or three shows under construction simultaneously and works in an advise-and-consent capacity with these houses. In civic theater organizations costume construction is generally either farmed out or done by volunteers

at night. Each situation requires a different work schedule. The civic theater usually needs the longest time, sometimes eight to twelve weeks for a musical.

In university situations three to six weeks is the general time requirement, depending on the show's complexity. Several repertory theaters work on a two to four week schedule. The commercial construction houses have the best of everything at their fingertips and are therefore the most flexible.

For the purposes of this example, let's stick with our previously-mentioned hypothetical production of *Amelia Goes To The Ball*.

Shopping Time

Chapter 8 discussed the gathering of samples. Of course, you should keep a notebook of data showing where you got each sample and how much it cost. Now you allow shopping time, which may be one or two days. If you are having fabrics shipped, be sure to allow the proper time. Never waste days. Be sure you have something to work on in the meantime. Your shopping time must be included in your scheduling.

Drafting and Cutting Time

Next is drafting time. You should have received or taken your measurements as soon as the play has been cast. It helps to use mass production techniques wherever possible. Draft and cut all the women's skirts together, then bodices, pants, coats, and so forth. As we stated in our labor estimates, it takes eight hours to draft four dresses, or about two hours per dress. If you are doing only one-of-a-kind items, that same two hours can include the cutting of the dress, as well. The only time you have to allow extra cutting time is when you are drafting a basic pattern to be used to cut several dresses alike, but adjusted for size. Then you should estimate one hour for each additional size. It takes four to eight hours to draft and cut a man's three-piece suit. Therefore, the drafting and cutting time for *Amelia* would be approximately six work days.

A word to the wise: If you have more than one cutter and are doing several costumes alike, it pays to have like costumes cut by the same person. The same holds true for sewing as well. In the university situation it is often wise to sew (as well as cut) all the skirts, then bodices, etc. It saves instruction and supervisory time.

Sewing Time

Naturally, as soon as the first items are cut, sewing can begin. Therefore, some of the sewing and cutting time runs concurrently. It takes one person eight hours to sew a dress from start to finish if it is relatively untrimmed. With *Amelia*, the maids' dresses (including caps and aprons) and the neighbor's nightgown and hat are considered this way. So it would be one work day for each of those. Amelia's fancy undergarments and dress are highly detailed, as is the dress of her friend. Better add an extra four hours to each of those, as well as the lady passerby's dress. Her bonnet would be another four hours. Therefore, those four outfits would comprise six work days

for one person. The gentlemen can be counted as sixteen hours each, times seven outfits = fourteen work days. So if one person were drafting, cutting, and building, the total of required eight-hour work days would be thirty-one. There are five work days to a week. That equals one day over six weeks.

Now this time can be cut down by the amount of skilled help available. Most of the New York houses have enough staff to complete this work in seven work days, including all the incidentals not mentioned.

In a repertory theater shop that has a drafter-cutter and four seamstresses, it comes to about ten to twelve work days. In the university situation it would be about twelve to fifteen work days with the same number of people of that level of proficiency. With learning students you either must double the work force or double the time allotted. In civic theater this latter rule also applies.

Dress Rehearsals

Also, the number of dress rehearsals must be agreed upon and added to the schedule. Therefore, a reasonable work schedule for *Amelia* in a university situation would be something close to this:

Sketches finally approved by	March 16
Shopping and gathering from stock completed by	March 18
Cutting begins	March 18
Sewing begins	March 19
1st dress rehearsal or dress parade	April 11
Opening night	April 15

Fitting Time

Somewhere in this construction time schedule there must be time for fittings, but it is also concurrent with sewing time.

Working Forward from Opening Night

Wardrobe Running Schedule

The next schedule you may have to worry about is the wardrobe running schedule. This is one area that the commercial designer does not have to think about. Repertory companies usually have a wardrobe schedule based on their particular needs, but in civic and university theater it should be overseen just to make matters run smoothly.

Every production has its own running time. Most shows run somewhere between one and one-half to three and one-half hours. They have act breaks, scene changes, and so forth. Your costume plot will tell you all of this. Work out a traffic pattern with the actors. Where do they exit and where do they go to make their next entrance? If they have a fast change, *be there*. Make a map of who is where and in what costume.

Repairs

Company call is usually one hour before curtain. Wardrobe should arrive for set up about one-half hour before company call. If curtain is at 8:30, wardrobe should arrive at 7:00. This half-hour gives time for small repairs and if small repairs are constantly looked after, there will not be any big ones.

Laundry and Dry Cleaning

In case of big jobs and laundry, daytime hours should be assigned, as well as the gathering and collecting of dry cleaning. Wardrobe needs to check in all costumes after every final curtain. That can take twenty minutes to an hour after curtain.

In a long-running commercial play there are often double sets of certain costumes that are worn the longest and require the most laundry and dry cleaning. Several shirts alike for men and several similar or alike blouses or dresses for the women are useful. This may not be economically possible for every show. Actor's Equity has certain rules concerning these matters.

The university and resident theater company often have laundry facilities right on the premises. Repertory theater has an off night for one play while another is on the boards, and this is uniquely helpful. Very often in civic theaters the play's run is not long enough to worry about laundry. They may have two consecutive dark days in the early part of the week, preferring to run on the weekends. This also solves the problem.

Each case is unique and requires its own schedule, but a schedule should be made, nonetheless. Leave as little to chance as possible.

18

The Fine Art of Scrounging

Although you can't make a silk purse out of a sow's ear, occasionally you can make a reasonable facsimile, if not from the ear, perhaps from something as equally unlikely. This can save time, as well as money. You can turn a '50s three-button, narrow-lapelled man's jacket into a four-button 1900s sack coat. The lapels can be widened with binding. An extra button and buttonhole, *"et voila!"* There is a great similarity between the baggy pants of the '60s and the "oxford bags" of the '20s.

Be a thrift-shop shopper. Also, second-hand clothing is helpful. Some of the items found are shoes, old hats, old purses, fur pieces, junk jewelry, to say nothing of regular clothes. If you reside in any area for a length of time and the shop owners get to know you, they will save extra goodies for you. Many thrift shops are run for charity. Sometimes if you are short of cash, you can even trade for items.

For example, I once traded two Gothic costumes for two derbies and an inverness cape. When that cape became totally recognizable to our audiences after two years, I traded it back for a beautifully embroidered Spanish shawl. (I had already cut a pattern from the cape.)

The next places of importance are your local antique stores; though they often want too much money for period clothing, they will generally let you borrow items for copy purposes. Victorian hatpins are becoming rare these days and they are essential for those large Victorian and Edwardian hats. These you must buy at antique stores. The same goes for old jewelry and costume props, such as parasols, canes, fans, old-fashioned eyeglasses, snuff boxes, reticules, and so forth.

Don't turn down that old umbrella whose silk has separated and the moths have successfully sieved it. Count all the spokes and check the handle. If it's all there, buy it. The fabric can always be replaced. Ditto with fans. It's the frame that counts. All you need for a cane is an attractive handle. You can always add it to a dowel.

Another excellent source for cane handles is decorative doorknobs. I've even made one out of a faucet handle that had lost its mate. It was hand-painted porcelain, French, circa 1900. I paid fifteen francs (about $3.00 in 1970). It made a beautiful parasol handle and the audience never saw the "C" on it for *chaude* (hot).

Always buy old shoes that have baby Louis heels or old high-top shoes. It doesn't matter if they are size 3. Both heels and tops can be used on other shoes.

If a fad oriented to a past period suddenly becomes popular, buy it in every size if you can afford it and store it. When you need it, it will not be "in." Several years ago the Arrow Shirt Company reissued their detachable round-collared striped shirt. I bought as many as I could find. I did the same when the high-throated cuban-heeled shoes were popular for men in the early '70s. Using red cellophane tape (3M) has given me the perfect Restoration heeled shoe. Without it they make excellent flamenco shoes and serve other purposes as well.

Have you priced silk flowers and feathers lately? Old '50s hats abounded with them and one can usually pick them up in thrift shops for ten to twenty-five cents, because no one wears hats anymore. (They are on their way back in fashion.) The big brimmed hats are also very versatile for making into period bonnets and so forth. (See the chapter on hat construction in Volume II.)

Junk jewelry is a necessary addition to any costume supply. Avoid '50s plastic if possible, particularly poppet beads, because they are unsewable. However, Mardi Gras strings are a great help. One must simply develop an eye for what can become something else. That rhinestone brooch with the three stones missing may look tacky up close, but over the footlights it might look like the Hope Diamond.

There are two maxims for the costume designer to live by: 1) Don't worry about it if you can't see it from three feet away; 2) You'll never see it on a moving horse (in our case, actor). An article in *Theater Crafts Magazine* described the construction of costumes for the BBC production of the *Six Wives of Henry VIII*. They literally made the heavy jewelry and ornamentation out of junk from the scene shop floor; nails, lug bolts, screws, washers, hooks, rope, etc.

Felt rug padding is a great help for armor and hat making. Felt stiffener is all very nice but requires an exceedingly well-ventilated work space. Plain old shellac does just as well. Also, felt takes fiberglassing resin beautifully. (See chapters on hat construction and construction of armor, Volume II.)

We are often required to do what I have termed over the years "a rag show." Some rag shows are *Fiddler on the Roof, The Good Woman of Szechwan,* and *Man of La Mancha*—in other words, shows that require costumes with a lived-in look. Often Shakespeare contrasts the rich and the poor, and the poor are always in rags. Nothing looks as used or worn as old fabric. No amount of dyeing, distressing, and/or bleaching can give quite the same effect. Therefore, save that old chenille bedspread and those tacky drapes that were once blue and are now purple in the folds. When black ages, it often gets either a brownish or greenish cast to it, which is almost impossible to duplicate.

There are a few sources for good rags, however. For heavy texture, burlap bags and meal sacks are excellent. So are Army and Navy surplus blankets. (This latter also makes excellent tailored great coats.) If you live near water, ships chandler stores are a great source for hemp rope, canvas, and netting in wide widths. Surplus stores usually sell cheap muslin mattress covers, an excellent source of inexpensive muslin if you are hard-pressed.

Unfortunately, the most fluttery of rags are made of natural silk, which is not cheap. Remember all those '50s formals with yards of chiffon held out by yards of net? They are very cheap these days and the chiffon (nylon usually) makes great rags. The net has umteen uses, and even the beaded top can be saved and reapplied onto something else.

There are a few things that are harder to scrounge. Sometimes it takes ingenuity and good salesmanship. I once scrounged a full-length mink for *Bye Bye Birdie* by going to the best (and naturally the most expensive) furrier in town and telling him what I wanted and that I would like it to have three interchangeable linings to go with each of Albert's mother's three outfits. Naturally, we gave him program credit. I also let him use the three outfits as a window display idea for four weeks before we opened, by which the production was advertised. He got orders for four full-length minks with interchangeable linings. We sold out at the box office (and he sent me a lovely mink scarf). Everyone was happy.

One of the best sources for any resident theater is the community at large. Put a blurb in your program that such and such a show is coming up and you will need the following items. Use your local newspaper. I once needed a peculiarly shaped pair of cow horns for a specific hat. After trying every dairy and local slaughterhouse, I finally asked the newspapers and got just what I needed within twenty-four hours of the paper's hitting the doorsteps. It was fast, free, and good publicity.

Always be on the alert. I have pulled some excellent costumes out of the actor's own wardrobe, but needless to say, you as the designer must do the selecting.

Always take good care of what you borrow and return it promptly! That's how you make friends who will call you and say, "I've got eleven Paris originals over here. I'll hold them and let you have first pick."

In conclusion there is the final maxim for the costume designer. Never throw anything away (unless it's flea-infested or shredding at the seams). Just as sure as you do, you'll need it in the next show.

19

How to Prepare a Portfolio

What to Include, How Much, and How to be Selective

Without a portfolio you will not get a job and without a job you can't build up a portfolio. It does sound a little like a "Catch 22." But in fact it really is not as bad as all that.

First of all, never confuse a resumé with a portfolio. Your resumé should always accompany your portfolio, but it should contain a summary of all your educational and job experiences. (The fledgling designer should include it all. The longer the career, the more selective you may be with the resumé.)

Your portfolio should show your ability to its best advantage. If you have delved into design through the higher educational process (either university or art school), you should begin preparing your portfolio from your very first art class, keeping each class's sketches, so that by graduation you have a body of work from which to choose the best. Those drawings that earned the best grades are always the most tempting, but they may not always be the most representative or helpful. Also, do not show only one side of your talent. You want as broad a per-

spective as possible. Even if you really care nothing about designing scenery, you should include a couple of set sketches to show your ideas, particularly in relation to costumes from the same show.

It is not necessary to have every costume from every show. Pick out several that are the most representative of a particular production. Show as many techniques of drawing and painting with which you are proficient as you can. If you enjoy using different styles for different plays, include several examples of these.

Not all sketches need swatches, but one group at least should have them. You should have one or two complete shows; pick nice compact ones. You should also include scaled patterns, draftings, and photographs of finished productions for some of the sketches. Show as great a variety of periods as possible.

I recently brought my own portfolio up to date and laughed as I remembered by first portfolio (which was to get into graduate school). It consisted of sketches for two operas and four musical comedies that I had actually done and sketched after the fact. Graduate school gave me time to sketch, but those sketches were for hypothetical productions, class assignments. After graduate school I added some production photos and was smart enough to put the sketches on slides. Now, thirteen years later, it is a case of *too much*. (My sketches now take up two closets and four cabinets.) So I began to weed out the dead wood.

This weeding process is very important and should be done as the years go by. It also helps to have a second opinion. I had a party to which I invited some of my theater associates, two designers, an actor buddy, and two directors I have worked with over the past eight years. I spread my favorite shows out over the living room and had each pick out choices. I kept a score card and then decided if I agreed with them. You might try this with your friends.

I have also helped my students as best I could by reviewing their body of work with them and telling them why I choose what I choose. Your professors would be most happy (and flattered) if you asked them. I also encourage my students to ask other faculty members as well. In the final analysis, however, the decision is still yours. You must develop your own criteria.

Perhaps a list from my present portfolio might give you some ideas, but please keep in mind that I have criteria that you might not want or need. (See end of chapter.) Besides those previously mentioned, I need to show a body of work that spans nineteen years and should (hopefully) show improvement with age. I have listed it by show or work of art, period, style, technique, place and date, and reason for choice. Also, I tried to include a little of everything I have designed—all types of theater, including musicals, operas, drama, tragedy, several types of comedy and dance, as well as glitzy items like nightclub show girls.

Most of us who paint costume sketches often paint other things. I do scenic murals and Chinese silk paintings. It's a good way to pick up extra cash. I've included a little of that, as well. If you do this sort of thing, you should include an example of it too. It adds interest and it helps to further identify you when you are one of a mass being interviewed for the same job. It's like your own personal trademark.

Your portfolio should be three things; neat, organized, and uniquely yours. The purpose of the sketch changes somewhat from that described in Chapter 8. It now becomes part of a body of illustrative work to show your talents to their best advantage. Matting can often help, as can a simple lined edge. Matting does not necessarily mean a black frame, however. The matting can be creative, and a means of preservation for certain lighter weight paper, especially charcoal or pastel paper, particularly when used with a clear acetate sheet.

Obviously if you use an illustration board, matting becomes superfluous. Use spray fixative to prevent blotching, smearing, and rubbing. (Hair spray is also an excellent fixative and often is cheaper than the artist variety.) Use clear plastic to cover sketches that humidity might ruin. Make sure all your work is properly identified by show, character, act, and scene. Make sure you sign all your sketches! Put your sketches in your portfolio in some semblance of order. If you are presenting your portfolio in person, rehearse your "spiel." If you are sending it, send a well-organized list with coordinated numbers, so that it can be viewed in a non-chaotic manner.

If you are presenting your portfolio in person, you, no less than any actor, must look your part. If you look like a gypsy just off the caravan, you might just as well not unzip the portfolio case. You are, after all, in the business of making people look their best; so should you.

Mailing your portfolio can cause great fear and trepidation. The U. S. mails seem to exist on Murphy's Law (if anything can happen, it will). My own private system is to send slides (duplicates at that). I always add that I would be happy to visit the prospective employer and bring my portfolio with me. Along with my slides, which are numbered, identified on an accompanying list, and sent with a *pocket viewer,* I may send Xeroxes of other items. Do you know about the new Xerox that sends color reproductions, even of slides? It currently costs about seventy-five cents a copy, but is *safer,* much *safer!*

In conclusion, let's talk about that extra special something "uniquely your own." Call it flair; call it style, panache, elegance, or what you will. It is to the designer what "star quality" is to an actor or actress—that extra sparkle. People cannot exactly put their fingers on it. It can't be taught. But when you find your own best style, stick with it.

Have you ever noticed that expression "It's a classic!" Its design looks as fabulous today as it did twenty years ago. Coco Chanel's "little black dress" is a classic. You could wear it today and look smashing at a disco. Time only enhances a classic. Look at the ageless beauty of Nefertiti or the shivering mystique of Garbo. Now there's style with a capital S.

Table 19–1.   Portfolio Example

Show or Work of Art	Period	Style	Technique	Place & Date	Reason for Choice
Midsummer Night's Dream rough sketches* a. Oberon b. Titania c. Peasblossom d. Cobweb *note: These were rejected by Director	Elizabethan with Art Nouveau detailing	à la Aubrey Beardsley	pen & ink on unprinted newspaper	intended for F.A.U. 1974	black & white
Romeo & Juliet all the guests and principals at the ball	Italian Renaissance	opulence	acrylic on toast matboard	F.A.U. 1975	did whole scene in black, white, and metals (gold, silver, copper)
Servant of Two Masters complete show plus swatches	Italian Rococo	à la Pietro Longhi	hard-edged watercolor	F.A.U. 1976	Rococo period & comedia overtones
The Boyfriend a. Polly & Tony b. Maise & her boyfriend	flapper English 1920s	cartoon	pen & ink & watercolor	F.A.U. 1977	style and musical comedy

Table 19–1. *(cont.)*

Show or Work of Art	Period	Style	Technique	Place & Date	Reason for Choice
Becket a. 4 barons b. Pope & Cardinal c. French King and Baron	Romanesque	stained glass window	acryllic on red mat board	Delray Beach Playhouse 1977	period and painting technique
A Flea in Her Ear a. Lucianne— Act II b. Don Carlos c. Yovanne— Act I d. Yovanne— Act II	French 1912–1914 hobbleskirt	high fashion	watercolor	F.A.U. 1977	period and style including pattern drafting
Sketch for Victorian Christmas Card	Victorian	Charles Dickens schmaltz	watercolor & coulauge	sold to greeting card company 1977	variety
Hedda Gabler complete show on four plates	Scandinavian Victorian 1880s	sepia tintypes	acrylic on gold matboard	F.A.U. 1978	got critics award for this; also Ibsen and type of realistic drama
Masque of the Red Death a ballet sets & costumes for the scene in the last room	Italian Renaissance	flowing	watercolor	Thesis project— graduate school—1966 Carnegie Tech— Pittsburgh, Pa.	only ballet I've sketched; also shows good movement
Tartuffe a. Marianne b. Valere	Cavalier	soft-edged	watercolor	University of Montana 1966	Molière— French Cavalier period
Rusalka a. Rusalka Act I b. Wasserman c. Jessicababa	Rococo fantasy	storybook illustrative	watercolor	Paris, France 1969	

Table 19–1.   *(cont.)*

Show or Work of Art	Period	Style	Technique	Place & Date	Reason for Choice
The Mikado costume sketches a. Koko & Katisha b. Nanki Poo and Yum Yum c. Peepbo & Poohbah set sketches—twelve sliding screens	Japanese	Japanese woodblock prints of 1700's	watercolor or pen & ink background	Musical Theater Guild—Butler, Pa. 1971	did both sets and costumes & painting style
Marat/Sade a. 4 clowns b. M. & Md Cummiere c. Corday d. Duperez e. inmates plus photo of clowns in production	mixture of periods	total theater	hard-edged watercolor	F.A.U. 1974	to show extreme variety within a given production; also to show the before and after effect with photographs
Lady's Not For Burning a. Jennet Jordg-mayne #1 b. Jennet Jordg-mayne #2	Gothic	old masters	oil paintings	F.A.U. 1973	my only sketches in oil paints
Midsummer Night's Dream finished sketches a. Hippolyta & Theseus b. Hermia & Lysander c. Demetrius & Helena	Elizabethan with Art Nouveau detailing	Arthur Rackham	hard-edged watercolor	F.A.U. 1974	Elizabethan period

Table 19–1.   *(cont.)*

Show or Work of Art	Period	Style	Technique	Place & Date	Reason for Choice
A Funny Thing (etc.)[1] a. Panacea b. Vibrata c. Gymnasia	loosely Roman	musical comedy	watercolor & pastel pencil	F.A.U. 1978	all the delightfully funny publicity the *fake* nudity caused, including newspaper articles and cartoons
Blood Wedding a. Death b. Leonardo	non-period	Frazetti	acryllic	F.A.U. 1978	way-out and truly bizarre concept
Two showgirl outfits for two different nightclubs	tits & glitz	razzle dazzle	pastel and coulauge	Miami, Fla. and Atlanta, Ga. 1978 and 1979	glitzy & fun
Sketch for church mural	based on *The Creation* by James Weldon Johnson	cartoon	watercolor	commissioned for church, Orlando, Fla.	variety

[1]The need for the previously-mentioned cow horns (Chapter 11) for Vibrata's hat and my crazy search got some delightful news coverage, including a cartoon in the paper. Also, the *nude* look caused some very funny "Letters to the Editor," which I have laminated and included.

Bibliography

History

Aristotle. *Aristotle's Theory of Poetry and the Fine Arts,* 4th edition. New York: Dover Press, 1951. Critical text and translation by S. H. Butcher.

Bridgewater, William (ed.). *The Columbia Viking Desk Encyclopedia.* New York: Viking Press, 1953.

Churchill, Winston. *A History of the English Speaking Peoples, Volume I: The Birth of Britain.* New York: Dodd Meade Edition, 1958.

———. *A History of the English Speaking Peoples, Volume II: The New World.* New York: Dodd Meade Edition, 1958.

———. *A History of the English Speaking Peoples, Volume III: The Age of Revolution.* New York: Dodd Meade Edition, 1958.

———. *A History of the English Speaking Peoples, Volume IV: The Great Democracies.* New York: Dodd Meade Edition, 1958.

New Larousse Encyclopedia of Mythology, 9th printing. London: Prometheus Press for The Hamlyn Publishing Group Limited, 1974.

Reishauer, Edwin O. and Fairbanks, John K. *East Asia: The Great Tradition.* Boston: Houghton Mifflin Company, 1960.

The World Book Encyclopedia. Chicago: 1979.

Theater History

Albright, H. D., Halstead, William P., and Mitchell, Lee. *Principles of Theater Art.* Boston, New York: Houghton Mifflin Company, 1955.

Brockett, Oscar G. *History of the Theater,* 3rd ed. Boston: Allyn and Bacon, 1978.

Cheney, Sheldon. *The Theater: Three Thousand Years of Drama, Acting, and Stagecraft,* rev. ed. New York: McKay Publisher, 1972.

Gassner, John. *Masters of the Drama,* 3rd ed. New York: Dover Publications, 1954.

Gassner, John and Quinn, E. (eds.). *The Reader's Encyclopedia of World Drama,* 3rd ed. New York: Crowell, 1969.

Green, Stanley. *The World of Musical Comedy.* New York: Ziff-Davis Publishing Company, 1960.

Roberts, Vera M. *On Stage: A History of Theater,* 2nd ed. New York: Harper & Row Publishers, 1974.

Music and Art History

Bridgeman, Harriet and Drury, Elizabeth (eds.). *The Encyclopedia of Victoriana.* London: Macmillan Publishing Company, 1975.

Grout, Donald Jay. *A History of Western Music,* rev. ed. New York: W. W. Norton & Company, Inc., 1973.

Janson, H. W. and Janson, Dora Jane. *The Picture History of Painting.* New York: Harry Nabrams, Inc., 1957.

Maillard, Robert (ed.). *Tudor History of Painting in 1000 Color Reproductions.* New York: Tudor Publishing Company, 1961.

New York Graphic Society. *Fine Art Reproductions of Old and Modern Masters.* New York: New York Graphic Society Publishers, 1968.

Pope, Arthur. *The Language of Painting and Drawing.* Cambridge, Massachusetts: Harvard University Press, 1949.

Read, Herbert (ed.) *Encyclopedia of the Arts.* London: Thames & Hudson, Limited, 1966.

Costume and Fashion History

Black, J. Anderson and Garland, Madge. *A History of Fashion.* New York: William Morrow & Company, Inc., 1975.

Boucher, Francois. *L'Histoire du Costume.* Paris: Flammarion, 1965.

Bradley, Carolyn G. *Western World Costume.* New York: Appleton-Century-Crofts, 1956.

Bradshaw, Angela. *World Costumes.* London: Adam & Charles Black, 1959.

Braun and Schneider (publishers of the original German plates between 1861 and 1890 in Munich, Germany). *Historic Costume in Pictures.* New York: Dover Publication, 1975.

Bruhn, Wolfgang and Tilke, Max. *A Pictorial History of Costume,* fourth printing. Tuebingen, Germany: Hastings House Publishers, 1955.

Contini, Mila. *Fashion.* New York: The Odyssey Press, 1965.

Cunnington, Phillis and Lucas, Catherine. *Occupational Costume in England.* London: Adam & Charles Black, 1967.

Davenport, Millia. *The Book of Costume,* fourth printing. New York: Crown Publishers, 1948.

Earle, Alice Morse. *Two Centuries of Costume in America, 1620–1820, Volumes I and II.* New York: Dover Publications, 1970.

Fairchild Publication. *Men's Wear, 75 Years of Fashion.* New York, June 1965.

Gorsline, Douglas. *What People Wore.* New York: Bonanza Books, 1952.

Hope, Thomas. *Costumes of the Greeks and Romans.* New York: Dover Publications, 1962.

Kelly, F. M. and Schwabe, R. *Historic Costume, 1490–1790,* 2nd ed. New York: Benjamin Blom, Inc., 1929.

Kretchmer, Albert and Rehrbach, Carl. *Die Trachten der Völker.* Leipzig, Germany: J. G. Bach's Verlag, 1882.

Kybalova, Ludmilla; Herbsenova, Olga; and Larmarova, Milena. *A Pictorial Encyclopedia of Fashion.* New York: Crown Publishers, Inc., 1968.

Laver, James. *Costume.* New York: Hawthorn Books, Inc., 1963.

———. *Costumes in Antiquity.* New York: Clarkson N. Potter, Inc., 1964.

———. *Costumes through the Ages, 1000 Illustrations.* New York: Simon & Schuster, 1963.

Selbie, Robert. *The Anatomy of Costume.* New York: Crescent, 1977.

Sichel, Marion. *Costume Reference #1 Roman Britain and the Middle Ages.* Boston: Plays, Inc., 1977.

———. *Costume Reference #2 Tudors and Elizabethans.* Boston: Plays, Inc., 1977.

———. *Costume Reference #3 Jacobean, Stuart, and Restoration.* Boston: Plays, Inc., 1977.

———. *Costume Reference #5 The Regency.* Boston: Plays, Inc., 1978.

———. *Costume Reference #6 The Victorians.* Boston: Plays, Inc., 1978.

Wilcox, R. Turner. *Folk and Festival Costumes of the World.* New York: Charles Scribner's Sons, 1965.

———. *The Mode in Costume.* New York: Charles Scribner's Sons, 1958.

———. *The Mode in Footwear.* New York: Charles Scribner's Sons, 1948.

———. *The Mode in Hats and Headdresses, including Hairstyle, Cosmetics, and Jewelry.* New York: Charles Scribner's Sons, 1959.

Costume Style, Design, and Patterns

Arnold, Janet. *Patterns of Fashion #1 English Women's Dresses and Their Construction 1660–1860.* London: Macmillan London, Limited, 1972

————. *Patterns of Fashion #2 English Women's Dresses and Their Construction 1860–1940.* London: Macmillan London, Limited, 1972.

Barton, Lucy. *Historic Costume for the Stage.* Boston: Walter H. Baker Company, 1963.

Barton, Lucy and Edson, Doris. *Period Patterns.* Boston: Walter H. Baker Company, 1942.

Carter, Ernestine. *The Changing World of Fashion.* New York: G. P. Putnam's Sons, 1977.

Hill, Margot Hamilton and Bucknell, Peter. *The Evolution of Fashion: Pattern and Cut from 1066–1930.* New York: Reinhold Publishing Co., 1967.

Motley. *Designing and Making Stage Costumes.* New York: Watson-Guptill Publications, 1964.

Payne, Blanche. *History of Costume.* New York: Harper & Row Publishers, 1965.

Pope, Arthur. *The Language of Drawing and Painting,* 2nd printing. Cambridge, Massachusetts: Harvard University Press, 1949.

Russel, Douglass A. *Period Style for the Theater.* Boston: Allyn & Bacon, 1980.

————. *Stage Costume Design Theory Technique and Style.* Englewood Cliffs, New Jersey: Prentice-Hall, Inc., 1973.

Tilke, Max. *Costume Patterns and Designs.* New York: Hastings House Publishers, 1957.

Trëster, Frantisek (ed.). *Costume on the Stage.* Prague, Czechoslovakia: Arita, 1962.

Heraldry, Armor, and Uniforms

Fox-Davies, Arthur. *The Art of Heraldry.* New York: Arno Press, 1976.

Franklyn, Julian. *Heraldry.* New Jersey: A. S. Barnes & Company, 1965.

Funcken, Fred and Funcken, Liliane. *Le Costume et les Armes des Soldats de Tous les Temps.* France: Casterman, 1967.

Kelly, F. M. and Schwabe, R. *A Short History of Costume and Armor, Volume I, 1066–1485.* Reissued 1968. New York: Benjamin Blom, Inc., 1931.

Martin, Paul. *European Military Uniforms.* Feltham, Great Britain: Spring Books, 1968.

Stone, George Cameron. *A Glossary of the Construction, Decoration and Use of Arms and Armor.* New York: Jack Brussel Publisher, 1961.

Index